Modern Critical Interpretations

Modern Critical Interpretations

William Shakespeare's
Romeo and Juliet

Edited and with an introduction by
Harold Bloom
Sterling Professor of the Humanities
Yale University

CHELSEA HOUSE PUBLISHERS
Philadelphia

© 2000 by Chelsea House Publishers, a subsidiary of
Haights Cross Communications.

Introduction © 2000 by Harold Bloom

Printed and bound in the United States of America

10 9 8 7 6 5 4 3 2

∞ The paper used in this publication meets the minimum
requirements of the American National Standard for
Permanence of Paper for Printed Library Materials,
Z39.48-1984

Library of Congress Cataloging-in-Publication Data

William Shakespeare's Romeo and Juliet/ edited and with an
introduction by Harold Bloom.
        p. cm.— (Modern critical interpretations)
    Includes bibliographical references and index.
    ISBN 0-7910-5662-7 (alk.paper)
    1. Shakespeare, William, 1564–1616. Romeo and Juliet.
2. Tragedy.   I. Title: Romeo and Juliet.   II. Bloom,
Harold.   III. Series.
PR2831. W55   2000
822.3'3—dc21
                                        99-049118
                                           CIP

Contributing Editor: Mirjana Kalezic

Contents

Editor's Note

This volume brings together a distinguished group of essays on Shakespeare's tragedy, *Romeo and Juliet*. I am grateful to Mirjana Kalezic for her skilled and devoted care in helping me edit this book.

My Introduction meditates upon the status of *Romeo and Juliet* among Shakespeare's tragedies.

The late Robert Penn Warren, poet-critic-novelist, considers *Romeo and Juliet* in the context of his own adage: "Poetry wants to be pure but poems do not."

Harold C. Goddard's essay is particularly helpful in its wariness towards Mercutio and the Nurse, two dangerously rancid entertainers, while John Lawlor's discussion emphasizes how powerfully consistent *Romeo and Juliet* is with the full range of Shakespeare's imagination.

Ruth Nevo centers upon the full articulation of Shakespeare's tragic structure in the play, after which Rosalie L. Colie juxtaposes "the problematics of love" in *Romeo and Juliet* and *Othello*.

For Sir Frank Kermode the complexity of *Romeo and Juliet* is crucial, while comic elements within the tragedy are stressed by Sysan Snyder.

Northrop Frye centers upon the alternation of light and dark imagery in the play, after which Thomas McAlindon locates *Romeo and Juliet*'s place in relevant cosmological contexts.

The concluding essay, by this volume's editor, gives primacy to Juliet's eloquence and largeness of spirit, and sees in them the abiding glory of this tragedy.

Introduction

Except for *Hamlet* and *Macbeth*, *Romeo and Juliet* seems the most popular of Shakespeare's tragedies, though it is necessarily dwarfed by the heroic sequence of *Hamlet*, *Othello*, *King Lear*, *Macbeth*, and *Antony and Cleopatra*. Some critics prefer *Coriolanus* to the High Romanticism of *Romeo and Juliet*, and I myself would rather reread *Julius Cesar* than turn again to *Romeo and Juliet*. Yet the massive, permanent popularity of *Romeo and Juliet* is well-deserved. Its appeal is universal and world-wide, and its effect upon world literature is matched among the tragedies only by *Hamlet*. Stendhal, who with Victor Hugo is the great partisan of Shakespeare in equivocal France, wrote his own sublime tribute to *Romeo and Juliet* in his last completed novel, *The Charterhouse of Parma*.

Since I write rather fully about *Romeo and Juliet* in the essay printed last in this volume, I desire here only to make some brief reflections upon the relative aesthetic eminence of the play in the full context of Shakespeare's achievement. So prodigal was Shakespeare's inventiveness, particularly in the creation of personalities, that I myself, in earlier years, tended to undervalue *Romeo and Juliet* in the full panoply of Shakespeare. There are perhaps twenty plays by him that I rated higher, even if some of them lacked the enormous popularity of *Romeo and Juliet*. I do not know whether I merely have aged, or have matured, but Juliet herself moves me now in many of the same ways that I find Desdemona and Cordelia to be almost unbearably poignant. What Robert Penn Warren called her "pure poetry" remains astonishingly vital and powerful, as when she wishes her lover's vow to Romeo could be inaugurated again:

> But to be frank and give it thee again;
> And yet I wish but for the thing I have.
> My bounty is as boundless as the sea,

1

> My love as deep: The more I give to thee
> The more I have, for both are infinite.

That is a transcendently persuasive utterance of love's reality, as rich as literature affords, so distant from vainglory or self-deception that Romeo is transfigured by receiving it. Shakespeare is reputed to have said that he had to kill off Mercutio lest Mercutio kill the play. I think it likelier that the full revelation of Juliet's greatness made it necessary to dispose of the prurient Mercutio, whose lively blasphemies against the splendors of Juliet's love might well have wearied us.

Juliet's is a difficult role to play, for the curse of our theaters are "high-concept" directors, and some of them do not seem to know clearly the difference between Juliet and the Cressida of *Troilus and Cressida*! Properly performed, or adequately interpreted by a sensitive reader, Juliet is an essential part of Shakespeare's unmatched invention of the human.

ROBERT PENN WARREN

Pure and Impure Poetry

Critics are rarely faithful to their labels and their special strategies. Usually the critic will confess that no one strategy—the psychological, the moralistic, the formalistic, the historical—or combination of strategies, will quite work the defeat of the poem. For the poem is like the monstrous Orillo in Boiardo's *Orlando Innamorato*. When the sword lops off any member of the monster, that member is immediately rejoined to the body, and the monster is as formidable as ever. But the poem is even more formidable than the monster, for Orillo's adversary finally gained a victory by an astonishing feat of dexterity: he slashed off both the monster's arms and quick as a wink seized them and flung them into the river. The critic who vaingloriously trusts his method to account for the poem, to exhaust the poem, is trying to emulate this dexterity: he thinks that he, too, can win by throwing the lopped-off arms into the river. But he is doomed to failure. Neither fire nor water will suffice to prevent the rejoining of the mutilated members to the monstrous torso. There is only one way to conquer the monster: you must eat it, bones, blood, skin, pelt, and gristle. And even then the monster is not dead, for it lives in you, is assimilated into you, and you are different, and somewhat monstrous yourself, for having eaten it.

So the monster will always win, and the critic knows this. He does not want to win. He knows that he must always play stooge to the monster. All

From *New and Selected Essays*. ©1989 Robert Penn Warren.

he wants to do is to give the monster—the poem—a chance to exhibit again its miraculous power, which is poetry.

With this fable, I shall begin by observing that poetry wants to be pure. And it always succeeds in this ambition. In so far as we have poetry at all, it is always pure poetry; that is, it is not non-poetry. The poetry of Shakespeare, the poetry of Pope, the poetry of Herrick, is pure, in so far as it is poetry at all. We call the poetry "higher" or "lower," we say "more powerful" or "less powerful" about it, and we are, no doubt, quite right in doing so. The souls that form the great rose of Paradise are seated in banks and tiers of ascending blessedness, but they are all saved, they are all perfectly happy; they are all "pure," for they have all been purged of mortal taint. This is not to say, however, that if we get poetry from only one source, say Shakespeare, such a single source ought to suffice us, in as much as we can always appeal to it; or that, since all poetry is equally pure, we engage in a superfluous labor in trying to explore or create new sources of poetry. No, for we can remember that every soul in the great rose is precious in the eyes of God. No soul is the substitute for another.

Poetry wants to be pure, but poems do not. At least, most of them do not want to be too pure. The poems want to give us poetry, which is pure, and the elements of a poem, in so far as it is a good poem, will work together toward that end, but many of the elements, taken in themselves, may actually seem to contradict that end, or be neutral toward the achieving of that end. Are we then to conclude that neutral or recalcitrant elements are simply an index to human frailty, and that in a perfect world there would be no dross in poems, which would, then, be perfectly pure? No, it does not seem to be merely the fault of our world, for the poems include, deliberately, more of the so-called dross than would appear necessary. They are not even as pure as they might be in this imperfect world. They mar themselves with cacophonies, jagged rhythms, ugly words and ugly thoughts, colloquialisms, clichés, sterile technical terms, headwork and argument, self-contradictions, clevernesses, irony, realism—all things which call us back to the world of prose and imperfection.

Sometimes a poet will reflect on this state of affairs, and grieve. He will decide that he, at least, will try to make one poem as pure as possible. So he writes:

> Now sleeps the crimson petal, now the white;
> Nor waves the cypress in the palace walk;
> Nor winks the gold fin in the porphyry font.
> The fire-fly wakens; waken thou with me.

We know the famous garden—the garden in Tennyson's "Princess." We know how all nature conspires here to express the purity of the moment: how the milk-white peacock glimmers like a ghost, and how like a ghost the unnamed "she" glimmers on to her tryst; how earth lies "all Danaë to the stars," as the beloved's heart lies open to the lover; and how, in the end, the lily folds up her sweetness, "and slips into the bosom of the lake," as the lovers are lost in the sweet dissolution of love.

And we know another poet and another garden. Or perhaps it is the same garden, after all, viewed by a different poet, Shelley.

> I arise from dreams of thee
> In the first sweet sleep of night,
> When the winds are breathing low,
> And the stars are shining bright.
> I arise from dreams of thee,
> And a spirit in my feet
> Hath led me—who knows how?
> To thy chamber window, Sweet!

We remember how, again, all nature conspires, how the wandering airs "faint," how the Champak's odors "pine," how the nightingale's complaint "dies upon her heart," as the lover will die upon the beloved's heart. Nature here strains out of nature, it wants to be called by another name, it wants to spiritualize itself by calling itself another name. How does the lover get to the chamber window? He refuses to say how, in his semi-somnambulistic daze, he got there. He blames, he says, "a spirit in my feet," and hastens to disavow any knowledge of how that spirit operates. In any case, he arrives at the chamber window. Subsequent events and the lover's reaction toward them are somewhat hazy. We know only that the lover, who faints and fails at the opening of the last stanza and who asks to be lifted from the grass by a more enterprising beloved, is in a condition of delectable passivity, in which distinctions blur out in the "purity" of the moment.

Let us turn to another garden: the place, Verona; the time, a summer night, with full moon. The lover speaks:

> But, soft! what light through yonder
>   window breaks?
> It is the east . . .

But we know the rest, and know that this garden, in which nature for the moment conspires again with the lover, is the most famous of them all, for the scene is justly admired for its purity of effect, for giving us the very essence of young, untarnished love. Nature conspires beneficently here, but we may remember that beyond the garden wall strolls Mercutio, he can celebrate Queen Mab, but who is always aware that nature has other names as well as the names the pure poets and pure lovers put upon her. And we remember that Mercutio, outside the wall, has just said:

> . . . 'twould anger him
> To raise a spirit in his mistress' circle
> Of some strange nature, letting it there stand
> Till she had laid it and conjured it down.

Mercutio has made a joke, a bawdy joke. That is bad enough, but worse, he has made his joke witty and, worst of all, intellectually complicated in its form. Realism, wit, intellectual complication—these are the enemies of the garden purity.

But the poet has not only let us see Mercutio outside the garden wall. Within the garden itself, when the lover invokes nature, when he spiritualizes and innocently trusts her, and says,

> Lady, by yonder blessed moon I swear,

the lady herself replies,

> O! Swear not by the moon, the inconstant moon,
> That monthly changes in her circled orb.

The lady distrusts "pure" poems, nature spiritualized into forgetfulness. She has, as it were, a rigorous taste in metaphor, too; she brings a logical criticism to bear on the metaphor which is too easy; the metaphor must prove itself to her, must be willing to subject itself to scrutiny beyond the moment's enthusiasm. She injects the impurity of an intellectual style into the lover's pure poem.

And we must not forget the voice of the nurse, who calls from within, a voice which, we discover, is the voice of expediency, of half-measures, of the view that circumstances alter cases—the voice of prose and imperfection.

It is time to ask ourselves if the celebrated poetry of this scene, which as poetry is pure, exists despite the impurities of the total composition, if the effect would be more purely poetic were the nurse and Mercutio absent and the lady a more sympathetic critic of pure poems. I do not think so. The effect might even be more vulnerable poetically if the impurities were purged away. Mercutio, the lady, and the nurse are critics of the lover, who believes in pure poems, but perhaps they are necessary. Perhaps the lover can be accepted only in their context. The poet seems to say: "I know the worst that can be said on this subject, and I am giving fair warning. Read at your own risk." So the poetry arises from a recalcitrant and contradictory context; and finally involves that context.

Let us return to one of the other gardens, in which there is no Mercutio or nurse, and in which the lady is more sympathetic. Let us mar its purity by installing Mercutio in the shrubbery, from which the poet was so careful to banish him. You can hear his comment when the lover says:

> And a spirit in my feet
> Hath led me—who knows how?
> To thy chamber window, Sweet!

And we can guess what the wicked tongue would have to say in response to the last stanza.

It may be that the poet should have made early peace with Mercutio, and appealed to his better nature. For Mercutio seems to be glad to co-operate with a poet. But he must be invited; otherwise, he is apt to show a streak of merry vindictiveness about the finished product. Poems are vulnerable enough at best. Bright reason mocks them like sun from a wintry sky. They are easily left naked to laughter when leaves fall in the garden and the cold winds come. Therefore, they need all the friends they can get, and Mercutio, who is an ally of reason and who himself is given to mocking laughter, is a good friend for a poem to have.

On what terms does a poet make his peace with Mercutio? There are about as many sets of terms as there are good poets. I know that I have loaded the answer with the word *good* here, that I have implied a scale of excellence based, in part at least, on degree of complication. I shall return to this question. For the moment, however, let us examine an anonymous sixteenth-century poem whose apparent innocence and simple lyric cry should earn it a place in any anthology of "pure poetry."

> Western wind, when will thou blow,
> The small rain down can rain?
> Christ, if my love were in my arms
> And I in my bed again!

The lover, grieving for the absent beloved, cries out for relief. Several kinds of relief are involved in the appeal to the wind. First, there is the relief that would be had from the sympathetic manifestation of nature. The lover, in his perturbation of spirit, invokes the perturbations of nature. He invokes the beneficent perturbation,

> Western wind, when will thou blow,

as Lear invokes the destructive,

> Blow, winds, and crack your cheeks! rage! blow!

Second, there is the relief that would be had by the fulfillment of grief—the frost of grief, the drought of grief broken, the full anguish expressed, then the violence allayed in the peace of tears. Third, there is the relief that would be had in the excitement and fulfillment of love itself. There seems to be a contrast between the first two types of relief and the third type; speaking loosely, we may say that the first two types are romantic and general, the third type realistic and specific. So much for the first two lines.

In the last two lines, the lover cries out for the specific solace of his case: reunion with his beloved. But there is a difference between the two lines. The first is general, and romantic. The phrase "in my arms" does not seem to mean exactly what it says. True, it has a literal meaning, if we can look close at the words, but it is hard to look close because of the romantic aura—the spiritualized mist about them. But with the last line the perfectly literal meaning suddenly comes into sharp focus. The mist is rifted and we can look straight at the words, which, we discover with a slight shock of surprise, do mean exactly what they say. The last line is realistic and specific. It is not even content to say,

> And I in bed again!

It is, rather, more scrupulously specific, and says,

> And I in *my* bed again!

All of this does not go to say that the realistic elements here are to be taken as canceling, or negating, the romantic elements. There is no ironical leer. The poem is not a celebration of carnality. It is a faithful lover who speaks. He is faithful to the absent beloved, and he is also faithful to the full experience of love. That is, he does not abstract one aspect of the experience and call it the whole experience. He does not strain nature out of nature; he does not over-spiritualize nature. This nameless poet would never have said, in the happier days of his love, that he had been led to his Sweet's chamber window by "a spirit in my feet"; and he certainly would not have added the coy disavowal, "who knows how?" But because the nameless poet refused to overspiritualize nature, we can accept the spirituality of the poem.

Another poem gives us another problem.

> Ah, what avails the sceptered race!
>   Ah, what the form divine!
> What every virtue, every grace!
>   Rose Aylmer, all were thine.
>
> Rose Aylmer, whom these wakeful eyes
>   May weep, but never see,
> A night of memories and sighs
>   I consecrate to thee.

This is another poem about lost love: a "soft" subject. Now, to one kind of poet the soft subject presents a sore temptation. Because it is soft in its natural state, he is inclined to feel that to get at its poetic essence he must make it softer still, that he must insist on its softness, that he must render it as "pure" as possible. At first glance, it may seem that Landor is trying to do just that. What he says seems to be emphatic, unqualified, and open. Not every power, grace, and virtue could avail to preserve his love. That statement insists on the pathetic contrast. And in the next stanza, wakefulness and tearfulness are mentioned quite unashamedly, along with memories and sighs. It is all blurted out, as pure as possible.

But only in the paraphrase is it "blurted." The actual quality of the first stanza is hard, not soft. It is a chiseled stanza, in which formality is insisted upon. We may observe the balance of the first and second lines; the balance of the first half with the second half of the third line, which recapitulates the structure of the first two lines; the balance of the two parts of the last line, though here the balance is merely a rhythmical and not a sense balance as in the preceding instances; the binders of discreet alliteration, repetition, and assonance. The stanza is built up, as it were, of units which are firmly defined and sharply separated, phrase by phrase, line by line. We have the formal control of the soft subject, ritual and not surrender.

But in the second stanza the rigor of this formality is somewhat abated, as the more general, speculative emphasis (why cannot pomp, virtue, and grace avail?) gives way to the personal emphasis, as though the repetition of the beloved's name had, momentarily, released the flood of feeling. The first line of the second stanza spills over into the second; the "wakeful eyes" as subject find their verb in the next line, "weep," and the *wake-weep* alliteration, along with pause after *weep*, points up the disintegration of the line, just as it emphasizes the situation. Then with the phrase "but never see" falling away from the long thrust of the rhetorical structure to the pause after *weep*, the poem seems to go completely soft, the frame is broken. But, even as the poet insists on "memories and sighs," in the last two lines he restores the balance. Notice the understatement of "A night." It says: "I know that life is a fairly complicated affair, and that I am committed to it and to its complications. I intend to stand by my commitment, as a man of integrity, that is, to live despite the grief. Since life is complicated, I cannot, if I am to live, spare too much time for indulging grief. I can give *a* night, but not all nights." The lover, like the hero of Frost's poem "Stopping by Woods on a Snowy Evening," tears himself from the temptation of staring into the treacherous, delicious blackness, for he, too, has "promises to keep." Or he resembles the Homeric heroes who, after the perilous passage is made, after their energy has saved their lives, and after they have beached their craft and eaten their meal, can then set aside an hour before sleep to mourn the comrades lost by the way—the heroes who, as Aldous Huxley says, understand realistically a whole truth as contrasted with a half-truth.

Is this a denial of the depth and sincerity of the grief? The soft reader, who wants the poem pure, may be inclined to say so. But let us look at the last line to see what it gives us in answer to this question. The answer seems to lie in the word *consecrate*. The meter thrusts this word at us; we observe that two of the three metrical accents in the line fall on syllables of this word, forcing it beyond its prose emphasis. The word is important and importance is justified, for the word tells us that the single night is not merely a lapse into weakness, a trivial event to be forgotten when the weakness is overcome. It is, rather, an event of the most extreme and focal importance, an event formally dedicated, "set apart for sacred uses," an event by which other events are to be measured. So the word *consecrate* formalizes, philosophizes, ritualizes the grief; it specifies what in the first stanza has been implied by style.

But here is another poem of grief, grief at the death of a child. It is "Bells for John Whiteside's Daughter," by John Crowe Ransom.

> There was such speed in her little body,
> And such lightness in her footfall,
> It is no wonder her brown study
> Astonishes us all.
>
> Her wars were bruited on our high window.
> We looked among orchard trees and beyond,
> Where she took arms against her shadow,

Or harried unto the pond

The lazy geese, like a snow cloud
Dripping their snow on the green grass,
Tricking and stopping, sleepy and proud,
Who cried in goose, Alas,

For the tireless heart within the little
Lady with rod that made them rise
From their noon apple-dreams, and scuttle
Goose-fashion under the skies!

But now go the bells, and we are ready;
In one house we are sternly stopped
To say we are vexed at her brown study,
Lying so primly propped.

Another soft subject, softer, if anything, than the subject of "Rose Aylmer," and it presents the same problem. But the problem is solved in a different way.

The first stanza is based on two time-honored clichés: first, "Heavens, won't that child ever be still, she is driving me distracted"; and second, "She was such an active, healthy-looking child, who would've ever thought she would just up and die?" In fact, the whole poem develops these clichés, and exploits, in a backhand fashion, the ironies implicit in their interrelation. And in this connection, we may note that the fact of the clichés, rather than more original or profound observations at the root of the poem, is important; there is in the poem the contrast between the staleness of the clichés and the shock of the reality. Further, we may note that the second cliché is an answer, savagely ironical in itself, to the first: the child you wished would be still *is* still, despite all that activity which had interrupted your adult occupations.

But such a savage irony is not the game here. It is too desperate, too naked, in a word, too pure. And ultimately, it is, in a sense, a meaningless irony if left in its pure state, because it depends on a mechanical, accidental contrast in nature, void of moral content. The poem is concerned with modifications and modulations of this brute, basic irony, modulations and modifications contingent upon an attitude taken toward it by a responsible human being, the speaker of the poem. The savagery is masked, or ameliorated.

In this connection, we may observe, first, the phrase "brown study." It is not the "frosted flower," the "marmoreal immobility," or any one of a thousand such phrases which would aim for the pure effect. It is merely the brown study which astonishes—a phrase which denies, as it were, the finality of the situation, underplays the pathos, and merely reminds one of those moments of childish pensiveness into which the grownup cannot penetrate. And the phrase itself is a cliché—the common now echoed in the uncommon.

Next, we may observe that stanzas two, three, and four simply document, with a busy, yet wavering rhythm (one sentence runs through the three stanzas), the tireless naughtiness which was once the cause of rebuke, the naughtiness which disturbed the mature goings-on in the room with the "high window." But the naughtiness is now transmuted into a kind of fanciful story-book dream world, in which geese are whiter than nature, and the grass greener, in which geese speak in goose language, saying "Alas," and have apple-dreams. It is a drowsy, delicious world, in which the geese are bigger than life, and more important. It is an unreal (now unreal because lost), stylized world. Notice how the phrase "the little lady with rod" works: the detached primness of "little lady"; the formal, stiff effect gained by the omission of the article before *rod*; the slightly unnatural use of the word *rod* itself, which sets some distance between us and the scene (perhaps with the hint of the fairy story, a magic wand, or a magic rod—not a common, everyday stick). But the stanzas tie back into the premises of the poem in other ways. The little girl, in her excess of energy, warred against her shadow. Is it crowding matters too hard to surmise that the shadow here achieves a sort of covert symbolic significance? The little girl lost her war against her "shadow," which was always with her. Certainly the phrase "tireless heart" has some rich connotations. And the geese which say "Alas" conspire with the family to deplore the excessive activity of the child. (They do not conspire to express the present grief, only the past vexation—an inversion of the method of the pastoral elegy, or of the method of the first two garden poems.)

The business of the three stanzas, then, may be said to be twofold. First, they make us believe more fully in the child and therefore in the fact of the grief itself. They "prove" the grief, and they show the deliciousness of the lost world which will never look the same from the high window. Second, and contrariwise, they "transcend" the grief, or at least give a hint of a means for transcending immediate anguish: the lost world is, in one sense, redeemed out of time; it enters the pages of the picture book where geese speak, where the untrue is true, where the fleeting is fixed. What was had cannot, after all, be lost. (By way of comparison—a comparison which, because extreme, may be helpful—we may think of the transcendence in *A la Recherche du Temps Perdu*.) The three stanzas, then, to state it in another way, have validated the first stanza and have prepared for the last.

The three stanzas have made it possible for us to say, when the bell tolls, "we are ready." Some kind of terms, perhaps not the best terms possible but some kind, has been made with the savage underlying irony. But the terms arrived at do not prevent the occasion from being a "stern" one. The transcendence is not absolute, and in the end is possible only because of an exercise of will and self-control. Because we control ourselves, we can say "vexed" and not some big word. And the word itself picks up the first of the domestic clichés on which the poem is based—the outburst of impatience at the naughty child who, by dying, has performed her most serious piece of naughtiness. But now the word comes to us charged with the burden of the poem, and further, as re-echoed here by the phrase "brown study," charged by the sentence in which it occurs: we are gathered formally, ritualistically, sternly together to say the word *vexed*. *Vexed* becomes the ritualistic, the summarizing word.

I have used the words *pure* and *impure* often in the foregoing pages, and I confess that I have used them rather loosely. But perhaps it has been evident that I have meant something like this: the pure poem tries to be pure by excluding, more or less rigidly, certain elements which might qualify or contradict its original impulse. In other words, the pure poems want to be, and desperately, all of a piece. It has also been evident, no doubt, that the kinds of impurity which are admitted or excluded by the various little anthology pieces which have been presented, are different in the different poems. This is only to be expected, for there is not one doctrine of "pure poetry"—not one definition of what constitutes impurity in poems—but many.

And not all of the doctrines are recent. When, for example, one cites Poe as the father of *the* doctrine of pure poetry, one is in error; Poe simply fathered *a* particular doctrine of pure poetry. One can find other doctrines of purity long antedating Poe. When Sir Philip Sidney, for example, legislated against tragicomedy, he was repeating a current doctrine of purity. When Ben Jonson told William Drummond that Donne, for not keeping of accent, deserved hanging, he was defending another kind of purity; and when Dryden spoke to save the ear of the fair sex from metaphysical perplexities in amorous poems, he was defending another kind of purity, just as he was defending another when he defined the nature of the heroic drama. The eighteenth century had a doctrine of pure poetry, which may be summed up under the word *sublimity*, but which involved two corollary doctrines, one concerning diction and the other concerning imagery. But at the same time that this century, by means of these corollary doctrines, was tidying up and purifying the doctrine derived by Longinus, it was admitting into the drama certain impurities which the theorists of the heroic drama would not have admitted.

But when we think of the modern doctrine of pure poetry, we usually think of Poe, as critic and poet, perhaps of Shelley, of the Symbolists, of the Abbé Bremond, perhaps of Pater, and certainly of George Moore and the

Imagists. We know Poe's position: the long poem is "a flat contradiction in terms," because intense excitement, which is essential in poetry, cannot be long maintained; the moral sense and the intellect function more satisfactorily in prose than in poetry, and, in fact, "Truth" and the "Passions," which are for Poe associated with the intellect and the moral sense, may actually be inimical to poetry; vagueness, suggestiveness are central virtues, for poetry has for "its object an *indefinite* instead of a *definite* pleasure"; poetry is not supposed to undergo close inspection, only a cursory glance, for it, "above all things, is a beautiful painting whose tints, to minute inspection, are confusion worse confounded, but start out boldly to the cursory glance of the connoisseur"; poetry aspires toward music, since it is concerned with "indefinite sensations, to which music is *essential*, since the comprehension of sweet sound is our most indefinite conception"; melancholy is the most poetical effect and enters into all the higher manifestations of beauty. We know, too, the Abbé Bremond's mystical interpretation, and the preface to George Moore's anthology, and the Imagist manifesto.

But these views are not identical. Shelley, for instance, delights in the imprecision praised and practiced by Poe, but he has an enormous appetite for "Truth" and the "Passions," which are, except for purposes of contrast, excluded by Poe. The Imagist manifesto, while excluding ideas, endorses precision rather than vagueness in rendering the image, and admits diction and objects which would have seemed impure to Poe and to many poets of the nineteenth century, and does not take much stock in the importance of verbal music. George Moore emphasizes the objective aspect of his pure poetry, which he describes as "something which the poet creates outside his own personality," and this is opposed to the subjective emphasis in Poe and Shelley; but he shares with both an emphasis on verbal music, and with the former a distaste for ideas.

But more recently, the notion of poetic purity has emerged in other contexts, contexts which sometimes obscure the connection of the new theories with the older theories. For instance, Max Eastman has a theory. "Pure poetry," he says in *The Literary Mind*, "is the pure effort to heighten consciousness." Mr. Eastman, we discover elsewhere in his book, would ban idea from poetry, but his motive is different from, say, the motive of Poe, and the difference is important: Poe would kick out the ideas because the ideas hurt the poetry, and Mr. Eastman would kick out the ideas because the poetry hurts the ideas. Only the scientist, he tells us, is entitled to have ideas on any subject, and the rest of the citizenry must wait to be told what attitude to take toward the ideas which they are not permitted to have except at second-hand. Literary truth, he says, is truth which is "uncertain or comparatively unimportant." But he does assign the poet a function—to heighten consciousness. In the light of this context we would have to rewrite his original definition: pure poetry is the pure effort to heighten consciousness, but the consciousness which is heightened must not have any connection with ideas, must involve no attitude toward any ideas.

Furthermore, to assist the poet in fulfilling the assigned function, Mr. Eastman gives him a somewhat sketchy doctrine of "pure" poetic diction. For instance, the word *bloated* is not admissible into a poem because it is, as he testifies, "sacred to the memory of dead fish," and the word *tangy* is, though he knows not exactly how, "intrinsically poetic." The notion of a vocabulary which is intrinsically poetic seems, with Mr. Eastman, to mean a vocabulary which indicates agreeable or beautiful objects. So we might rewrite the original definition to read: pure poetry is the pure effort to heighten consciousness, but the consciousness which is heightened must be a consciousness exclusively of agreeable or beautiful objects—certainly not a consciousness of any ideas.

In a recent book, *The Idiom of Poetry*, Frederick Pottle has discussed the question of pure poetry. He distinguishes another type of pure poetry in addition to the types already mentioned. He calls it the "Elliptical," and would include in it symbolist and metaphysical poetry (old and new) and some work by poets such as Collins, Blake, and Browning. He observes—without any perjorative implication, for he is a critical relativist and scarcely permits himself the luxury of evaluative judgments—that the contemporary product differs from older examples of the elliptical type in that "the modern poet goes much further in employing private experiences or ideas than would formerly have been thought legitimate." To the common reader, he says, "the prime characteristic of this kind of poetry is not the nature of its imagery but its obscurity: its urgent suggestion that you add something to the poem without telling you what that something is." This omitted "something" he interprets as the prose "frame"—to use his word—the statement of the occasion, the logical or narrative transitions, the generalized application derived from the poem, etc. In other words, this type of pure poetry contends that "the effect would be more powerful if we could somehow manage to feel the images fully and accurately without having the effect diluted by any words put in to give us a 'meaning'—that is, if we could expel all the talk *about* the imaginative realization and have the pure realization itself."

For the moment I shall pass the question of the accuracy of Mr. Pottle's description of the impulse of Elliptical Poetry and present the question which ultimately concerns him. How pure does poetry need to be in practice? That is the question which Mr. Pottle asks. He answers by saying that a great degree of impurity *may* be admitted, and cites our famous didactic poems, *The Faerie Queene, An Essay on Man, The Vanity of Human Wishes, The*

Excursion. That is the only answer which the relativist, and nominalist, can give. Then he turns to what he calls the hardest question in the theory of poetry: What kind of prosaism is acceptable and what is not? His answer, which he advances very modestly, is this:

> . . . the element of prose is innocent and even salutary when it appears as—take your choice of three metaphors—a background on which the images are projected, or a frame in which they are shown, or a thread on which they are strung. In short, when it serves a *structural* purpose. Prose in a poem seems offensive to me when . . . the prosaisms are sharp, obvious, individual, and ranked coordinately with the images.

At first glance this looks plausible, and the critic has used the sanctified word *structural.* But at second glance we may begin to wonder what the sanctified word means to the critic. It means something rather mechanical—background, frame, thread. The structure is a showcase, say a jeweler's showcase, in which the little jewels of poetry are exhibited, the images. The showcase shouldn't be ornamental itself ("sharp, obvious, individual," Mr. Pottle says), for it would then distract us from the jewels; it should be chastely designed, and the jewels should repose on black velvet and not on flowered chintz. But Mr. Pottle doesn't ask what the relation among the bright jewels should be. Not only does the showcase bear no relation to the jewels, but the jewels, apparently, bear no relation to each other. Each one is a shining little focus of heightened interest, and all together they make only such a pattern, perhaps, as may make it easier for the eye to travel from one little jewel to the next, when the time comes to move on. Structure becomes here simply a device of salesmanship, a well-arranged showcase.

It is all mechanical. And this means that Mr. Pottle, after all, is himself an exponent of pure poetry. He locates the poetry simply in the images, the nodes of "pure realization." This means that what he calls the "element of prose" includes definition of situation, movement of narrative, logical transition, factual description, generalization, ideas. Such things, for him, do not participate in the poetic effect of the poem; in fact, they work against the poetic effect, and so, though necessary as a frame, should be kept from being "sharp, obvious, individual."

I have referred to *The Idiom of Poetry*, first, because it is such an admirable and provocative book, sane, lucid, generous-spirited, and second, because, to my mind, it illustrates the insidiousness with which a doctrine of pure poetry can penetrate into the theory of a critic who is suspicious of such a doctrine. Furthermore, I have felt that Mr. Pottle's analysis might help me to define the common denominator of the various doctrines of pure poetry.

That common denominator seems to be the belief that poetry is an essence that is to be located at some particular place in a poem, or in some particular element. The exponent of pure poetry persuades himself that he has determined the particular something in which the poetry inheres, and then proceeds to decree that poems shall be composed, as nearly as possible, of that element and of nothing else. If we add up the things excluded by various critics and practitioners, we get a list like this:

1. ideas, truths, generalizations, "meaning"
2. precise, complicated, "intellectual" images
3. unbeautiful, disagreeable, or neutral materials
4. situation, narrative, logical transition
5. realistic details, exact descriptions, realism in general
6. shifts in tone or mood
7. irony
8. metrical variation, dramatic adaptations of rhythm, cacophony, etc.
9. meter itself
10. subjective and personal elements

No one theory of pure poetry excludes all of these items, and, as a matter of fact, the items listed are not on the same level of importance. Nor do the items always bear the same interpretation. For example, if one item seems to be central to discussions of pure poetry, it is the first: "ideas," it is said, "are not involved in the poetic effect, and may even be inimical to it." But this view can be interpreted in a variety of ways. If it is interpreted as simply meaning that the paraphrase of a poem is not equivalent to the poem, that the poetic gist is not to be defined as the statement embodied in the poem with the sugar-coating as bait, then the view can be held by opponents as well as exponents of any theory of pure poetry. We might scale down from this interpretation to the other extreme interpretation that the poem should merely give the sharp image in isolation. But there are many complicated and confused variations possible between the two extremes. There is, for example, the interpretation that "ideas," though they are not involved in the poetic effect, must appear in poems to provide, as Mr. Pottle's prosaisms do, a kind of frame, or thread, for the poetry—a spine to support the poetic flesh, or a Christmas tree on which the baubles of poetry are hung. T. S. Eliot has said something of this sort:

> The chief use of the "meaning" of a poem, in the ordinary sense, may be (for here again I am speaking of some kinds of poetry and not all) to satisfy one habit of the reader, to keep his mind diverted and quiet, while the poem does its work upon him: much as the imaginary burglar is always provided with a bit of nice meat for the house-dog.

Here, it would seem, Mr. Eliot has simply inverted the old sugar-coated-pill theory: the idea becomes the sugar-coating and the "poetry" becomes the medicine. This seems to say that the idea in a poem does not participate in the poetic effect, and seems to commit Mr. Eliot to a theory of pure poetry. But to do justice to the quotation, we should first observe that the parenthesis indicates that the writer is referring to some sort of provisional and superficial distinction and not to a fundamental one, and second observe that the passage is out of its context. In the context, Mr. Eliot goes on to say that some poets "become impatient of this 'meaning' [explicit statement of ideas in logical order] which seems superfluous, and perceive possibilities of intensity through its elimination." This may mean either of two things. It may mean that ideas do not participate in the poetic effect, or it may mean that, though they do participate in the poetic effect, they need not appear in the poem in an explicit and argued form. And this second reading would scarcely be a doctrine of pure poetry at all, for it would involve poetic casuistry and not poetic principle.

We might, however, illustrate the second interpretation by glancing at Marvell's "Horatian Ode" on Cromwell. Marvell does not give us narrative; he does not give us an account of the issues behind the Civil War; he does not state the two competing ideas which are dramatized in the poem, the idea of "sanction" and the idea of "efficiency." But the effect of the poem does involve those two factors; and the reserved irony, scarcely resolved, which emerges from the historical situation, is an irony derived from unstated materials and ideas. It is, to use Mr. Pottle's term again, a pure poem in so far as it is elliptical in method, but it is anything but a pure poem if by purity we mean the exclusion of idea from participation in the poetic effect. And Mr. Eliot's own practice implies that he believes that ideas do participate in the poetic effect. Otherwise, why did he put the clues to his ideas in the notes at the end of *The Waste Land* after so carefully excluding any explicit statement of them from the body of the poem? If he is regarding those ideas as mere bait—the "bit of nice meat for the house-dog"—he has put the ideas in a peculiar place, in the back of the book—like giving the dog the meat on the way out of the house with the swag, or giving the mouse the cheese after he is in the trap.

All this leads to the speculation that Marvell and Mr. Eliot have purged away statement of ideas from their poems, not because they wanted the ideas to participate less in the poetry, but because they wanted them to participate more fully, intensely, and immediately. This impulse, then, would account for the characteristic types of image, types in which precision, complication, and complicated intellectual relation to the theme are exploited; in other words, they are trying—whatever may be their final success—to carry the movement of mind to the center of the process. On these grounds they are the exact opposite of poets who, presumably on grounds of purity, exclude the movement of mind from the center of poetic process—from the internal structure of the poem—but pay their respects to it as a kind of footnote, or gloss, or application coming at the end. Marvell and Eliot, by their cutting away of frame, are trying to emphasize the participation of ideas in the poetic process. Then Elliptical Poetry is not, as Mr. Pottle says it is, a pure poetry at all; the elliptical poet is elliptical for purposes of inclusion, not exclusion.

But waiving the question of Elliptical Poetry, no one of the other theories does—or could—exclude all the items on the list above. And that fact may instruct us. If all of these items were excluded, we might not have any poem at all. For instance, we know how some critics have pointed out that even in the strictest Imagist poetry idea creeps in—when the image leaves its natural habitat and enters a poem, it begins to "mean" something. The attempt to read ideas out of the poetic party violates the unity of our being and the unity of our experience. "For this reason," as Santayana puts it, "philosophy, when a poet is not mindless, enters inevitably into his poetry, since it has entered into his life; or rather, the detail of things and the detail of ideas pass equally into his verse, when both alike lie in the path that has led him to his ideal. To object to theory in poetry would be like objecting to words there; for words, too, are symbols without the sensuous character of the things they stand for; and yet it is only by the net of new connections which words throw over things, in recalling them, that poetry arises at all. Poetry is an attenuation, a rehandling, an echo of crude experience; it is itself a theoretic vision of things at arm's length."

Does this not, then, lead us to the conclusion that poetry does not inhere in any particular element but depends upon the set of relationships, the structure, which we call the poem?

Then the question arises: what elements cannot be used in such a structure? I should answer that nothing that is available in human experience is to be legislated out of poetry. This does not mean that anything can be used in *any* poem, or that some materials or elements may not prove more recalcitrant than others, or that it might not be easy to have too much of some things. But it does mean that, granted certain contexts, any sort of material, a chemical formula for instance, might appear functionally in a poem. It also may mean that, other things being equal, the greatness of a poet depends upon the extent of the area of experience which he can master poetically.

Can we make any generalizations about the nature of the poetic structure? First, it involves resistances, at various levels. There is the tension between the rhythm of the poem and the rhythm of speech (a tension which is very low at the extreme of free verse and at the extreme of verse such as that of "Ulalume," which verges toward a walloping doggerel); between the formality of the rhythm and the informality of the language; between the particular and the general, the concrete and the abstract; between the elements of even the simplest metaphor; between the beautiful and the ugly; between ideas (as in Marvell's poem); between the elements involved in irony (as in "Bells for John Whiteside's Daughter" or "Rose Aylmer"); between prosaism and poeticisms (as in "Western Wind").

This list is not intended to be exhaustive; it is intended to be merely suggestive. But it may be taken to imply that the poet is like the jujitsu expert; he wins by utilizing the resistance of his opponent—the materials of the poem. In other words, a poem, to be good, must earn itself. It is a motion toward a point of rest, but if it is not a resisted motion, it is motion of no consequence. For example, a poem which depends upon stock materials and stock responses is simply a toboggan slide, or a fall through space. And the good poem must, in some way, involve the resistances; it must carry something of the context of its own creation: it must come to terms with Mercutio.

This is another way of saying that a good poem involves the participation of the reader; it must, as Coleridge puts it, make the reader into "an active creative being." Perhaps we can see this most readily in the case of tragedy: the determination of good or evil is not a "given" in tragedy, it is something to be earned in the process, and even the tragic villain must be "loved." We must kill him, as Brutus killed Caesar, not as butchers but as sacrificers. And all of this adds up to the fact that the structure is a dramatic structure, a movement through action toward rest, through complication toward simplicity of effect.

In the foregoing discussion, I have deliberately omitted reference to another type of pure poetry, a type which tends to become dominant in an age of political crisis and social disorientation. Perhaps the most sensible description of this type can be found in an essay by Herbert Muller:

> If it is not the primary business of the poet to be eloquent about these matters [faith and ideals], it still does not follow that he has more dignity or wisdom than those who are, or that

he should have more sophistication. At any rate the fact is that almost all poets of the past did freely make large, simple statements, and not in their prosy or lax moments.

Mr. Muller then goes on to illustrate by quoting three famous large, simple statements:

> *E'n la sua volontade è nostra pace*

and

> We are such stuff
> As dreams are made on; and our little life
> Is rounded with a sleep.

and

> The mind is its own place, and in itself
> Can make a heaven of hell, a hell of heaven.

Mr. Muller is here attacking the critical emphasis on ironic tension in poetry. His attack really involves two lines of argument. First, the poet is not wiser than the statesman, philosopher, or saint, people who are eloquent about faith and ideals and who say what they mean, without benefit of irony. This Platonic line of argument is, I think, off the point in the present context. Second, the poets of the past have made large, simple affirmations, have said what they meant. This line of argument is very much on the point.

Poets *have* tried very hard, for thousands of years, to say what they mean. Not only have they tried to say what they mean, they have tried to prove what they mean. The saint proves his vision by stepping cheerfully into the fires. The poet, somewhat less spectacularly, proves his vision by submitting it to the fires of irony—to the drama of his structure—in the hope that the fires will refine it. In other words, the poet wishes to indicate that his vision has been earned, that it can survive reference to the complexities and contradictions of experience. And irony is one such device of reference.

In this connection let us look at the first of Mr. Muller's exhibits. The famous line occurs in Canto III of the *Paradiso*. It is spoken by Piccarda Donati, in answer to Dante's question as to why she does not desire to rise higher than her present sphere, the sphere of the moon. But it expresses, in unequivocal terms, a central theme of the *Commedia*, as of Christian experience. On the one hand, it may be a pious truism, fit for sampler work, and on the other hand, it may be a burning conviction, tested and earned. Dante, in his poem, sets out to show how it has been earned and tested.

One set of ironic contrasts which centers on this theme concerns, for instance, the opposition between the notion of human justice and the notion of divine justice. The story of Paolo and Francesca is so warm, appealing, and pathetic in its human terms, and their punishment so savage and unrelenting, so incommensurable, it seems, with the fault, that Dante, torn by the conflict, falls down as a dead body falls. Or Farinata, the enemy of Dante's house, is presented by the poet in terms of his human grandeur, which now, in Hell, is transmuted into a superhuman grandeur,

com' avesse l'inferno in gran dispitto.

Ulysses remains a hero, a hero who should draw special applause from Dante, who defined the temporal end of man as the conquest of knowledge. But Ulysses is damned, as the great Brutus is damned, who hangs from the jaws of the fiend in the lowest pit of traitors. So divine justice is set over against human pathos, human dignity, human grandeur, human intellect, human justice. And we recall how Virgil, more than once, reminds Dante that he must not apply human standards to the sights he sees. It is this long conflict, which appears in many forms, this ironic tension, which finally gives body to the simple eloquence of the line in question; the statement is meaningful, not for what it says, but for what has gone before. It is earned. It has been earned by the entire poem.

I do not want to misrepresent Mr. Muller. He does follow his quotations by the sentence: "if they are properly qualified in the work as a whole, they may still be taken straight, they *are* [he italicizes the word] taken so in recollection as in their immediate impact." But how can we take a line "straight," in either "recollection" or "immediate impact," unless we ignore what "properly qualified" the line in "the work as a whole"? And if we do take it so, are we not violating, very definitely, the poet's meaning, for the poet means the *poem*, he doesn't mean the line.

It would be interesting to try to develop the contexts of the other passages which Mr. Muller quotes. But in any case, he is simply trying, in his essay, to guard against what he considers to be, rightly or wrongly, a too narrow description of poetry; he is not trying to legislate all poetry into the type of simple eloquence, the unqualified statement of "faith and ideals." But we have also witnessed certain, probably preliminary, attempts to legislate literature into becoming a simple, unqualified, "pure" statement of faith and ideals. We have seen the writers of the 1920s called the "irresponsibles." We have seen writers such as Proust, Eliot, Dreiser, and Faulkner called writers of the "death drive." Why are these writers condemned? Because they have tried, within the limits of their gifts, to remain faithful to the complexities of the problems with which they are dealing, because they have refused to take the easy statement as solution, because they have tried to define the context in which, and the terms by which, faith and ideals may be earned.

This method, however, will scarcely satisfy the mind which is hot for certainties; to that mind it will seem merely an index to lukewarmness, indecision, disunity, treason. The new theory of purity would purge out all complexities and all ironies and all self-criticism. And this theory will forget that the hand-me-down faith, the hand-me-down ideals, no matter what the professed content, is in the end not only meaningless but vicious. It is vicious because, as parody, it is the enemy of all faith.

HAROLD C. GODDARD

Romeo and Juliet

One word has dominated the criticisms of *Romeo and Juliet:* "star-cross'd."

> From forth the fatal loins of these two foes,

says the Prologue-Chorus,

> A pair of star-cross'd lovers take their life.

"Star-cross'd" backed by "fatal" has pretty much surrendered this drama to
the astrologers. "In this play," says one such interpreter, "simply the Fates
have taken this young pair and played a cruel game against them with loaded
dice, unaided by any evil in men." That is merely an extreme expression of
the widely held view that makes *Romeo and Juliet,* in contrast with all Shakespeare's later tragedies, a tragedy of accident rather than of character and on
that account a less profound and less universal work. That this play betrays
signs of immaturity and lacks some of the marks of mastery that are common
to the other tragedies may readily be granted. But that its inferiority is due
to the predominance of accident over character ought not to be conceded
without convincing demonstration. The burden of proof is certainly on those
who assert it, for nowhere else does Shakespeare show any tendency to

From *The Meaning of Shakespeare.* © 1951 University of Chicago.

believe in fate in this sense. The integrity of his mind makes it highly unlikely that in just one instance he would have let the plot of the story he was dramatizing warp his convictions about freedom.

The theme of *Romeo and Juliet* is love and violence and their interactions. In it these two mightiest of mighty opposites meet each other squarely—and one wins. And yet the other wins. This theme in itself makes *Romeo and Juliet* an astrological play in the sense that it is concerned throughout with Venus and Mars, with love and "war," and with little else. Nothing ever written perhaps presents more simply what results from the conjunction of these two "planets." But that does not make it a fatalistic drama. It all depends on what you mean by "stars." If by stars you mean the material heavenly bodies exercising from birth a predestined and inescapable occult influence on man, Romeo and Juliet were no more star-crossed than any lovers, even though their story was more unusual and dramatic. But if by stars you mean—as the deepest wisdom of the ages, ancient and modern, does—a psychological projection on the planets and constellations of the unconsciousness of man, which in turn is the accumulated experience of the race, then Romeo and Juliet and all the other characters of the play are star-crossed as every human being is who is passionately alive.

> In tragic life, God wot,
> No villain need be! Passions spin the plot,
> We are betrayed by what is false within.

The "villain" need not be a conspicuous incarnation of evil like Richard III or Iago; the "hero" himself may be the "villain" by being a conspicuous incarnation of weakness as was another Richard or a Troilus. Or the "villain" may consist in a certain chemical interplay of the passions of two or more characters. To seek a special "tragic flaw" in either Romeo or Juliet is foolish and futile. From pride down, we all have flaws enough to make of every life and of life itself a perpetual and universal tragedy. Altering his source to make the point unmistakable, Shakespeare is at pains to show that, however much the feud between Capulets and Montagues had to do with it incidentally, the tragedy of this play flowed immediately from another cause entirely. But of that in its place. Enough now if we have raised a suspicion that the "star-cross'd" of the Prologue should be taken in something other than a literal sense, or, better, attributed to the Chorus, not to the poet. The two are far from being the same.

In retrospect, Shakespeare's plays, which in one sense culminate in *King Lear* and in another in *The Tempest*, are seen to deal over and over with the same underlying subject that dominates the Greek drama: the relation of the generations. *Romeo and Juliet*, as the first play of its author in which this subject is central, assumes a profound seminal as well as intrinsic interest on that account. It points immediately in this respect to *Henry IV* and *Hamlet*, and ultimately to *King Lear* and *The Tempest*.

This theme of "the fathers" is merely another way of expressing the theme of "the stars." For the fathers are the stars and the stars are the fathers in the sense that the fathers stand for the accumulated experience of the past, for tradition, for authority, and hence for the two most potent forces that mold and so impart "destiny" to the child's life. Those forces, of course, are heredity and training, which between them create that impalpable mental environment, inner and outer, that is even more potent that either of them alone. The hatred of the hostile houses in *Romeo and Juliet* is an inheritance that every member of these families is born into as truly as he is born with the name Capulet or Montague. Their younger generations have no more choice in the matter than they have choice of the language they will grow up to speak. They suck in the venom with their milk. "So is the will of a living daughter curbed by the will of a dead father," as Portia puts it in *The Merchant of Venice*. The daughter may be a son and the father may be living, but the principle is the same. Thus the fathers cast the horoscopes of the children in advance—and are in that sense their stars. If astrology is itself, as it is, a kind of primitive and unconscious psychology, then the identity of the stars and the fathers becomes even more pronounced.

Now there is just one agency powerful enough in youth to defy and cut across this domination of the generations, and that is love. Love also is a "star" but in another and more celestial sense. Romeo, of the Montagues, after a sentimental and unrequited languishing after one Rosaline, falls in love at first sight with Juliet, of the Capulets, and instantly the instilled enmity of generations is dissipated like mist by morning sunshine, and the love that embraces Juliet embraces everything that Juliet touches or that touches her.

> My bounty is a boundless as the sea,
> My love as deep; the more I give to thee,
> The more I have, for both are infinite.

The words—music, imagery, and thought uniting to make them as wonderful as any ever uttered about love—are Juliet's, but Romeo's love is as deep—almost. It is love's merit, not his, that his enemies suddenly become glorified with the radiance of the medium through which he now sees every-thing. Hostility simply has nothing to breathe in such a transcendental atmosphere. It is through this effect of their love on both lovers, and the poetry in which they spontaneously embody it, that Shakespeare convinces us it is no mere infatuation, but love indeed in its divine sense. Passion it is, of course, but that contaminated term has in our day become helpless to express it. Purity would be the perfect word for it if the world had not forgotten that purity is simply Greek for fire.

II

Shakespeare sees to it that we shall not mistake this white flame of Romeo's love, or Juliet's, for anything lower by opposing to the lovers two of the impurest characters he ever created, Mercutio and the Nurse. And yet, in spite of them, it has often been so mistaken. Mercutio and the Nurse are masterpieces of characterization so irresistible that many are tempted to let them arrogate to themselves as virtue what is really the creative merit of their maker. They are a highly vital pair, brimming with life and fire—but fire in a less heavenly sense than the one just mentioned. Juliet, at the most critical moment of her life, sums up the Nurse to all eternity in one word. When, in her darkest hour, this woman who has acted as mother to her from birth goes back on her completely, in a flash of revelation the girl sees what she is, and, reversing in one second the feeling of a lifetime, calls her a fiend ("most wicked fiend"). She could not have chosen a more accurate term, for the Nurse is playing at the moment precisely the part of the devil in a morality play. And Juliet's "ancient damnation" is an equally succinct description of her sin. What more ancient damnation is there than sensuality—and all the other sins it brings in its train? Those who dismiss the Nurse as just a coarse old woman whose loquacity makes us laugh fail hopelessly to plumb the depth of her depravity. It was the Nurse's desertion of her that drove Juliet to Friar Laurence and the desperate expedient of the sleeping potion. Her cowardice was a link in the chain that led to Juliet's death.

The Nurse has sometimes been compared with Falstaff—perhaps the poet's first comic character who clearly surpassed her. Any resemblance between them is superficial, for they are far apart as the poles. Falstaff was at home in low places but the sun of his imagination always accompanied him as a sort of disinfectant. The Nurse had no imagination in any proper sense. No sensualist—certainly no old sensualist—ever has. Falstaff loved Hal. What the Nurse's "love" for Juliet amounted to is revealed when she advises her to make the best of a bad situation and take Paris (bigamy and all). The man she formerly likened to a toad suddenly becomes superior to an eagle.

Go, counsellor,

cries Juliet, repudiating her Satan without an instant's hesitation,

Thou and my bosom henceforth shall be twain.

It is the rejection of the Nurse. But unlike Falstaff, when he is rejected, she carries not one spark of our sympathy or pity with her, and a pathetic account of her death, as of his, would be unthinkable. We scorn her as utterly as Juliet does.

III

The contrast between Friar Laurence and the Nurse even the most casual reader or spectator could scarcely miss. The difference between the spiritual adviser of Romeo and the worldly confidant of Juliet speaks for itself. The resemblance of Mercutio to the Nurse is more easily overlooked, together with the analogy between the part he plays in Romeo's life and the part she plays in Juliet's. Yet it is scarcely too much to say that the entire play is built around that resemblance and that analogy.

The indications abound that Shakespeare created these two to go together. To begin with, they hate each other on instinct, as two rival talkers generally do, showing how akin they are under the skin. "A gentleman, nurse," says Romeo of Mercutio, "that loves to hear himself talk, and will speak more in a minute than he will stand to in a month." The cap which Romeo thus quite innocently hands the Nurse fits her so perfectly that she immediately puts it on in two speeches about Mercutio which are typical examples of *her* love of hearing herself talk and of saying things *she* is powerless to stand by:

> An a' speak any thing against me, I'll take him down, an 'a were lustier than he is, and twenty such Jacks; and if I cannot, I'll find those that shall. Scurvy knave! I am none of his flirt-gills; I am none of his skains-mates. (*Turning to* PETER, *her man*) And thou must stand by too, and suffer every knave to use me at his pleasure! . . . Now, afore God, I am so vexed, that every part about me quivers. Scurvy knave!

That last, and the tone of the whole, show that there was a genuinely vicious element in the Nurse under her superficial good nature, as there invariably is in an old sensualist; and I do not believe it is exceeding the warrant of the text to say that the rest of the speech in which she warns

Romeo against gross behavior toward her young gentlewoman—quite in the manner of Polonius and Laertes warning Ophelia against Hamlet—proves that in her heart she would have been delighted to have him corrupt her provided she could have shared the secret and been the go-between. "A bawd, a bawd, a bawd!" is Mercutio's succinct description of her.

But, as usual, when a man curses someone else, he characterizes himself. In what sense Mercutio is a bawd appears only too soon. In the meantime what a pity it is that he is killed off so early in the action to allow no full and final encounter between these two fountains of loquacity! "Nay, an there were two such, we should have none shortly." Mercutio himself says it in another connection, but it applies perfectly to this incomparable pair. Their roles are crowded with parallelisms even down to what seem like the most trivial details. "We'll to dinner thither," says Mercutio, for example, parting from Romeo in Act II, scene 4. "Go, I'll to dinner," says the Nurse on leaving Juliet at the end of scene 5. A tiny touch. But they are just the two who would be certain never to miss a meal. In Shakespeare even such trifles have significance.

The fact is that Mercutio and the Nurse are simply youth and old age of the same type. He is aimed at the same goal she has nearly attained. He would have become the same sort of old man that she is old woman, just as she was undoubtedly the same sort of young girl that he is young man. They both think of nothing but sex—except when they are so busy eating or quarreling that they can think of nothing. (I haven't forgotten Queen Mab; I'll come to her presently.) Mercutio cannot so much as look at the clock without a bawdy thought. So permeated is his language with indecency that most of it passes unnoticed not only by the innocent reader but by all not schooled in Elizabethan smut. Even on our own unsqueamish stage an unabridged form of his role in its twentieth-century equivalent would not be tolerated. Why does Shakespeare place the extreme example of this man's soiled fantasies precisely before the balcony scene? Why but to stress the complete freedom from sensuality of Romeo's passion? Place Mercutio's dirtiest words, as Shakespeare does, right beside Romeo's apostrophe to his "bright angel" and all the rest of that scene where the lyricism of young love reaches one of its loftiest pinnacles in all poetry—and what remains to be said for Mercutio? Nothing—except that he is Mercutio. His youth, the hot weather, the southern temperament, the fashion among Italian gentlemen of the day, are unavailing pleas; not only Romeo, but Benvolio, had those things to contend with also. And they escaped. Mercury is close to the sun. But it was the material sun, Sol, not the god, Helios, that Mercutio was close to. Beyond dispute, this man had vitality, wit, and personal magnetism. But personal magnetism combined with sexuality and pugnacity is one of the most dangerous mixtures that can exist. The unqualified laudation that Mercutio has frequently received, and the suggestion that Shakespeare had to kill him off lest he quite set the play's titular hero in the shade, are the best proof of the truth of that statement. Those who are themselves seduced by Mercutio are not likely to be good judges of him. It may be retorted that Mercutio is nearly always a success on the stage, while Romeo is likely to be insipid. The answer to that is that while Mercutios are relatively common, Romeos are excessively rare. If Romeo proves insipid, he has be wrongly cast or badly acted.

"But how about Queen Mab?" it will be asked. The famous description of her has been widely held to be quite out of character and has been set down as an outburst of poetry from the author put arbitrarily in Mercutio's mouth. But the judgment "out of character" should always be a last resort. Undoubtedly the lines, if properly his, do reveal an unsuspected side of Mercutio. The prankish delicacy of some of them stands out in pleasing contrast with his grosser aspects. The psychology of this is sound. The finer side of a sensualist is suppressed and is bound to come out, if at all, incidentally, in just such a digression as this seems to be. Shakespeare can be trusted not to leave such things out. Few passages in his plays, however, have been more praised for the wrong reasons. The account of Queen Mab is supposed to prove Mercutio's imagination: under his pugnacity there was a poet. It would be nearer the truth, I think, to guess that Shakespeare put it in as an example of what poetry is popularly held to be and is not. The lines on Queen Mab are indeed delightful. But imagination in any proper sense they are not. They are sheer fancy. Moreover, Mercutio's anatomy and philosophy of dreams prove that he knows nothing of their genuine import. He dubs them

> the children of an idle brain,
> Begot of nothing but vain fantasy.

Perhaps his are—the Queen Mab lines would seem to indicate as much. Romeo, on the other hand, hold that dreamers "dream things true," and gives a definition of them that for combined brevity and beauty would be hard to better. They are "love's shadows." And not only from what we can infer about his untold dream on this occasion, but from all the dreams and premonitions of both Romeo and Juliet throughout the play, they come from a fountain of wisdom somewhere beyond time. Primitives distinguish between "big" and "little" dreams. (Aeschylus makes the same distinction in *Prometheus Bound*.) Mercutio, with his aldermen and gnats and coachmakers and sweetmeats and parsons and drums and ambuscadoes, may tell us a little about the littlest of dreams. He thinks that dreamers are still in their day world at night. Both Romeo and Juliet know that there are dreams that come from as far below the surface of the world as was that prophetic tomb at the bottom of which she saw him "as one dead" at their last parting. Finally, how characteristic of Mercutio that he should make Queen Mab a midwife and blemish his description of her by turning her into a "hag" whose function it is to bring an end to maidenhood. Is this another link between Mercutio and the Nurse? Is Shakespeare here preparing the way for his intimation that she would be quite capable of assisting in Juliet's corruption? It might well be. When Shakespeare writes a speech that seems to be out of character, it generally, as in this case, deserves the closest scrutiny.

And there is another justification of the Queen Mab passage. Romeo and Juliet not only utter poetry; they are poetry. The loveliest comment on Juliet I ever heard expressed this to perfection. It was made by a girl only a little older than Juliet herself. When Friar Laurence recommends philosophy to Romeo as comfort in banishment, Romeo replies:

> Hang up philosophy!
> Unless philosophy can make a Juliet . . .
> It helps not, it prevails not. Talk no more.

"Philosophy can't," the girl observed, "but poetry can—and it did!" Over against the poetry of Juliet, Shakespeare was bound, by the demands of contrast on which all art rests, to offer in the course of his play examples of poetry in various verbal, counterfeit, or adulterate estates.

> This precious book of love, this unbound lover,
> To beautify him, only lacks a cover.

That is Lady Capulet on the prospective bridegroom, Paris. It would have taken the play's booby prize for "poetry" if Capulet himself had not outdone it in his address to the weeping Juliet:

> How now! a conduit, girl? What, still in tears?
> Evermore showering? In one little body
> Thou counterfeit'st a bark, a sea, a wind;
> For still thy eyes, which I may call the sea,
> Do ebb and flow with tears; the bark thy body is,
> Sailing in this salt flood; the winds, thy sighs;
> Who, raging with thy tears, and they with them,
> Without a sudden calm, will overset
> Thy tempest-tossed body.

It is almost as if Shakespeare were saying in so many words: That is how poetry is not written. Yet, a little later, when the sight of his daughter, dead as all suppose, shakes even this egotist into a second of sincerity, he can say:

> Death lies on her like an untimely frost
> Upon the sweetest flower of all the field.

There is poetry, deep down, even in Capulet. But the instant passes and he is again talking about death as his son-in-law—and all the rest. The Nurse's vain repetitions in this scene are further proof that she is a heathen. Her O-lamentable-day's only stress the lack of one syllable of genuine grief or love such as Juliet's father shows. These examples all go to show what Shakespeare is up to in the Queen Mab speech. It shines, and even seems profound, beside the utterances of the Capulets and the Nurse. But it fades, and grows superficial, beside Juliet's and Romeo's. It is one more shade of what passes for poetry but is not.

IV

The crisis of *Romeo and Juliet*, so far as Romeo is concerned, is the scene (just after the secret marriage of the two lovers) in which Mercutio and Tybalt are slain and Romeo banished. It is only two hundred lines long. Of these two hundred lines, some forty are introduction and sixty epilogue to the main action. As for the other hundred that come between, it may be doubted that Shakespeare to the end of his career ever wrote another hundred that surpassed them in the rapidity, inevitability, and psychologic truth of the succession of events that they comprise. There are few things in dramatic literature to match them. And yet I think they are generally misunderstood. The scene is usually taken as the extreme precipitation in the play of the Capulet-Montague feud; whereas Shakespeare goes out of his way to prove that at most the feud is merely the occasion of the quarrel. Its cause he places squarely in the temperament and character of Mercutio, and Mercutio, it is only too easy to forget, is neither a Capulet nor a Montague, but a kinsman of the Prince who rules Verona, and, as such, is under special obligation to preserve a neutral attitude between the two houses.

This will sound to some like mitigating the guilt of Tybalt. But Tybalt has enough to answer for without making him responsible for Mercutio's sins.

The nephew of Lady Capulet is as dour a son of pugnacity as Mercutio is a dashing one:

> What, drawn, and talk of peace! I hate the word,
> As I hate hell.

These words—almost the first he speaks in the play—give Tybalt's measure. "More than prince of cats," Mercutio calls him, which is elevated to "king of cats" in the scene in which he mounts the throne of violence. (It is a comment on the Nurse's insight into human nature that she speaks of this fashionable desperado as "O courteous Tybalt! honest gentleman!") Mercutio's contempt for Tybalt is increased by the latter's affectation of the latest form in fencing: "He fights as you sing prick-song, keeps time, distance, and proportion. . . . The pox of such antic, lisping, affecting fantasticoes; these new tuners of accents!" Yet but a moment later, in an exchange of quips with Romeo, we find Mercutio doing with his wit just what he has scorned Tybalt for doing with his sword. For all their differences, as far as fighting goes Mercutio and Tybalt are two of a kind and by the former's rule are predestined to extinction: "an there were two such, we should have none shortly, for one would kill the other." When one kills the other, there is not one left, but none. That is the arithmetic of it. The encounter is not long postponed.

Tybalt is outraged when he discovers that a Montague has invaded the Capulet mansion on the occasion of the ball when Romeo first sees Juliet. But for his uncle he would assail the intruder on the spot:

> Patience perforce with wilful choler meeting
> Makes my flesh tremble in their different greeting.
> I will withdraw; but this intrusion shall
> Now seeming sweet convert to bitter gall.

He is speaking of the clash between patience and provocation in himself. But he might be prophesying his meeting with Romeo. As the third act opens, he is hunting his man.

Tybalt is not the only one who is seeking trouble. The first forty lines of the crisis scene are specifically devised to show that Mercutio was out to have a fight under any and all circumstances and at any price. As well ask a small boy and a firecracker to keep apart as Mercutio and a quarrel. Sensuality and pugnacity are the poles of his nature. In the latter respect he is a sort of Mediterranean Hotspur, his frank southern animality taking the place of the idealistic "honour" of his northern counterpart. He is as fiery in a literal as Romeo is in a poetic sense.

The scene is a public place. Enter Mercutio and Benvolio. Benvolio knows his friend:

I pray thee, good Mercutio, let's retire.
The day is hot, the Capulets abroad,
And, if we meet, we shall not 'scape a brawl,
For now, these hot days, is the mad blood stirring.

Mercutio retorts with a description of the cool-tempered Benvolio that makes him out an inveterate hothead:

> Thou! why, thou wilt quarrel with a man that hath a hair more, or a hair less, in his beard, than thou hast. Thou wilt quarrel with a man for cracking nuts, having no other reason but because thou hast hazel eyes. What eye but such an eye would spy out such a quarrel? Thy head is as full of quarrels as an egg is full of meat, and yet thy head hath been beaten as addle as an egg for quarrelling. Thou hast quarrelled with a man for coughing in the street, because he hath wakened thy dog that hath lain asleep in the sun. Didst thou not fall out with a tailor for wearing his new doublet before Easter? with another, for tying his new shoes with old riband?

This, the cautious and temperate Benvolio! As Mercutio knows, it is nothing of the sort. It is an ironic description of himself. It is he, not his friend, who will make a quarrel out of anything—out of nothing, rather, and give it a local habitation and a name, as a poet does with the creatures of his imagination. Mercutio is pugnacity in its pure creative state. At the risk of the Prince's anger, he makes his friend Romeo's cause his own and roams the streets in the hope of encountering some Capulet with whom to pick a quarrel. The feud is only a pretext. If it hadn't been that, it would have been something else. The Chorus may talk about "stars," but in this case Mars does not revolve in the skies on the other side of the Earth from Venus, but resides on earth right under the jerkin of this particular impulsive youth, Mercutio. Or if this "fate" be a god rather than a planet, then Mercutio has opened his heart and his home to him with unrestrained hospitality. So Romeo is indeed "star-cross'd" in having Mercutio for a friend.

Mercutio has no sooner finished his topsy-turvy portrait of Benvolio than Tybalt and his gang come in to reveal which of the two the description fits. Tybalt is searching for Romeo, to whom he has just sent a challenge, and recognizing Romeo's friends begs "a word with one of you." He wishes, presumably, to ask where Romeo is. But Mercutio, bent on provocation, retorts, "make it a word and a blow." Benvolio tries in vain to intervene. Just as things are getting critical, Romeo enters, and Tybalt turns from Mercutio to the man he is really seeking:

> Romeo, the love I bear thee can afford
> No better term than this,—thou art a villain.

Here is the most direct and galling of insults. Here are Mercutio, Benvolio, and the rest waiting to see how Romeo will take it. The temperature is blistering in all senses. And what does Romeo say?

> Tybalt, the reason that I have to love thee
> Doth much excuse the appertaining rage
> To such a greeting; villain am I none;
> Therefore farewell; I see thou know'st me not.

We who are in the secret know that "the reason" is Juliet and that his love for her is capable of wrapping all Capulets in its miraculous mantle, even "the king of cats."

But Tybalt is intent on a fight and will not be put off by kindness however sincere or deep. "Boy," he comes back insolently,

> this shall not excuse the injuries
> That thou hast done me; therefore turn and draw.

Romeo, however, is in the power of something that makes him impervious to insults:

> I do protest I never injur'd thee,
> But love thee better than thou canst devise
> Till thou shalt know the reason of my love;
> And so, good Capulet,—which name I tender
> As dearly as my own,—be satisfied.

The world has long since decided what to think of a man who lets himself be called a villain without retaliating. Romeo, to put it in one word, proves himself, according to the world's code, a mollycoddle. And indeed a mollycoddle might act exactly as Romeo appears to. But if Romeo is a mollycoddle, then Jesus was a fool to talk about loving one's enemies, for Romeo, if anyone ever did, is doing just that at this moment. And Juliet was demented to talk about love being boundless and infinite, for here Romeo is about to prove that faith precisely true. Those who think that Jesus, and Juliet, and Romeo were fools will have plenty of backing. The "fathers" will be on their side. They will have the authority of the ages and the crowd. Only a philosopher or two, a few lovers, saints, and poets will be against them. The others will echo the

> O calm, dishonourable, vile submission!

with which Mercutio draws his rapier and begins hurling insults at Tybalt that make Tybalt's own seem tame:

> MER.: Tybalt, you rat-catcher, will you walk?
> TYB.: What wouldst thou have with me?
> MER.: Good king of cats, nothing but one of your nine
> lives.

And Mercutio threatens to stick him before he can draw if he does not do so instantly. What can Tybalt do but draw? "I am for you," he cries, as he does so.

Such, however, is the power of Romeo's love that even now he attempts to prevent the duel:

> Gentle Mercutio, put thy rapier up.

But Mercutio pays no attention and the two go to it. If ever a quarrel scene defined the central offender and laid the responsibility at one man's door, this is the scene and Mercutio is the man. It takes two to make a quarrel. Romeo, the Montague, will not fight. Tybalt, the Capulet, cannot fight if Romeo will not. With Mercutio Tybalt has no quarrel. The poet takes pains to make that explicit in a startling way. "Peace be with you, sir," are the words Tybalt addresses to Mercutio when Romeo first enters. *That* from the man who once cried,

> peace! I hate the word,
> As I hate hell.

Now we see why Shakespeare had him say it. It was in preparation for this scene. Thus he lets one word exonerate Tybalt of the responsibility for what ensues between himself and Mercutio.

And now, condensed into the fractional part of a second, comes the crisis in Romeo's life. Not later, when he decides to kill Tybalt, but now. Now is the moment when two totally different universes wait as it were on the turning of a hand. There is nothing of its kind to surpass it in all Shakespeare, not even in *Hamlet* or *King Lear*, not, one is tempted to think, in all the drama of the world. Here, if anywhere, Shakespeare shows that the fate we attribute to the stars lies in our own souls.

> Our remedies oft in ourselves do lie,
> Which we ascribe to heaven: the fated sky
> Gives us free scope.

Romeo had free scope. For, if we are free to choose between two compulsions, we are in so far free. Romeo was free to act under the compulsion of force or under the compulsion of love—under the compulsion of the stars, that is, in either of two opposite senses. Granted that the temptation to surrender to the former was at the moment immeasurably great, the power of the latter, if Juliet spoke true, was greater yet:

> My bounty is as boundless as the sea,
> My love as deep; the more I give to thee,
> The more I have, for both are *infinite.*

Everything that has just preceded shows that the real Romeo wanted to have utter faith in Juliet's faith. "Genius trusts its faintest intimation," says Emerson, "against the testimony of all history." But Romeo, whose intimations were not faint but strong, falls back on the testimony of all history that only force can overcome force. He descends from the level of love to the level of violence and attempts to part the fighters with his sword.

> Draw, Benvolio; beat down their weapons.
> Gentlemen, for shame, forbear this outrage!
> Tybalt, Mercutio, the prince expressly hath
> Forbidden bandying in Verona streets.
> Hold, Tybalt! good Mercutio!

Here, if anywhere, the distinction between drama and poetry becomes clear. Drama is a portrayal of human passions eventuating in acts. Poetry is a picture of life in its essence. On the level of drama, we are with Romeo absolutely. His purpose is noble, his act endearingly impulsive. We echo that purpose and identify ourselves with that act. In the theater we do, I mean, and under the aspect of time. But how different under the aspect of eternity! There the scene is a symbolic picture of life itself, of faith surrendering to force, of love trying to gain its end by violence—only to discover, as it soon does, and as we do too, that what it has attained instead is death. A noble motive never yet saved a man from the consequences of an unwise act, and Romeo's own words to Mercutio as he draws his sword are an unconscious confession in advance of his mistake. Having put aside his faith in Juliet's faith, his appeal is in the name of law rather than of love: "The prince expressly hath forbidden." That, and his "good Mercutio," reveal a divided soul. And it is that divided soul, in a last instant of hesitation, that causes an awkward and uncoördinated motion as he interferes and gives the cowardly Tybalt his chance to make a deadly thrust at Mercutio under Romeo's arm. If Romeo had only let those two firebrands fight it out, both might have lost blood with a cooling effect on their heated tempers, or, if it had gone to a finish, both might have been killed, as they ultimately were anyway, or, more likely, Mercutio would have killed Tybalt. ("An there were two such, we should have none shortly, for one would kill the other.") In any of these events, the feud between the two houses would not have been involved. As it is, the moment of freedom passes, and the rest is fate.

The fallen Mercutio reveals his most appealing side in his good humor at death. But why his reiterated "A plague o' both your houses?" He is one more character in Shakespeare who "doth protest too much." Four times he repeats it, or three and a half to be exact. How ironical of Mercutio to attribute his death to the Capulet-Montague feud, when the Capulet who killed him had plainly been reluctant to fight with him, and the chief Montague present had begged and begged him to desist. That "plague o' both your houses" is Mercutio's unwitting confession that his own intolerable pugnacity, not the feud at all, is responsible. And if that be true, how much that has been written about this tragedy must be retracted.

What follows puts a final confirmation on Romeo's error in trying to part the duelists by force. With Mercutio dead as a direct result of his interference, what can Romeo say? We heard him fall from love to an appeal to law and order while the fight was on. Now it is over, he descends even lower as he bemoans his "reputation stain'd with Tybalt's slander." Reputation! Iago's word.

> O sweet Juliet,
> Thy beauty hath made me effeminate
> And in my temper soften'd valour's steel!

Were ever words more tragically inverted? That fire should soften metal must have seemed a miracle to the man who first witnessed it. How much greater the miracle whereby beauty melts violence into love! That is the miracle that was on the verge of occurring in *Romeo and Juliet*.

Instead, Benvolio enters to announce Mercutio's death. Whereat Romeo, throwing the responsibility of his own mistake on destiny, exclaims:

> This day's black fate on more days doth depend;
> This but begins the woe others must end.

Could words convey more clearly the fact that the crisis has passed? Freedom has had its instant. The consequences are now in control.

Tybalt re-enters. Does Romeo now remember that his love for Juliet makes every Capulet sacred? Does he recall his last words to her as he left the orchard at dawn?—

> Sleep dwell upon thine eyes, peace in thy breast!
> Would I were sleep and peace, so sweet to rest!

Does he now use his sword to prevent bloodshed?

> Away to heaven, respective lenity,

he cries, implying without realizing it the infernal character of his decision,

> And fire-ey'd fury be my conduct now!

Fury! Shakespeare's invariable word for animal passion in man gone mad. And in that fury Romeo's willingness to forgive is devoured like a flower in a furnace:

> Now, Tybalt, take the villain back again
> That late thou gav'st me; for Mercutio's soul
> Is but a little way above our heads,
> Staying for thine to keep him company.
> Either thou, or I, or both, must go with him.

The spirit of Mercutio does indeed enter Romeo's body, and though it is Tybalt who is to go with the slain man literally, it is Romeo who goes with him in the sense that he accepts his code and obeys his ghost. Drawing his rapier, he sends Tybalt to instant death—to the immense gratification of practically everyone in the audience, so prone are we in the theater to surrender to the ancestral emotions. How many a mother, suspecting the evil influence of some companion on her small son, has put her arms about him in a desperate gesture of protection. Yet that same mother will attend a performance of *Romeo and Juliet*, and, seduced by the crowd, will applaud Romeo's capitulation to the spirit of Mercutio to the echo. So frail is the tenderness of the mothers in the face of the force of the fathers.

In this respect the scene is like the court scene in *The Merchant of Venice* when we gloat over Shylock's discomfiture. Here, as there, not only our cooler judgment when we are alone but all the higher implications of the tragedy call for a reversal of our reaction when with the crowd. In this calmer retrospect, we perceive that between his hero's entrance and exit in this scene Shakespeare has given us three Romeos, or, if you will, one Romeo in three universes. First we see him possessed by love and a spirit of universal forgiveness. From this he falls, first to reason and an appeal to law, then to violence—but violence in a negative or "preventive" sense. Finally, following Mercutio's death, he passes under the control of passion and fury, abetted by "honour," and thence to vengeance and offensive violence. In astrological terms, he moves from Venus, through the Earth, to Mars. It is as if Dante's *Divine Comedy* were compressed into eighty lines and presented in reverse— Romeo in an inverted "pilgrimage" passing from Paradise, through Purgatory, to the Inferno.

This way of taking the scene acquits Romeo of doing "wrong," unless we may be said to do wrong whenever we fail to live up to our highest selves. Love is a realm beyond good and evil. Under the aspect of time, of common sense, possibly even of reason and morality, certainly of "honour," Romeo's conduct in the swift succession of events that ended in Tybalt's death was unexceptionable. What else could he have done? But under the aspect of eternity, which is poetry's aspect, it was less than that. We cannot blame a man because he does not perform a miracle. But when he offers proof of his power, and the very next moment has the opportunity to perform one, and does not, the failure is tragic. Such was the "failure" of Romeo. And he himself admits it in so many words. Death, like love, lifts us for a moment above time. Just before he drinks the poison, catching sight of the body of Tybalt in the Capulet vault, Romeo cries, "Forgive me, cousin." Why should he ask forgiveness for what he did in honor, if honor be the guide to what is right?

Romeo as an honorable man avenges his friend. But in proving himself a man in this sense, he proves himself less than the perfect lover. "Give all to love," says Emerson:

> Give all to love . . .
> 'Tis a brave master;
> Let it have scope:
> Follow it utterly,
> Hope beyond hope . . .
> Heartily know,
> When half-gods go,
> The gods arrive.

Juliet's love had bestowed on Romeo power to bring down a god, to pass even beyond the biblical seventy times seven to what Emily Brontë calls the "first of the seventy-first." But he did not. The play is usually explained as a tragedy of the excess of love. On the contrary it is the tragedy of a deficiency of it. Romeo did not "follow it utterly," did not give quite "all" to love.

V

Romeo's mental condition following the death of Tybalt is proof of the treason he has committed against his own soul. Up to this point in the scene, as we saw, Shakespeare has given us three Romeos. Now he gives us a fourth: the man rooted to the spot at the sight of what he has done. The citizens have heard the tumult and are coming. "Stand not amaz'd," cries Benvolio—and it is a case where one poet's words seem to have been written to illuminate another's. Wordsworth's lines are like a mental stage direction for the dazed Romeo:

> Action is transitory—a step, a blow,
> The motion of a muscle—this way or that—
> 'Tis done; and in the after-vacancy
> We wonder at ourselves like men betrayed:
> Suffering is permanent, obscure and dark,
> And has the nature of infinity.

"O! I am Fortune's fool," cries Romeo. "Love's not Time's fool," says Shakespeare, as if commenting on this very scene, in that confession of his own faith, the 116th sonnet:

> O, no! it is an ever-fixed mark,
> That looks on tempests and is never shaken;
> It is the star to every wandering bark,
> Whose worth's unknown, although his height be taken.

There is an astrology at the opposite pole from that of the Chorus to this play. Romeo's love looked on a tempest—and it was shaken. He apparently has just strength enough left to escape and seek refuge in Friar Laurence's cell, where, at the word of his banishment, we find him on the floor,

> Taking the measure of an unmade grave,

in a fit of suicidal despair that so often treads on the heels of "fury." It is not remorse for having killed Tybalt that accounts for his condition, nor even vexation with himself for having spoiled his own marriage, but shame for having betrayed Juliet's faith in the boundlessness of love.

Meanwhile, at the scene of the duels, citizens have gathered, followed by the Prince with Capulets and Montagues. Lady Capulet, probably the weakest character in the play, is the first to demand more blood as a solution of the problem:

> Prince, as thou art true,
> For blood of ours, shed blood of Montague.

But the Prince asks first for a report of what happened.

> Benvolio, who began this bloody fray?

Benvolio mars what is otherwise a remarkably accurate account of the affair by failing utterly to mention Mercutio's part in instigating the first duel, placing the entire blame on Tybalt.

> He is kinsman to the Montague,

cries Lady Capulet,

> Affection makes him false; he speaks not true.
> Some twenty of them fought in this black strife,
> And all those twenty could but kill one life.

Her sense of reality and character are on level with her courage.

In Capulet's orchard, the Nurse brings to Juliet the rope ladder by which her husband is to reach her chamber—and with it the news of Tybalt's death and Romeo's banishment.

> O serpent heart, hid with flowering face!
> Did ever dragon keep so fair a cave?

cries Juliet,

> O nature, what hadst thou to do in hell,
> When thou didst borrow the spirit of a fiend
> In mortal paradise of such sweet flesh?

Even in the exaggeration of her anguish, Juliet diagnoses what has happened precisely as Shakespeare does: a fiend—the spirit of Mercutio—has taken possession of her lover-husband's body. Contrast her insight at such a moment with the Nurse's drivellings:

> There's no trust,
> No faith, no honesty in men; all perjur'd,
> All forsworn, all naught, all dissemblers.
> Ah, where's my man?

A fair sample of how well her inane generalizations survive the test of a concrete need.

Back in Friar Laurence's cell, the stunned Romeo is like a drunken man vaguely coming to himself after a debauch. When he draws his sword to make away with himself, the Friar restrains him not by his hand, as Romeo had once sought to restrain Mercutio at a similarly critical moment, but by the force of his words:

> Hold thy desperate hand!
> Art thou a man?

And he seeks to sting him back to manhood by comparing his tears to those of a woman and his fury to that of a beast.

> Thou hast amaz'd me. . . .
> Why rail'st thou on thy birth, the heaven, and earth?
> Since birth, and heaven, and earth, all three do meet
> In thee at once, which thou at once wouldst lose.

No nonsense about "star-cross'd lovers" for Friar Laurence. Shakespeare, like Dante before him and Milton after him, knew where the stars are, knew that heaven and hell, and even earth, are located within the human soul. Romeo is the "skilless soldier" who sets afire the powder in his own flask.

VI

Juliet too in her despair can think of death. But with what relative calmness and in what a different key! The contrast between the two lovers at this stage is a measure of the respectively innocent and guilty states of their souls.

Their meeting at night is left to our imagination, but their parting at dawn is Shakespeare's imagination functioning at its highest lyrical intensity, with interwoven symbols of nightingale and lark, darkness and light, death and love. Then follow in swift succession the mother's announcement of her daughter's impending marriage with Paris, Juliet's ringing repudiation of the idea, the rejection of her, in order, by her father, her mother, and the Nurse—the first brutal, the second supine, the third Satanic. And then, with an instantaneousness that can only be called divine, Juliet's rejection of the Nurse. In a matter of seconds the child has become a woman. This is the second crisis of the drama, Juliet's, which, with Romeo's, gives the play its shape as certainly as its two foci determine the shape of an ellipse. If ever two crises were symmetrical, and opposite, these are.

Romeo, in a public place, lured insensibly through the influence of Mercutio to the use of force, falls, and as a direct result of his fall, kills Tybalt. Juliet, in her chamber, deserted by father and mother and enticed to faithlessness by the Nurse, child as she is, never wavers for an instant, puts her tempter behind her, and consents as the price of her fidelity to be "buried" alive. Can anyone imagine that Shakespeare did not intend this contrast, did not build up his detailed parallelism between Mercutio and the Nurse to effect it? Romeo, as we said, does not give quite "all" for love. But Juliet does. She performs her miracle and receives supernatural strength as her reward. He fails to perform his and is afflicted with weakness. But eventually her spirit triumphs in him. Had it done so at first, the tragedy would have been averted. Here again the heroine transcends the hero. And yet Romeo had Friar Laurence as adviser while Juliet was brought up by the Nurse! The profounder the truth, the more quietly Shakespeare has a habit of uttering it. It is as if he were saying here that innocence comes from below the sources of pollution and can run the fountain clear.

To describe as "supernatural" the strength that enables Juliet "without fear or doubt" to undergo the ordeal of the sleeping potion and the burial vault does not seem excessive:

> Give me, give me! O! tell me not of fear!

Long before—in the text, not in time—when she had wondered how Romeo had scaled the orchard wall below her balcony, he had said:

> With love's light wings did I o'erperch these walls;
> For stony limits cannot hold love out,
> And what love can do that dares love attempt.

Juliet is now about to prove the truth of his words, in a sense Romeo never dreamed of, "in that dim monument where Tybalt lies." The hour comes, and after facing the terrors her imagination conjures up, Juliet goes through her "dismal scene" alone, is found "dead," and following a scene that anticipates but reverses *Hamlet* in that the wedding is turned into a funeral, is placed in the Capulet vault in accordance with Friar Laurence's desperate plan. But after force has had its instant way, fate in the guise of fear usually has its protracted way, and to oppose it is like trying to stay an avalanche with your hand.

VII

The pestilence prevents the Friar's messenger from reaching Romeo. Instead, word is brought to him that Juliet is dead, and, armed with a drug of an apothecary who defies the law against selling poison, he ends his banishment to Mantua and starts back to Verona to seek beside Juliet the eternal banishment of death. The fury with which he threatens his companion Balthasar, on dismissing him when they reach the churchyard, if he should return to pry, reveals Romeo's mood:

> By heaven, I will tear thee joint by joint
> And strew this hungry churchyard with thy limbs.
> The time and my intents are savage-wild,
> More fierce and inexorable far
> Than empty tigers or the roaring sea.

And when he encounters and slays Paris, the contrast between his death and that of Mercutio, or even Tybalt, shows that we are dealing here not so much with the act of a free agent choosing his course in the present as with the now fatal consequences of an act in the past, of an agent then free but now no longer so. Paris is little more than the branch of a tree that Romeo pushes aside—and his death affects us almost as little. It is all like a dream, or madness. Finding the sleeping—as he supposes the dead—Juliet, Romeo pours out his soul in words which, though incomparable as poetry, err in placing on the innocent heavens the responsibility for his own venial but fatal choice:

>   O, here
> Will I set up my everlasting rest,
> And shake the yoke of inauspicious stars
> From this world-wearied flesh.

And then, by one of those strokes that, it sometimes seems, only Shakespeare could achieve, the poet makes Romeo revert to and round out, in parting from Juliet forever, the same metaphor he had used when she first gazed down on him from her balcony and he had tried to give expression to the scope and range of his love. How magically, placed side by side, the two passages fit together, how tragically they sum up the story:

> I am no pilot; yet, wert thou as far
> As that vast shore wash'd with the farthest sea,
> I would adventure for such merchandise.

> Come, bitter conduct, come, unsavoury guide!
> Thou desperate pilot, now at once run on
> The dashing rocks thy sea-sick weary bark!
> Here's to my love! (*Drinks.*) O true apothecary!
> Thy drugs are quick. Thus with a kiss I die. (*Dies.*)

Enter Friar Laurence—a moment too late. That fear is with him Shakespeare shows by another echo. "Wisely and slow; they stumble that run fast," the Friar had warned Romeo on dismissing him after his first confession of his love for Juliet, and now he says:

> How oft to-night
> Have my old feet stumbled at graves! . . .
> . . . Fear comes upon me.

He discovers the dead Romeo. Just then Juliet awakes. But at the same moment he hears a noise. The watch is coming! He cannot be found here.

> Come, go, good Juliet, I dare no longer stay,

and when she refuses to follow, he deserts her. With a glance into the empty cup in Romeo's hand and a kiss on the lips that she hopes keep poison for her own—anticipating touches at the deaths of both Hamlet and Cleopatra—she snatches Romeo's dagger and kills herself.

Why did Shakespeare, after building up so noble a character as Friar Laurence, permit him to abandon Juliet at so fatal a moment? Why add *his* name to the so different ones of Capulet, Lady Capulet, and the Nurse, no matter how much better the excuse for his desertion of her? For two reasons, I think: first, to show how far the infection of fear extends that Romeo's use of force had created. "Here is a friar, that trembles, sighs, and weeps," says the Third Watchman, and Laurence himself confesses, when he tells his story,

> But then a noise did scare me from the tomb.

And then, to show that Juliet, abandoned *even by religion*, must fall back for courage finally on love alone.

The pestilence plays a crucial part toward the end of the action. It is a symbol. Whatever literal epidemic there may have been in the region, it is plain that fear is the real pestilence that pervades the play. It is fear of the code of honor, not fate, that drives Romeo to seek vengeance on Tybalt. It is fear of the plague, not accident, that leads to the miscarriage of Friar Laurence's message to Romeo. It is fear of poverty, not the chance of his being on hand at the moment, that lets the apothecary sell the poison. It is fear of the part he is playing, not age, that makes Friar Laurence's old feet stumble and brings him to the tomb just a few seconds too late to prevent Romeo's death. It is fear of being found at such a spot at such a time, not coincidence, that lets him desert Juliet at last just when he does. Fear, fear, fear, fear, fear. Fear is the evil "star" that crosses the lovers. And fear resides not in the skies but in the human heart.

VIII

The tragedy ends in the reconciliation of the two houses, compensation, it is generally held, for the deaths of the two lovers. Doubtless the feud was not renewed in its former form. But much superfluous sentiment has been spent on this ending. Is it not folly to suppose that Capulet or Lady Capulet was spiritually transformed by Juliet's death? And as for Montague, the statue of her in pure gold that he promised to erect in Verona is proof in itself how incapable he was of understanding her spirit and how that spirit alone, and not monuments or gold, can bring an end to feuds. (Lady Montague, who died of a broken heart, was far and away the finest of the four parents.) Shakespeare's happy endings are, almost without exception, suspect. Or rather they are to be found, if at all, elsewhere than in the last scene and final speeches, and are "happy" in a quite untheatrical sense.

Cynics are fond of saying that if Romeo and Juliet had lived their love would not have "lasted." Of course it wouldn't—in the cynic's sense. You can no more ask such love to last than you can ask April to last, or an apple blossom. Yet April and apple blossoms do last and have results that bear no resemblance to what they come from—results such as apples and October—and so does such love. Romeo, in his last words, referred to the phenomenon known as "a lightning before death." Here is that lightning, and here, if it have one, is the happy ending of *Romeo and Juliet:*

Rom.:   If I may trust the flattering truth of sleep,
My dreams presage some joyful news at hand.
My bosom's lord sits lightly on his throne,
And all this day an unaccustom'd spirit
Lifts me above the ground with cheerful thoughts.
I dreamt my lady came and found me dead—
Strange dream, that gives a dead man leave to think!—
And breath'd such life with kisses in my lips,
That I reviv'd and was an emperor.
Ah me! how sweet is love itself possess'd,
When but love's shadows are so rich in joy!

Enter Balthasar—with news of Juliet's death.

Dreams go by contraries, they say, and this seems to be an example. But is it?

JOHN LAWLOR

Romeo and Juliet

It is perhaps impossible to approach any play of Shakespeare's without strong, if latent, preconception; and this may be especially so with his first major incursion into tragedy. *Romeo and Juliet* is not Shakespeare's first attempt at tragic writing; but it is the first of his plays to excite and sustain any deep concern with humanity in the ills that befall it. This concern, however, it appears to be generally held, is other than that evoked by later tragedies; and since in them we have an insistent probing of the connections between what men are and what may befall them, it is easy to make a distinction between the tragedy of fortune and the tragedy of character; and, referring the first to a medieval inheritance, find in *Romeo and Juliet* an experiment, in greater or less degree unsuccessful, towards a second and greater mode. It is these terms that G. I. Duthie, an editor of the *New Cambridge Shakespeare*, introduces the play. The feud between Montague and Capulet is 'quite unconvincing'; Fate is thus 'nothing more important than a matter of sheer bad luck'; and the protagonists have 'weakness of character' (principally a lack of 'mature poise and balance') which are yet not related to their doom. In this Duthie follows two principal critics, H. Charlton in the first point and D. Stauffer in the second. 'What we actually have then,' he concludes, 'is a drama of Fate involving the destruction of two innocent

From *Early Shakespeare, Stratford-Upon-Avon Studies* 3 © 1961 Edward Arnold (Publishers).

victims who have defects of character which are not properly worked into the pattern.' Unless we follow J. W. Draper in his belief that these lovers are literally 'star-cross'd) so that the play illustrates astrological determinism), it is difficult to see where any 'system or governing purpose' may lie. *Romeo and Juliet* may yet appear to be saved by its poetry: Shakespeare, though lacking a true 'grasp of the foundations of tragedy' (Charlton) is 'totally successful' in expressing the triumph of a love over which 'Death has no power' (Duthie). It is a fair expression of the majority view: the dramatist has failed 'to convey a certain great tragic conception (which points forward to his maturity)'; and Duthie localizes that failure in an imperfect relation between the story of the two lovers, as embodying 'a certain well-known traditional conception of tragedy', and the story of the two families which prompts 'quite another conception of tragedy—a more deeply satisfying conception'. Much, evidently, depends on certain assumptions about the tragic. It will be best to begin with the 'traditional conception' inherited by the Elizabethan.

Medieval tragedy—it may make for clarity if it is called hereafter *tragedie*—is perhaps more often understood in terms of its characteristic working than its final effect. It is as though criticism of the more familiar kind of tragedy were to fasten wholly upon its mechanism—the 'passions' that 'spin the plot'—and ignore its distinctive effect upon the spectator. That effect is one in which apparent opposites are reconciled; a balance is struck between pity and terror, the logic of events and whatever we may mean by an inscrutable Fate—'the necessary' as opposed to 'the probable'. There is an end of any merely mechanistic notion (a quasi-causal relation between what men are and what may befall them), and, at the same time, of a wholly inscrutable Fate. It is a dual perception, affirming a system as finally myste-rious while revealing it in part of its ordered working. Against this, *tragedie* is, from one point of view, less complex; it calls forth no dual perception, for it needs none. Its central truth is that Fortune knows nothing of human deserving. But her activities are not, in the end, inscrutable; for those who are minded to learn, a greater good is in prospect. Similarly, on the level of 'plot'—the sequence of events in the external world—*tragedie* may be said to have beginning and end, but no distinctive middle. The beginning is in 'prosperitee', a happiness unshadowed by imminent reversal; the end in apparent disaster, as unalterable as unpredictable. The formula, then, is simple; but the experience available to us in these terms is a more complex matter. It is certainly not 'profoundly pessimistic', as Duthie, following a general persuasion, would have us believe. Fortune's 'delight' in her opera-tions is the illusion of the sufferer, clinging to his belief in a retributive justice and protesting, like Chaucer's Troilus, 'I have it nat deserved'. Certainly, where the dominant type of tragic writing strongly asserts connection

between 'character' and calamity, then what apparently runs counter to this
will seem merely arbitrary:

> As flies to wanton boys are we to the gods—
> They kill us for their sport.

But it is in fact this universal misunderstanding of Fortune's operations
which *tragedie* exists to challenge, and to alter. When disaster has come in
tragedie, we find man lamenting as uncovenanted the harm that has befallen
him. Fortune's operations are thus, as they were in the archetype, Boethius's
Consolation of Philosophy, a manifest cruelty: *satis eminet fortunae in nos saevi-
entis asperitas*. But the tragic design puts a period to fruitless lament: we may
rise to an understanding that

> All is best, though we oft doubt
> What th' unsearchable dispose
> Of highest wisdom brings about,
> And ever best found in the close.

The 'close' of *tragedie* enables the spectator to look beyond a limited time of
inexplicable suffering to happiness beyond time's reach. In the close, we, like
Troilus, repair 'home'; another dimension of time, an eternal present, is
entered upon in *tragedie*, as it was in Boethius's philosophical questioning of
Divine foreknowledge and free will.

We may trace this characteristic progress of the spectator in Dante's
inquiry concerning Fortune, the first of a series of major discourses in which
'the plan of the spiritual and physical universe', as the medieval mind appre-
hended it, is unfolded. Dante must learn that she is reviled who ought to be
praised; but, being in bliss, she hears it not (*Ma ella s'è beata, e ciò non ode*). His
approach had been to her as having the good things of the world in her
control (*che i ben del mondo ha sì tra branche*). It is the typical standpoint of
mortals; and as such it calls forth a general rebuke upon foolish and ignorant
humanity (*O creature sciocche, quanta ignoranza è quella che vi offende!*). The
argument must take us beyond possessions, the creature-comforts and empty
'goods' of this life (*li ben vani*). Fortune, the presiding intelligence of our
sphere, has her task allotted from on high; and she conducts her operations
'beyond the hindrance of human wisdom' (*oltre la difension de' senni umani*).
In the close of *tragedie* we see, as Boethius saw at the end of a long and hard
road, that things are what they seemed at the outset. The spectator,
beholding the tragic sufferer, attains to that insight which, in its fullness, is
the Divine prerogative: *Manet etiam spectator desuper cunctorium* . . . The aerial
ascent of Troilus's spirit in the close of Chaucer's poem is appropriate to this

order of exalted vision. It is the definitive experience of *tragedie*, corresponding to the *katharsis* of nemesis-type tragedy. Where such tragedy returns us to the real world, *tragedie* takes us beyond it. The important consideration is that the one is not an imperfect form of the other; where causal connection interests the Greek, what absorbs the medieval mind is the absence of a rationale in any terms less than an unsearchable Divine wisdom. Refused all proximate solutions, we must confront man as the patient of forces beyond his control. Through lesser disasters we are drawn to a greater good; and this, so far from being pessimistic, can touch the deeps of happiness—the landfall long postponed, and lately despaired of, is at last in view. Our final perspective may even offer the wry comedy of wilful blindness and thus a painful journeying. Like Boethius we may observe man's erratic progress towards the greatest good, stumbling to it like a drunken man who knows not the way home (*velut ebrius domum quo tramite revertatur ignorat*). We shall go very far astray if we think of the 'tragedy of fortune' as pessimistic in giving an apparent victory to Death. Its distinctive capacity is in fact the awakening to understanding of a greater good. Not all the feeble *exempla* of mere reversal, the turning of her wheel by the strumpet Fortune, should distract us from this distinctive capacity of *tragedie* in the hands of a master-poet. In Chaucer it is *Troilus and Criseyde* we attend to, not the Monk's Tale.

A stereotype of cruel Fortune is, of course, abundantly evident in later medieval and Elizabethan 'tragic' writing, and it constitutes the central image of that 'Gothic' tragedy which W. E. Farnham soundly contrasts with the Greek in its unwillingness 'to confine its scope to the action that immediately brings catastrophe'. There are two major reactions to this notion of cruel Fortune's sway. The first is a strongly moral protest, asserting the superiority of Virtue over Fortune. Thus, in George Wither's *Emblemes* we see not only the strumpet Fortune but Zeus hastening to the captive's aid, the whole set within the encouraging legend *Sors non obest Virtuti*—

> *Though* Fortune *prove true* Vertues *Foe,*
> *It cannot overwork her Overthrowe.*

This is to resolve the matter by pronouncement: certainly virtue itself may not be overthrown; but all else may be. More timorous spirits may appeal for protection against Fortune. Only the gods can,

> In general synod, take away her power;
> Break all the spokes and fellies from her wheel,
> And bowl the round nave down the hill of heaven,

As low as to the fiends.

It is precisely because Shakespeare wishes us to feel Hamlet's destiny as mysterious that the image of implacable Fortune is given over to ridicule in these earnest histrionics of the First Player. The centre of attention in any serious drama must be the over-burdened human figure who is yet an *agent*. In Elizabethan terms this must mean one who achieves an end which does not minimize, much less cancel, Fortune's power, but which denies her an entire victory. That Death has no final power over the lovers of *Romeo and Juliet* is therefore not 'an impression' differing from 'the tragic design that Shakespeare obviously intended to produce' (Duthie). Whatever may be discoverable about Shakespeare's intentions, it is wholly consistent with *tragedie* that out of evil comes not good merely but a greater good. What we see in the close of *Romeo and Juliet* is not simply a renewal of a pattern disturbed, but its re-ordering; life is not continued merely; it is regenerated. Only thus do we experience the quality of a 'Beauty too rich for use, for earth too dear'. It is earth, the realm of Fortune, that is the loser. We see it as 'unworthy' of the lovers, a world of 'less generous passions'⟨G. Bullough⟩; so this love is placed, fittingly, at once beyond reach and beyond change. Shakespeare, in this at least, has not broken with but rather has reaffirmed the distinctive quality of *tragedie*. But is this perhaps at the cost of 'a more deeply satisfying conception' of tragedy? To answer this question we must begin by considering the tragic plays written before *Romeo and Juliet*.

Titus Andronicus is Shakespeare's first essay in tragic writing; and it portrays a conscious and purposeful evil. Aaron the Moor knows himself evil and delights in the knowledge. What is noteworthy is that this evil overflows into a spontaneous mischief: if at one end of the scale it embraces 'murders, rapes, and massacres', at the other it includes burning hay-stacks and luring cattle to their destruction:

> Make poor men's cattle break their necks;
> Set fire on barns and hay-stacks in the night,
> And bid the owners quench them with their tears.
>
> (V. i. 132)

These offences, too, it appears, must be itemized in a general confession of 'Acts of black night, abominable deeds'. It is as though the conscious agent of evil is a figure releasing in the Shakespearian imagination associations of diabolical enmity to man—an enmity which includes impish irresponsibility as well as more lurid disasters. The forest of II. iii and iv is a region of darkly unlimited possibility; and here type and antitype seem very close if we compare the horrors of *Titus Andronicus* with the perils safely overpassed of *A Midsummer Night's Dream*. Shakespeare's art in each play is to place between the spectator and the dire or fantastic events of the stage a *cordon sanitaire*; and this effect in *Titus Andronicus* is reinforced by its rhetoric, an oratory which, as K. Muir remarks, 'acts as a shield between the horrors and our hearts'. In *Richard III* we are again concerned with the conscious agent of evil; and here the popular tradition of a murderous Machiavel relieves the dramatist of any necessity for subtle characterization. We concentrate upon a progress to the Crown which cuts down all in its path. But here, again, we may see in the dramatist's working imagination something which is distinctive. The barrenness that Richard makes around him is, in the end, realized in wholly individual terms. The lament for the absence of friends may come 'too late to humanize an essentially melodramatic character': but in the self-knowledge that accepts this exclusion—

> I myself
> Find in myself no pity to myself—
>   (V. iii. 202)

the circle of 'Richard loves Richard' is fatally complete. Richard's punishment is to have achieved his aim; he is, unmistakably and finally, alone. These two treatments of the conscious agent of evil express the same truth. If the evil-doer is not, like Aaron, outrageously immune to all self-reproach, he must be finally subject to the knowledge that his success, the fulfilment of his original aims, is a total failure in human terms. Cut off, excluded, cast out—this is the final predicament of the one who wills the world of 'I am I'; and his punishment is to know that this is unalterably so.

With *Richard II* we turn from conscious evil to unconscious weakness; and with this shift there comes an access of creative power. As Muir has pointed out, Shakespeare had learnt from Marlowe 'the trick of concentrating on his hero's weakness and vice before his downfall, and on his better qualities afterwards'. This allows the dramatist to make a skilful balance of sympathy, between insurrection against misgovernment and the sin of usurpation. It is a kind of hindsight which perfectly corresponds with real experience. Once impatience and anger are discharged in action, there inevitably arise not only feelings of revulsion and pity but also a new understanding of the victim. We may remember Macbeth's soliloquy before the intended murder of a wholly virtuous ruler: Duncan's death is certain to awaken realization of his virtues, a realization new-born with pity. A similar understanding grows for a Richard who survives to be the spectator of his own deposition. The design of the play—'the disposition of the fable'—thus corresponds with the actual movement of the audience's feelings; and it answers to the greater change, a shift from the hero as conscious agent of evil to the hero as unwitting author of his own undoing. The important consideration is not that the disasters which come upon Richard are ultimately attributable to his 'character'. The dramatist's real opportunity occurs when the progress of the play is not to convict the hero of failure by the manifest ruin of his plans, but when failure receives the hero's full assent as an unalterable human lot. Richard, certainly, has a wisdom after the event; but it lies in the recognition of an even-handed justice ('I wasted time, and now doth time waste me') and a steady refusal of the fiction that man can unmake himself. It is easy to recognize and allow that 'sweet' must turn to 'sour' 'When time is broke and no proportion kept'. But what shall we say of failure to know the self? The focus of Richard's understanding is upon man as the subject of illusion:

> here have I the daintiness of ear
> To check time broke in a disorder'd string;
> But for the concord of my state and time
> Had not an ear to hear my true time broke.
> > (V. v. 45)

It is a momentous step. In such a play there is ample room for one obvious appeal of *tragedie*: the fall of a prince mirrors the uncertainty of this world's estate. But Richard's conclusion upon the matter deepens the conception of *tragedie*. We see the human condition as unchanging, incurable of illusion while life lasts:

> whate'er I be,
> Nor I nor any man that but man is,
> With nothing shall be pleased, till he be eased
> With being nothing.
> > (V. v. 38)

The development in *Richard II* is not away from *tragedie*, but rather to take that fulfilment of design which *tragedie* characteristically emphasizes, the recognition of a greater good, out of the region of dramatic fiction, placing it beyond the bounds of life. The tragic fable must work to the 'easing' of man by his 'being nothing' before we can speak of a greater good. Here we have perhaps a reason why when the old story of Leir comes to be retold it must drive beyond the truth of 'unaccommodated man' to the nothingness of death. At all events, we may see from these early tragic plays that the conscious agent of evil is touched with melodrama; the unwitting author of his own undoing is invested with dignity and his death has a sacrificial quality. It is with this experience behind him that Shakespeare comes to the makings of *Romeo and Juliet*: in this light we may examine its alleged shortcomings.

The feud between Montague and Capulet is certainly introduced to us in undignified terms. Parallel with the vulgar delight of a serving-man in his master's quarrel is the senile eagerness of Capulet calling for his 'long sword', testily answered by his wife, 'A crutch, a crutch!' 'Old Montague', we are told, 'flourishes his blade in spite of me'. It is the very language of childish pique; and the foolishness of the whole proceeding is appropriately berated by the Prince. 'Verona's ancient citizens' have been made to

> Cast by their grave beseeming ornaments,
> To wield old partisans, in hands as old.
> (I. i. 100)

The note of absurdity is common in references to the old men of the play. But before the feud itself is dismissed as 'all . . . rather trivial, rather silly' ⟨Duthie⟩ we must place it in its full setting. There is not only the common-place brawling of the servants and the undignified caperings of the old men; there is also Tybalt's grim acceptance of the feud, and Mercutio's valiantly embracing it. We shall refer to the play of coincidence below; for the moment, the bearing of the feud on 'Fate' calls for some consideration. Romeo, we see, is placed in a world of untroubled assumptions; and it is these which, defining his situation, become the unalterable constraints upon him when he would pass beyond them. Thus, as to the point of honour, the behaviour expected of a young Montague, Romeo stands between the murderous Tybalt and the chivalrous Mercutio. It is a situation like that of Hamlet, opposed to the unhesitating vengefulness of Laertes, and put to shame at the sight of the honourable Fortinbras, whose example teaches what it is 'Rightly to be great'. At the turning-point for Romeo—as for Hamlet—the revenge code exacts obedience. But it is important not to mistake the desperate quality of Romeo's action. It is certainly not the dignified self-possession which we could infer from some critical accounts:

> Alive, in triumph! and Mercutio slain!
> Away to heaven, respective lenity,
> And fire-eyed fury be my conduct now!
> (III. i. 127)

This is the language of an avenger; one step more and it will be like Laertes's italianate defiance:

To hell, allegiance! Vows, to the blackest devil! . . .
I dare damnation.

(*Hamlet*, IV. v. 131–3)

Romeo's is an honourable part, in taking it upon himself to requite a death incurred on his behalf. But the hot blood cannot be gainsaid; the rant of the revenge theme, though made appropriate to an honourable avenger, is still in sharpest contrast to the mild speech of the first encounter between Romeo and Tybalt; and now Romeo takes occasion to requite the insult ('villain') he had himself received. Romeo is indeed 'Fortune's fool': as his love for Juliet had raised him to a height far above 'respective lenity' (Capulet had been a name to tender as dearly as his own) so now he sinks—not to the level merely of the revenge-code, but to an offence against the Prince's law, a 'bandying in Verona streets'. Shakespeare has certainly made the feud undignified; but we must not miss the real point of its being so. After the first scene, with the Prince's angry intervention, 'honourable' courses can mean only public brawling. To say that Romeo disposes of Tybalt 'in the name of all that is manly and honest' is to ignore the higher understanding that had come to Romeo; and this, too, we must observe in its full setting.

The love which prompts this understanding in Romeo is a new thing in the world of the play. It differs, most obviously, from his own conventional passion for Rosaline, and from Mercutio's light-hearted sensuality. But it differs, too, from everything else we see in Verona where 'love' is in question—from the attitudes of a masterful father; a match-making mother; a match-approving and therefore variable Nurse; a managing Friar, concerned to minimize risk and promote reconciliation; even—perhaps most of all—from the affections of a simple and likeable suitor, Paris. Every commentator has noticed that Shakespeare's Juliet is even younger than the Juliet of Brooke's poem. If we are to speak of maturity and immaturity, we must not fail to notice the decisive turning, in both Romeo and Juliet, away from the 'mature' viewpoints of all around to them, to a new thing. The point of characterization will concern us below: for the moment, we must observe that whatever may be said of the opposition of the stars, the Fate which 'so enviously debars' this love is plainly evident in a world where love is known to the bystanders as many things—all different from the experience of love as we see it in the two central figures. In this respect at least *Romeo and Juliet* is true to a cardinal principle of Shakespearian drama—it might almost be called the authenticating mark of his authorship. Whatever is profoundly true (true in that mystery of things which the drama in part reveals) is always literally true, true in terms of unalterable human disposition. It is not merely that the one answers as a deeper echo to the other, the operations of a myste-

rious Fate giving an authoritative significance to mortal acts and entangle-
ments. It is rather that, seeing more clearly into humanity we perceive both
its unchanging limits and its incalculable possibilities; so that Fate and
Chance become significant terms.

To this end, an initial 'immaturity' in the lovers is essential. In both we
meet youth on the hither side of experience; and in Romeo, entirely subject
to a hopeless love, we may see the false maturity in which all youthful inex-
perience would hide itself. Certainly, when we have heard his declaration of
woeful love ('Mis-shapen chaos of well-seeming forms') we can echo his
declaration: 'This is not Romeo, he's some other where' (I. i. 204). But when
we see Romeo in torment at Friar Lawrence's cell (III. iii) we are not to
assume that the antithetical flights in which he laments the sentence of
banishment are a return to the first Romeo. His outcry parallels, as Miss
Mahood has noted, that in the preceding scene, where Juliet has fought
against the belief that Romeo is slain; each episode must be placed among
Shakespeare's 'first attempts to reveal a profound disturbance of mind by the
use of quibbles'. This is an 'immaturity' in the lovers, if we will; but it is also
the dramatist's means of showing us the inadequacy of settled and ordered
language (as that of Friar Lawrence, with his confidence in 'armour to keep
off [the] word') to deal with the bewildering reversals in which Romeo and
Juliet find themselves. If the Friar must persist in speaking of what he cannot
'feel', this is the only language that the sufferers themselves can find to meet
the first impact of disaster:

> Hath Romeo slain himself? Say thou but '*I*',
> And that bare vowel '*I*' shall poison more
> Than the death-darting *eye* of cockatrice:
> *I* am not *I*, if there be such an *I* . . .
>
> (III. ii. 45)

Juliet's tormented iteration is perfectly consonant with Romeo's own
anguish:

> Flies may do this, but I from this must fly . . .
>
> (III. iii. 41)

It is a language which, embracing contradiction, is truer to reality than the
single standpoints expressed by Nurse and Friar. We may add that this
language sharpens into a more simple wordplay when a world that will not
be changed is steadfastly accepted. When, in the end, Romeo has learned
that 'philosophy' cannot

> make a Juliet,
> Displant a town, reverse a prince's doom—

then alternatives are no longer balanced; for opposites become one:

> O true apothecary!
> Thy drugs are *quick*. Thus with a kiss I *die*.

The speed of the poison unites life with death: and Juliet answers, as it were, in the same mode. She will kiss Romeo's lips, sharing what remains of the drug,

> To make me die with a restorative.

Romeo, like Hamlet, is young, gifted, sensitive—and all but unequal to a situation which he cannot change. It is essential to our understanding that we see him grow from these beginnings to a final maturity which outsoars all else in the play. The gentleness proffered to Tybalt appears to Mercutio 'calm, dishonourable, vile submission'; but it is a profounder quality than any yielding to 'honour's' demands. It is matched by the first forebearance shown to Paris at the tomb—

> By heaven, I love thee better than myself;
> For I come hither arm'd against myself—

and by the noble epitaph for a fallen opponent seen as a fellow-victim,

> One writ with me in sour misfortune's book.

Romeo has come to a maturity that is but a short time distant from his lying 'on the ground, with his own tears made drunk'. These young lovers (for 'Even so' Juliet lies—'Blubbering and weeping, weeping and blubbering') grow to a final forgetfulness of self. Romeo obeys the Nurse's bidding to 'be a man': but the course taken by both lovers is other than any the Nurse and Friar can foresee in their concern with practical arrangements. Romeo's maturity is first evident in the comfort he gives Juliet, subject to foreboding, at their parting:

> all these woes shall serve
> For sweet discourses in our time come.
>
> (III. v. 52)

A moment later, Lady Capulet's arrival calls forth all Juliet's powers of dissimulation:

> I never shall be satisfied
> With Romeo, till I behold him—dead—
> Is my poor heart so for a kinsman vex'd.
>   (III. v. 94)

This prepares us, as Miss Mahood has noted, for the determination with which Juliet is to fight down her fears in pursuing the plan of a feigned death. The soliloquy ('Farewell! God knows when we shall meet again . . . ,' IV. iii. 14 ff.) is at once the test and vindication of her maturity. The characterization of Juliet is all Shakespeare's own, and it is based on the essential alteration in his material—her extreme youthfulness, which authorizes both the simple certainty of premonition and the artless candour of her first dealings with Romeo, where it is particularly noticeable that, at their meeting after the ball, the 'jejune fears and long speeches' of Brooke's Julietta are 'turned to innocent frankness' and the untutored Juliet's withdrawing and returning, 'irresistibly drawn back to her lover', gives variety and urgency to Brooke's lengthy dialogue ⟨Bullough⟩. These two children, as the managing adults of their world see them, are, truly, innocents abroad. But they are quick to learn; in Romeo's attempted consolation of Juliet at their final leave-taking (III. v) we see the beginning of maturity in the man, while Juliet's improvised but spirited dissimulation of her true feelings (when reproved for grief by her mother) is evidence of her purpose, growing in its turn. Their love has been truly consummated; in the exchanges before parting there is a sharing of the burden of consolation. To this effect the earlier immaturity of the lovers is essential. We are to feel the prematurity of their love, their response to demands thrust upon them ahead of the ordinary process of time. Before Juliet is united with her lover, time works as it does in 'old folks'—'Unwieldy, slow, heavy, and pale as lead'. Now, at their parting, Juliet's earlier invocation to the 'fiery-footed steeds' is sadly fulfilled, as daylight comes irresistibly on: 'More light and light it grows'. Time will have its revenge when, separated, the lovers are to find 'in a minute there are many days'.

The relation of the lovers' youth and thus unformed character to the process of time is vital, for it involves the great and challenging contrast between age without maturity and youth called to premature 'estate' (to use Friar Laurence's word). The paradoxical, conceited poetry with which we begin—a poetry appropriate to 'immature' love, if we will—is essential to our understanding of the ends to which the lovers drive; for in that love-poetry the Elizabethan imagination had hitherto made its most frequent contact with the antithesis of change and permanence. It is, peculiarly, the subject of Renaissance poetry as a whole; for who but the poet can bind time—in the very act of declaring time's apparent victories? And for the dramatist, time is not so much a 'subject' as his essential medium. Before the play is done, the conventional antitheses of young love give place to 'the finest poetry which had yet been heard on the English stage'. To see the dramatist's imagination at its work of selecting, shaping and transcending we must look, however briefly, at the sources of this play.

The paradoxical nature of Elizabethan love-poetry is, as more than one critic has noted, peculiarly adapted to a drama of sudden alternations. Thus, Bullough observes that Shakespeare 'modulates from the public to the private theme' when he 'makes Romeo's conventional passion express itself in contradictions and paradoxes suited to the pattern of the whole play'. It is a fruitful remark. We may study these contradictions and para-doxes, evident in Shakespeare's general handling of his source-material, under several heads: as, contrast of tempo; the play of coincidence; and the conquering of all-conquering time (where, especially, the 'conceits' of traditional poetry are important). Only the outstanding instances can be noticed here; and we must admit that the remarkable achievement in this early play is not the managing of striking moments but the unity of the whole. We have, in the end, to consider a balance which subsumes all antitheses.

The onward drive of events that concern the lovers, as against the slower pace of a world going about its habitual business—so that the nine months' action of Brooke's *Tragicall Historye* is crowded into a few days—is nowhere clearer than in the handling of the first three scenes of the play. As Bullough notes, by the end of I. iii both Romeo and Juliet are going to the ball—'one to see the woman he thinks he loves; the other to see . . . the man her parents want her to love. Both are soon to change.' Inevitable cross-purpose is thus communicated; and in I. v the changefulness of Romeo, hith-erto the conventionally undying lover of Rosaline, is paralleled by Juliet's awakening to the truth of conventional poetry:

> Prodigious birth of love it is to me,
> That I must love a loathed enemy.

But what is this to an inquiring world? Curiosity is neatly turned aside; it is only

> A rhyme I learn'd even now

Of one I danced withal.

The turning-point for Romeo alters all that has gone before:

Did my heart love till now? Forswear it, sight!
For I ne'er saw true beauty till this night.

It is an intended farewell to the fictions of poetry: and, immediately, the hostile world makes the first move against the lovers. Past time is not to be abolished, whatever Romeo may purpose. It is not merely a theatrical effect that is gained by Shakespeare postponing the unmasking (which in Brooke occurs before the meeting of Romeo and Juliet), so that the very words of love awaken unyielding enmity:

This, by his voice, should be a Montague . . .

That not Romeo himself but his lineage is identified speaks directly to our deeper sense that there can be no escape for him. The second great instance of time-alteration is, of course, the brawl taking place between the marriage and its consummation (instead of 'a month or twain' afterwards). It is an alteration which deepens a fundamental difference from Brooke's lovers. Their living together in clandestine happiness risks the reader's sympathy; as G. A. Bonnard shrewdly observes 'in spite of their being married according to the rites of Holy Church their love assumes the aspect of an illicit affair'. Shakespeare's Romeo and Juliet must consummate their marriage in the knowledge that the morning brings separation; and, as we have seen, the time that had moved too slowly now hastens against them, just as the coming of light in the world outside brings only darkness to the lovers in their private world:

More light and light; more dark and dark our woes!
(III. v. 36)

The play of coincidence may be seen most clearly in the alterations that lead to the brawl and thus the banishment of Romeo and all that follows from it. Mercutio plays no part in the brawl in *The Tragicall Historye*. There it is a general encounter which Romeus, summoned by the uproar, endeavours to stop; and even when attacked by Tybalt he refuses to return the blow, appealing for Tybalt's 'helpe these folke to parte'. Only when Tybalt strikes again does Romeus slay him. That Shakespeare's Romeo is unable to stop a duel between Tybalt and Mercutio—for the code of honour is common ground between them—defines, as we have seen, his unique position. But that in the end we are back at worse than the beginning—the Mercutio who had avenged a laggard Romeo must himself be avenged—illustrates as nothing else could the turning of Fortune's wheel. It is futility upon futility, and Shakespeare has made accident—Romeo's entering upon the scene and then his thrusting between the contestants—play the decisive part. Shakespeare knows, too, when to rely on silence—as, notably, when, unlike Brooke, he leaves the hostility of Montague and Capulet unexplained—just as he knows when to make coincidence beautifully exact: as, the entire naturalness of Juliet meeting Paris at Friar Lawrence's cell, when she has come there to seek a means of escaping marriage with him; or the father's natural delight in her apparent submission which causes him to advance the date of the wedding—so that Friar Lawrence, that exponent of 'Wisely and slow', must act in haste, while for Juliet there can be no postponement of decision; and, in the end, the coming of Paris to the tomb, which ratifies in death a love as disinterested as Romeo's own, bringing a worthy guest to a vault made 'a feasting presence full of light'.

Shakespeare's wordplay gives us the most direct approach to that conquering of time which is at the play's centre. The ambiguities which we may be tempted to pass over as mere conceits have their own contribution to make. Thus Romeo's language in the orchard at sight of Juliet "above" plays delightedly with the impossible, that which is contrary to nature:

> her eyes in heaven
> Would through the airy region stream so bright
> That birds would sing and think it were not night.
> (II. ii. 20)

It is a passage which, as Miss Mahood has noted, is parallel with Juliet's apostrophe to night:

> Give me my Romeo; and, when he shall die,
> Take him and cut him out in little stars,
> And he will make the face of heaven so fine
> That all the world will be in love with night
> And pay no worship to the garish sun.
> (III. ii. 21)

The love of Romeo and Juliet is in fact to transform the world they live in—but only when the order of time is not arrested or inverted but made powerless. That Death has no final power over the lovers is the great truth to which we are directed by their own rapturous hyperboles and by the central fact of their love, its freedom from any taint of the merely clandestine—which derives immediately from its swiftness and brevity, making it certain that they can have 'no share in the evil of their world' ⟨G. A. Bonnard⟩. In the 'fearful passage' of this 'death-mark'd love' we can therefore see and accept apparent opposites; and this acceptance is required from the outset, where both 'fearful' and 'death-mark'd' mean, not only 'pathetic' and 'doomed', but also 'terrifying' and 'deathward bound,' journeying to Death as to a destination ⟨Mahood⟩.

In this, *Romeo and Juliet* fulfills an essential condition of all experience which warrants the term 'tragic', no matter what the special design and scope of the tragic form attempted. Whether 'tragedy' or *tragedie* in the major distinction discussed earlier, all must turn on the spectator perceiving not one meaning preponderating over its opposite, but both present, the more vividly for their interaction, in an experience where understanding can be full since such intervention, the imaginative taking of sides, is totally inhibited. In tragedy of the causal-connective kind, opposites are transcended in an experience which is accepted as 'thus, and only thus' in its working. In *tragedie* these ordinary opposites yield before a greater good. The situation that we encounter in *Romeo and Juliet* is big with promise in the Shakespearian imagination—man caught in a world that tolerates no questions, knowing only reasons for action. *Hamlet*, as was said above, is the obvious instance. But the plight of the honourable man, owing a duty to 'the stock and honour' of his 'kin' may suggest also the situation of Prince Hal, placed between the firebrand Hotspur and the prudent Falstaff; between, too, the unargued confidence of the old in appearances—and thus their confidence in problems 'solved' which yet lie in wait for the young—and a time of reckoning which comes inexorably on. The tragic potentiality is the questioning of what will not yield to question, so that the situation is unalterable save by sacrificial death. In the tetralogy completed in *Henry V* all unwarranted confidence must be destroyed—literally so in Falstaff's death, metaphorically in the young King on the eve of battle—before the new order can be established. In *Hamlet* the old revenge-tragedy, 'Blood will have blood', comes face to face with the new: 'O cursed spite, That ever I was born to set it right!' Birth must lead directly to death in a world which cannot be otherwise altered. *Romeo and Juliet*, like *Richard II*, offers a meeting-place of the old *tragedie* of ineluctable doom and a newer thing—the plain truth that man will not willingly relinquish his transitory happiness (*li ben vani*). The tragedy must drive to man's dispossession, his being 'eased With being nothing'; but then we may see a final triumph. The real significance of 'character' in such a drama is not in terms of 'flaws', nor in any more general emphasis upon causal connection (as the 'impetuosity' of the lovers in *Romeo and Juliet*). It is rather in the intensity of contrast between initial immaturity and the prematurity forced upon the protagonists. In that light we see man confronting and in the end dominating the ends to which he is brought—not by a fighting withdrawal but by accepting and going to meet his destiny. The 'ripeness' or readiness, especially as it is manifest between fellow-sufferers in the bond of love, is all. If that tie holds, Death is robbed of the greater glory; the ending is triumph, a transcending the limits of mortality by holding fast, in the union of suffering, to what is best in the mortal condition.

If this is the shape of tragedy in some early works of Shakespeare, including *Romeo and Juliet*, what status shall we accord it in the whole body of Shakespearian insights? In *A Midsummer Night's Dream*, following hard upon *Romeo and Juliet*, the story of Pyramus and Thisbe affords 'very tragical mirth'. The 'concord of this discord' is to be found in belated reconciliation, with Bottom starting up from the grave to assure us that

> the wall is down that parted their fathers.

Does Shakespeare's mature vision, in comedy and tragedy alike, leave aside the striking fiction of reconciliation purchased by death, to dwell on the sober truth that

> Love, friendship, charity, are subjects all
> To envious and calumniating time?

In the plays which A. C. Bradley selected for special attention there is an ample scope for the things we have seen in these early tragedies—notably, the play of accident; the reversals of Fortune; time as not to be bound; an unalterable contrast between the old for whom reality is immovably settled and the young who needs must change it. These themes and motifs contribute organically to tragedies in which there is none the less a primary emphasis upon the character of the protagonists, and a continuing, though subtle, relationship between manifest failings in character and the disasters which befall. But this is yet consonant with something which conceptions of tragic grandeur—and notably the high compliment of Shakespeare 'restoring to tragedy the sceptred pall of its ancient dignity and place'—may cause us to overlook. There are remarkable developments in Shakespeare's art; but it is perhaps even more remarkable that in the whole range from Richard Crookback to Macbeth the essential status of the evil-doer remains the same. In the latest tragic portrayal of a conscious evil, that evil is not worse than a terrifying *naïveté*, which thinks to do the impossible—to arrest the course of time—and laments in the end the isolation that has been achieved. The greatest punishment in the Shakespearian tragic universe appears to be constant: it is to realize that the world of 'I am I' has in fact been attained. But what is conveyed is less the note of grandeur than of ineffaceable stupidity—the absurdity of isolation. For opposed to wilful individualism is an utter simplicity of goodness, expressed as unity between human beings, especially in the blessed relationship of love. Johnson held that Shakespeare's 'tragedy seems to be skill, his comedy to be instinct'. What perhaps makes for 'comedy' is a profound sense of the reality of human loyalty—that to aim beyond the human condition in these terms, the interdependence of the human family, is to err, and to err foolishly. In the later tragedies mortals err to their own destruction; in the early tragedies we have been considering, especially in *Richard II* and *Romeo and Juliet*, where the links with *tragedie* are strong, they err to the destruction of others. In *Romeo and Juliet*, the limits within which the human figure can be treated as agent are clear in the activity of mortals—Nurse and Friar, father and mother, friend and clan-enemy— who would bend others to their designs. For this activity serves only to leave those others more clearly the victims of mischance when it comes, without raising problems of character-connection, the relation between what they are and what they must suffer.

The great difference between *Romeo and Juliet* and later tragedies is the exploration of this connection: and Shakespeare's entry upon it is in terms of purposeful evil, an evil which would seek not merely the downfall but the extinction of all that is other than itself; Aaron is the crude but substantial prototype of Iago. It is therefore true that Shakespeare's tragic development 'does not exactly proceed through *Romeo and Juliet*', though the elements common to earlier and later tragic plays should not be overlooked in any simplified account of the 'tragedy of character'. If we seek the line of development from *Romeo and Juliet* we may find it not in the later tragedies but in the antitype of *tragedie*, those last plays of Shakespeare where the scope of accident includes the truth of fortunate accident, so that ancient wrongs are righted and the old make way for the newness of life in the young; where fulfilment is achieved in this world and not in a region beyond the stars, even death itself being cancelled and the exile returned to his native land; where all, in fine, is subject to a Time which is not envious or calumniating but, joining with mortal designs, 'Goes upright with his carriage', Such dramatic work, like *Romeo and Juliet* itself, is not to be dismissed by easy reference to 'the magic of Shakespeare's poetic genius' and 'the intermittent force of his dramatic power' as against any 'grasp of the foundations' of dramatic art. In *Macbeth* a sure grasp of the foundations of tragedy reaffirms that the attempt to bind time is an inherent impossibility: and there all a mature playwright's understanding of his art persuades us of the folly of any who would 'mock the time with fairest show'. If this is characteristically the dramatist's emphasis, drawing upon his deepest sense of the very medium in which he works, in both *Romeo and Juliet* and the last plays there is evident an Elizabethan poet's sense of paradox, of inherent impossibility only to be cancelled when love is triumphant. Romeo's boast—'love devouring death do what he dare . . .'— and Juliet's defiance of time are not tragic errors. They are not less than statements of the incompatibility between man and time when man would reach beyond time. We must not let our preconceptions blind us to the real drift and emphasis in Shakespeare, more particularly when there are involved ideas of drama and poetry with which we are relatively unfamiliar. That theme of reconciliation which is strongest and most constant of all in Shakespeare has a higher place in the Elizabethan imagination than we ordinarily may be prepared to allow.

The poetry which, in tragedy and romance alike, expresses these values, is fully charged with oblique meaning. Shakespeare's Friar Lawrence expatiating on the properties of herbs goes beyond the text Brooke had written for him, a simple discourse upon the right and wrong uses of knowledge, to the nature of man, himself the subject of contending forces of 'grace and rude will'. In doing so, Friar Lawrence speaks more than he knows. His herbs will, in the event, lie in no separate and opposed categories; but, like the Apothecary's poison, they will at once heal and destroy. Friar Lawrence's is a world of firmly distinct properties. In this he is like Perdita of *The Winter's Tale*, another who discourses upon Nature's gifts of the earth: and it is a similar irony that the case for crossing these categories, by grafting different stocks, is something Perdita indignantly refuses while it is yet the destiny to which she must be brought, in a final order of reconciliation where all distinction between natural and artificial disappears in an art which 'itself is nature'. For the true placing of *Romeo and Juliet* we must look to Shakespeare's whole development, including those romances which offer a final check to any merely 'connective' drama; and which, allowing a free play of apparent opposites, exhibit the full context in which we are to place Elizabethan exploration of what man is and what may befall him. Shakespeare's course is not simple, but it is distinctive. Rejecting the stereotype of cruel Fortune's blows—man as merely the weak subject of heaven's stratagems— he reinvests *tragedie* with the sense of greater good. But it is a profound fidelity to the fact which places the attainment of that good on the further side of life. Man must be forcibly dispossessed before he can discover a power of bearing it out even to the edge of doom. Love is then transcendent, itself a 'Beauty too rich for use, for earth too dear'. Manifestly, such a climax is a triumph of poetic drama; the lovers outsoar the shadow of our night. The last act of this play, standing on the eve of the tragic sequence that begins with *Julius Caesar*, is surpassed in intensity only by the close of *Antony and Cleopatra*, where that sequence ends. But there, as here, we see that the drama is dependent on no mere fiction. The lovers purchase a final unity at the only true cost; and it is a cost exacted from them by the onward drive of events. If we can lay aside our preconceived notions alike of the 'tragedy of character' and the 'tragedy of fortune' we may see that *Romeo and Juliet* is profoundly consistent with the longer run of the Shakespearian imagination.

RUTH NEVO

Tragic Form in Romeo and Juliet

Embedded in the tragedy of *Romeo and Juliet*, in the characters of the Friar and of Romeo himself, are two opposing traditional views concerning the origin of suffering, hence of tragedy, in human life. The play however eludes both the "providential" and the "fatal" formulae and offers us an early, but fully articulated Shakespearean tragic structure. This is marked by a characteristic emphasis on the opacity of appearances which the protagonists fail to penetrate, by tragic heroes whose high distinction is to be understood in terms of their embodiment of the forces whose collision provides the dynamic of the action; by a finely turned peripeteia in which coincidence and inevitability meet in a nexus of ironies; and by the evolving affirmation, made both dramatically (through action and character contrast) and poetically (through the light imagery) of the high value of idealized sexual love.

The plot of *Romeo and Juliet* stresses the accidental. The fortuitous meeting of Romeo and Benvolio with Capulet's illiterate messenger bearing the invitations he cannot decipher, the chance encounter between Romeo and Tybalt at a most unpropitious moment, the outbreak of the plague which quarantines Friar John, the meeting of Romeo and Paris at the Capulet tomb are instances which come at once to mind. Shakespeare, so far from mitigating the effect of unfortunate coincidence is evidently concerned to draw

From *Studies in English Literature 1500–1900*, Vol. IX, No. 1 © 1969 William Marsh Rice University.

our attention to it. Bad luck, misfortune, sheer inexplicable contingency is a far from negligible source of the suffering and calamity in human life which is the subject of tragedy's mimesis; while of all the ancient and deep-seated responses of man to the world which he inhabits the fear of some force beyond his control and indifferent, if not positively inimical, to his desires is one of the most persistent. Accident, therefore, mischance, all that arouses a fearful and rebellious sense of the unintelligible and the non-necessitated, powerfully suggests to human anxiety a spectrum of the darker possibilities, whether these be interpreted as a universe dominated by meaningless, mindless vicissitude—the senseless hurrying of atoms, or as a devil-ridden chaos, the satanic void itself. *Lear* is the play in which Shakespeare presents the anguish of a mind fully facing the threat of chaos, a mind hovering above the void; in *Romeo and Juliet* when he sets out to dramatize the vulnerability of young love, he places his young lovers not too great a distance from that terrifying terrain.

Romeo and Juliet opens with the casual ruffianism of the Capulet servants, their idle chatter, their random bawdry, their haphazard impulses of sex and aggression. What is represented is the perennial fret and froth of lust and anger. This is indicated by Gregory's attempt to keep Sampson's eye upon the masculine target of enmity: "The quarrel is between our masters and us their men," and the nonchalant reply of the omnivorous Sampson:

> S: 'Tis all one. I will show myself a tyrant. When I have
> fought with the men, I will be cruel with the maids: I will
> cut off their heads.
> G: The heads of the maids?
> S: Ay, the heads of the maids, or their maidenheads;
> take it in what sense thou wilt.
>
> (I.i.17–23)

The comic-braggart style of these exchanges and of the subsequent thumb-biting denies seriousness or consequentiality to these petty swashbucklers, so that in what follows the masters find themselves in full scale collision as a result of a chance encounter, the most random, casual circumstances. Yet, since the impulses touched off in Sampson and Gregory are human constants, there is an inevitability about it as well. This is the quotidien reality of the street and it is in Shakespeare an image of the unstable, fluctuating, precarious, potentially explosive, potentially even demonic reality in which the protagonists' lives are set. In *Julius Caesar* and in *Coriolanus* it erupts in the mob violence of the death of Cinna and the lynching of Coriolanus. In *Romeo and Juliet* it is less terrifying if only because it is canalized into the conventional form of the feud—it is not therefore utterly anarchic.

In Mercutio's Queen Mab speech the irrational, uncontrollable forces, the intractable and mischievous "other" that thwarts the will, or enters into subversive alliance with the anarchic appetites, is rendered as no more than impish; but at two of the crucial points in the play's chain of events—Mercutio's death and Friar John's incarceration—it is a plague which Mercutio invokes upon "both your houses," and an outbreak of plague which keeps the Friar a prisoner. And thus the tone and the degree of seriousness accorded to the ever present threat of mischief deepen in consonance with the tragic shaping of events. Evil in *Romeo and Juliet* is not accorded the diabolic status it has in the great tragedies, never invades experience, nor undermines the possibilities of existence to the same degree. It is nevertheless present in the very fabric of events, in the interplay of the bad luck which dogs the lovers with the bad habits of ingrown pride in the Capulets and the Montagues.

The conventionalized aggressions of Verona's feuding families mask a violent and intractable will. Capulet's "Hang, beg, starve, die in the street" is Lear in little though it is not that particular relation which is pressed to an issue in this play. In *King Lear* it is pressed to an issue. But in *King Lear* random events—spontaneous, unplanned, unprepared for—press towards good, for example, the meeting between Edgar and the blinded Gloucester or Edgar and Oswald; the evil of the will is correspondingly thrown into relief. In *Romeo and Juliet* random events press towards evil while the willed actions of the protagonists are radically innocent.

Romeo and Juliet is less tragic than *Lear*, not because it is different in kind, a "tragedy of chance" rather than a "tragedy of character." It is "less" tragic because the vision of evil in it is less deep, less complex, less comprehensive, less profoundly imprinted upon the consciousness of the characters. Its answer to the question all tragedy asks—Unde Malum?—is more hesitant, more eclectic. Here all is at a lower pitch; nearer to the commonplace and ordinary. Such fools, such daughters, such tempests of the soul as there are in *Lear* we would go far in life to find. But such fathers, such nurses, such young gallants are at all our doorsteps, within everyone's experience; not rare at all, though rarely depicted. This realism is the play's charm, the particular delight of its mimesis; but it is also the measure of its reach. It is all perfectly accomplished, within its comparatively limited scope, its comparatively limited perception.

It is worth noting, too, that of all the experiences of life which heighten sensibility and bestow gifts of the imagination, youthful love is the classic and common instance; while the familial enmity of elders is the classic obstacle of lovers. It is as much as anything this aspect of the natural and the universally available which is rendered by the largely Anglo-Saxon and almost monosyllabic simplicity of so many of the lovers' exchanges, a refinement of common speech which captures its very essence. "I would I were your bird"; "Dry sorrow drinks our blood"; "But to be frank and give it thee again"; "I am content, so thou wilt have it so."

A dramatization of accident in human life may fail to achieve tragic form in two opposite ways: by way of melodrama in the dramaturgy of the playwright, or by way of intrusive morality in the interpretation of the spectator. With respect to the former way Aristotle's demand for the necessary or the probable, as opposed to the merely possible and hence insignificant, is palpably relevant.

Intelligibility, that which distinguishes form from phenomenon, requires the perception of consequence. Too high a proportion therefore of incidents totally uncaused—of coincidence, sheer, random chance—would be one way to render a plot untragic. Aristotle's dictum—those incidents have the greatest effect on the mind which "occur unexpectedly and at the same time in consequence of one another"—sets us on the right path, though his example (Mitys's statue falling upon Mitys's murderer) strikes us as over-contrived and far inferior to the complex Elizabethan dramaturgy.

What is required is an interlocking, an intersection of opposing aspects of reality: the fore-ordained and the fortuitous, the inevitable and the arbitrary, choice and chance, will and the world. Tragedy will properly convey, with varying degrees of rigor, the inextricability in events of the given and the open; but with each knot that is tied, certain avenues are closed, and causes are made, so to speak, to yield up their calamitous consequences. The central knot which is tied in the plot of tragedy, as Aristotle indicates, is to be sought in the reversal, or peripeteia—the point which articulates the recoil of the action. This will characteristically present a nexus of ironies and the paradoxical effect of a coincidence which impresses us as an inevitability.

In the peripeteia of *Romeo and Juliet* this paradox is powerfully realized. Once again the streets are abrawl, the mad blood stirring, heads as full of quarrels as an egg is of meat. Romeo, aglow from his marriage ceremony, a vessel of good will, happens by the sheerest accident upon the truculent Mercutio and the irate Tybalt, his kinsman of an hour, precisely at the moment when Mercutio's contemptuous dismissal of him—"Alas, poor Romeo, he is already dead! stabbed with a white wench's black eye . . . is he a man to encounter Tybalt?" (II.iv.14–17)—has become true in a sense undreamt of by Mercutio. The good will with which he is filled becomes the cause of the death of his friend and of his own "calm, dishonourable, vile submission" as he then too interprets his behavior. Thus the conventional code of honor vanquishes the good will and Romeo, alone of the participants, suffers the anguish of knowing "what might have been" supplanted by "what must now be," and of enacting the fatal transformation of the one into the other. Given the circumstances—the companionship of young hotheads acting in ignorant and conventional truculence, given his own character as young man of honor—then what happens as a result of Mercutio's death under his arm *must* happen, is completely intelligible. Shakespeare's craft has given us a finely turned peripeteia in which the protagonist is responsible for his actions, though he is not accountable for the circumstances in which he must act, and in which these actions recoil ironically upon his own head. His despairing cry "O, I am fortune's fool" richly expresses his sense of the uncalled for, unchosen, outrageous event; of his helplessness in the face of the forces which are ranged against him, which include his own acceptance of the code of honor, and his own grief and self-reproach at the death of his friend "under his arm."

It is clear that what transforms Aristotle's mere "possibility" in these events into "necessity" is character. And this brings us to the second of the ways in which the dramatization of the accidents of life may fail to achieve tragic effect. It is important to perceive that Romeo's challenge of Tybalt is not merely an instance, as in the stock moralizing interpretation, of a rashness which fatally flaws his character and brings about his doom. If this were so, then the consequences in the play, though certainly possible, would be considerably less moving. The play would be morally exemplary but without tragic significance. Romeo would be too simply to blame, as indeed he has often been held to be, and the great tragic error too simply moralized. And in point of dramatic fact Romeo's action in challenging Tybalt is precisely not rash, though it puts him into great danger. On the contrary it is an action first avoided, then deliberately undertaken, and it is entirely expected of him by his society's code. Indeed by dramatic character properly conceived is meant precisely that propensity in conduct towards the very action imitated by the drama. Some such continuity between action and character is always to be discovered in Shakespearean characterization however richly individualized, diversified, discriminated in the details of idiom or gesture his personages may be. As Fergusson puts it, paraphrasing Aristotle:

> The dramatist imitates the action he has in mind, first by means of the plot, then in the characters, and finally in the media of language, music and spectacle. In a well-written play, if we understood it thoroughly, we should perceive that plot, character, and diction, and the rest spring from the same source, or, in other words, realize the same action or motive in the forms appropriate to their various media.

Thus his tragic heroes are precisely such as will be subject to, or embody, the collision of forces envisioned by the dramatist as the soul of his action.

II

What the play tells us of Romeo throughout Acts I and II is that he is a young Veronese possessed of honor and imagination, high spirit and amorous melancholy. As such he is one among his companions, but he is set apart from them by his capacity, and his readiness, to be fired by a high passion. The orchard scene (II.i—without the artificial break at l. 45) may be taken as emblematic of this relationship: Mercutio's jesting bawdry, in which Romeo joins with a will when he "is sociable"; his separation from his fellows, as he leaps the garden wall; and his consciousness of what separates them as he observes "He jests at scars that never felt a wound."

His being one of them in this way and set apart from them in this way is definitive of his tragic role: in his very character is represented a collision between blind conventional uniformity and imaginative specificity. It is a poignant awareness of this collision that Juliet expresses in her anguished question, "Wherefore art thou Romeo?" and through her sense of the irrelevance of the mere agreed name to the sweet immediate scent of the rose. It is this collision which defines the relations between the lovers and all Verona, the tragic results of which the drama exhibits. It is this collision which is the soul of the action, determining the form and substance of plot and character alike.

Romeo's sense of social identity and social commitment is greater than Juliet's; his sense therefore of the menace of the powers in whose face he flies, correspondingly greater. He is indeed exposed to the worst blows of Fortune, as any Stoic could have told him, when he makes his happiness dependent upon the unique individuality of another. And this he knows. Johnson wondered why Shakespeare gives Romeo a mood of involuntary cheerfulness immediately before his reception of Balthazar's news:

> I dreamt my lady came and found me dead. . .
> And breathed such life with kisses in my lips
> That I revived and was an emperor.
>
> (V.i.6–9)

Apart from the obvious pathos of the dramatic irony, the lines effectively underline by contrast the bondage of dread in which a man lives who has "given hostages to fortune," so that his deepest dream is of liberation and sovereignty.

At the crisis of the play, as we have seen, he expresses in the despairing cry "O, I am fortune's fool" his sense of his own impotence; and again when he takes the poison the notion of forced obedience to an intractable and hostile power is implicit in his imagery, in the "yoke" of inauspicious stars, and in the legal implications of "dateless bargain to engrossing death."

> O here
> Will I set up my everlasting rest;
> And shake the yoke of inauspicious stars
> From this world-wearied flesh. Eyes, look your last!
> Arms, take your last embrace! and, lips, O you,
> The doors of breath, seal with a righteous kiss
> A dateless bargain to engrossing death!
> Come, bitter conduct; come, unsavory guide!
> Thou desperate pilot, now at once run on
> The dashing rocks thy seasick weary bark!
>   (V.iii.109)

Whiter, pioneer of image critics, noted the "strange coincidence . . . between this last speech of Romeo and a former one in which he anticipates his misfortunes . . . the ideas drawn from the Stars, the Law, and the Sea succeed each other in both speeches, in the same order, though with a different application." The speech Whiter had in mind follows upon Mercutio's "talk of dreams," and expresses his premonition of disaster together with his hope for the successful weathering of it:

> my mind misgives
> Some consequence, yet hanging in the stars,
> Shall bitterly begin his fearful date
> With this night's revels, and expire the term
> Of a despised life closed in my breast,
> By some vile forfeit of untimely death:
> But He that hath the steerage of my course,
> Direct my sail!
>   (I.v.106–113)

Whiter is at a loss to discover the "latent association" in this accumulation of images, but the association is easily found when it is remembered that it is not so much the sea as the ship that sails the sea which is the crucial term, and that the sea voyage is an archetypal metaphor for life precisely for the reason that seamanship pits will and skill against that part of nature—the ocean—most challenging, and menacing, to man in its inextricable co-mingling of immutable stellar law and wild waves' chaos. The bark of love, of Tristan, Petrarch, and the sonneteers, and here, is a particular instance of this symbolism, where the great perturbation, the "mindless woe," has left the boat rudderless, or pilotless, or in some other way endangered its safe passage by rendering it vulnerable.

Romeo's dramatic development is indicated by the invocation, in the first speech, of God's providential guidance, whereas in the last speech he is his own "desperate pilot," past hope, and therefore resolved to run his seasick weary bark upon the dashing rocks. In Act V he hastens disaster by his very conviction of it. "Then I defy you, stars" expresses a consolation of his will, a determination to take the one finally free action left, in the Senecan-Stoic view, to a man in extremity. His self-control contrasts with his self-abandon-ment in the Friar's cell when told of his banishment, but, by a paradox which is only apparent, is the measure of his loss of all hope. Projected dramatically in action, the stubborn intensity of his desire to possess his happiness expresses itself as a sense of an inimical and omnipotent force by which he is doomed. Thus does he register his awareness of his own tragic role, against which he rebels, conjuring up a vision of a contrary role: "all these woes shall serve / For sweet discourses in our time to come" (III.v.54).

It is to be noted that he precisely does not identify his will with Fate as does Ford's Faustian Giovanni. He fights fortune, and defeat is not a fore-gone conclusion. But his "free" act in defiance of the forces which seem to be conspiring against him or which seem to be condemning his love, brings about an unnecessitated doom more definitively than any other action in the play. The powerful irony of his death scene is that as he swallows his fatal potion he is in fact nearer the fulfillment of his heart's desire than at any other moment in the course of the drama.

The opacity of events, the blindness, or ignorance, or failure to pene-trate appearances of the protagonists is, of course, a major tragic theme. It receives its greatest virtuosity of treatment in *Hamlet*. Here it is announced as early as I.ii when arrives Capulet's illiterate messenger with the invitation which precipitates the entire subsequent action. "I pray you," he inquires of Romeo, "can you read anything you see?" "Ay," replies Romeo, "if I know the letters and the language." In the familiar manner of Elizabethan stage-craft the fool's patter, ostensibly drawing a jest from the discrepancy in wisdom between the learned and the ignorant, actually serves as an ironic commentary upon all human ignorance in knowledge, on all that men do, not knowing what they do. The fool is one of two classic Elizabethan means of dramatizing the limitations of human knowledge. The arras is the other, providing, with its analogues and metaphorical equivalents profound and various images of unawareness. Here, in Iv.v. the arras hides the inert body of Juliet from the Nurse's sight as she potters about calling to a slugabed bride, as she believes, to arouse her for her wedding; nor when it is drawn is the truth disclosed.

Against the ebb and flow of Romeo's hope and fear—charted by the sequence of scenes—are juxtaposed the Friar's Christian forebodings and Christian hopes. The Friar fears the lovers' destruction from their very first abandonment, in his view, to unbridled passion, rash impetuosity, and head-strong will. The Friar's strictures are often regarded as having a choric func-tion in the play, of being, that is, indicative of the point of view properly to be taken of events; certainly his words at their marriage are richly prophetic:

> These violent delights have violent ends
> And in their triumph die, like fire and powder,
> Which, as they kiss, consume.
>
> (II.vi.9–11)

But it is after all, simply in character, perfectly natural and appropriate to the *persona*, for the Friar to preach to Romeo upon the disastrous consequences of unbridled passion. It would be a dereliction of his evident Christian duty not to do so. It is similarly the least we could expect of the purveyor of religious instruction to identify the "greater power than we can contradict" with Provi-dence, though he does not presume to know at that point in the play when he is stumbling at graves to what obscure end Providence is thus thwarting his intents; and it is sound Christian doctrine beautifully adapted to the style of reflection of a gentle hermit-apothecary which ascribes to the strange para-doxes of Providence the evil presence of poison in the good herbs of the earth:

> O, mickle is the powerful grace that lies
> In plants, herbs, stones, and their true qualities;
> For naught so vile that on the earth doth live
> But to the earth some special good doth give;
> Nor aught so good but, strained from that fair use,
> Revolts from true birth stumbling on abuse.
> Virtue itself turns vice, being misapplied,
> And vice sometime's by action dignified; . . .
> Two such opposed kings encamp them still
> In man as well as herbs—grace and rude will;
> And where the worser is predominant,
> Full soon the canker death eats up that plant.
>
> (II.iii.15–30)

Certainly the Friar's "grace and rude will" speech has a comprehensive, generalizing, and reverberating quality—the generalizing and reverberating quality of Christian doctrine. How much more bitter an irony is it then that the Friar's own benevolent, would-be "providential" and truly Christian interference in the course of events in fact precipitates the catastrophe as much as anything in the play. His drug is in the outcome, as deathly as that dispensed to Romeo by his dusty and down-at-heel Mantuan counterpart.

The Stoic-Christian conflict runs deep in Shakespeare, as in the entire Renaissance drama. There is no tragedy which is without its variant. Here it takes the relatively simple and obvious form of a confrontation between a humanistically educated young man and his Christian confessor. Nothing could be more perfectly and completely dramatized, more perfectly in character than the terms of their dialogue, the projection of their separate points of view. Both Romeo and the Friar view their acts and enact their views with a marvellous consistency and propriety. But if action is here being imitated, or realized, in the medium of character in truly Shakespearean fashion, the action which is being imitated represents that blindness to the real state of things which is perhaps Shakespeare's profoundest intuition of the origin of pain and evil.

The question at issue between Romeo and the Friar is the question of love, of that heightened excitement of the senses, emotions, and imagination which accompanies, or gives rise to, sexual passion. And love, in the sense of sexual passion, as Shakespeare well knew, has been the object of more scepticism, suspicion, and disapprobation than any other movement of the human spirit and is included as such in the scheme of neither Stoicism nor Christianity. It is to be noted that the lovers, though they respect and revere their spiritual father, and gladly take his practical advice, are totally impervious to his religious instruction. They do not defy or evade, as do Ford's Giovanni and Annabella; they simply betray no awareness, save for Juliet's single reference to the "god of my idolatry," of the application of religious-moral evaluation or judgment to themselves at all. Since, in their eyes, love is self-justifying, they and the Friar represent two autonomous and mutually exclusive orders of experience, each reflecting upon the other at their points of intersection.

One such pivotal point of intersection is the pilgrim sonnet: the grave and joyful pas-de-deux which is their discovery of each other. This passage, in its implications, is perfectly ambiguous. From the point of view of Christian Agape it is profanity; from the point of view of romantic Eros, epiphany. The two loves, psychologically and historically interdependent, stand to each other, as they have so often stood, in a relation of antithesis, and challenge. The marriage of the lovers is, similarly, a point of intersection. The junction of their desire to be married as quickly as possible and the Friar's anxiety to have them married as quickly as possible is purely coincidental. They are indifferent to the consecrating aspect of the ceremony. Romeo speaks for both when he says:

> Do thou but close our hands with holy words
> Then love-devouring death do what he dare,
> It is enough I may but call her mine.
>   (II.vi.6–8)

Whereas to the Friar it is the sacrament and the sacrament alone which can "incorporate two in one" and rescue love from vanity.

If Shakespeare offers no one-dimensional view of the higher possibilities of love it is nevertheless the higher possibilities that he is concerned to bring out. The dramaturgy of multiple reflection brings each of the characters into analogous and contrastive relationship with the lovers. Romeo is flanked by Friar Lawrence who, with all his own resigned tolerance for youth, regards his doting as a regrettable carnality. He is also flanked by the inimitable Mercutio, who regards the same phenomenon as a foolishness which men invent to torment themselves with when they would be better employed wenching—"a great natural that runs lolling up and down to hide his bauble in a hole" (II.iv.89). Juliet, on the other hand, is flanked by Capulet, whose concern is the very proper one, in a dutiful and affectionate paterfamilias, of prudential matchmaking; and by the Nurse, the epitome of the earthy, the base, the material, and the utterly unimaginative. As naturalist as Mercutio though of infinitely less wit, she is one of Shakespeare's finest creations in the mode of contrast between high and low, base and heroic, rare and common; between comedy and dignity. And in this mode she is the apogee of that view of love as simply either sex or matchmaking which is the bedrock contrast to the lovers' affirmation. To them love is an enlightenment of the human condition perfectly fulfilling all needs of flesh and spirit.

III

What emerges from the contrasts and the affirmation is related to the definitive importance of the light imagery in the play—is indeed the reason for the definitive importance of the light imagery. The play's rich profusion and variety of light images, generally taken to be symbolic of the natural beauty of youthful love, and of the play's theme of "brilliance swiftly quenched," can be seen to possess a stricter and more cogent relation to the entire dramaturgy of the play. In the steady radiance of the play's imagery there is a progression from the light which is a metaphor for beauty to the light which is a metaphor for knowledge; from that which is a grace of appearance to that which is a gift of insight. Even in "O she doth teach the torches to burn bright," there is a suggestion of the platonic; while the "feasting presence full of light" is, typologically, a symposium. There is a solemnity about certain of the light images, as opposed to the sensuous delight of others, which allows comparison with the identification of beauty and knowledge through the imagery of light of Marvell or the Milton of the early poems.

What it amounts to is that Romeo and Juliet are possessed of the light. And they alone are possessed of the light, in a Verona to whom the light is beyond comprehension—to whom love is irrelevant. These others indeed, unrecognizing, unknowing, acting out their natures, bring harm to the light bearers. But the two whose significant presence in the play is Shakespeare's addition to his source, Rosaline and Paris, are the subtlest reflectors of all. Less clearly modelled, further in the middle distance of the play, attenuated shadows out of courtly love, chaste and devoted respectively, they are cast like a snake's skin by the more robust reality of Romeo and Juliet.

Happy love, observes de Rougemont, has no history.

> Romance only comes into existence where love is fatal, frowned upon and doomed by life itself. What stirs lyrical poets to their finest flights is neither the delight of the senses nor the fruitful contentment of the settled couple; not the satisfaction of life, but its passion. And passion means suffering. There we have the fundamental fact.

Because there is so much truth in de Rougemont's view it is important to make distinctions. Romeo and Juliet do not "suffer love." They suffer because they love; they are exposed to pain and suffering on account of their love; but they do not "suffer love." Paradoxically enough it is Shakespeare's comedy heroes who suffer love: Titania, Berowne, even Beatrice and Benedick, Viola, because it is through the frustrations and involvements of love suffered that the comic plot weaves its way to make these odds all even in the end. And Troilus, Angelo, Imogen, the young man of the Dark Sonnets,—these all suffer love.

But in *Romeo and Juliet* Shakespeare is as revolutionary as Donne: his lovers too are "interassured of the mind," a mutual pair. Life does not allow them either "the delight of the senses" nor the "fruitful contentment of the settled couple," but Juliet's "Gallop apace" is remarkable because it contains the promise of both—it is purely erotic, without trace of the mysticism in which sex is mere symbol. And the chiastic formality, the mock-rhetorical reversals and substitutions of their parting aubade (III.v.), suggest not merely the reciprocity of their feelings but also the perspective of life, of jocund day, from which to take in his playful-serious "Come death, and welcome!" It is a parting of which it can be truly claimed that it is "not yet a breach but an expansion"; and the love which is "an interinanimation of two souls" because it is precisely not the "passion that wants darkness and triumphs in a trans-figuring Death." There is no naked sword between these lovers. Theirs is not a desire to die to the world but a most energetic desire to live in it, to survive crises and to have "all these woes . . . serve / For sweet discourses in our time to come" (III.v.54). And to this powerful complex of feelings their suffering stands in an almost tangential relation.

Their suffering is powerfully delineated. It is Romeo's despair at Friar Lawrence's cell; it is Juliet's horror as she contemplates the Friar's drug; and her greater horror as she contemplates her betrothal to Paris. It is Romeo's realizing his betrayal of Mercutio; it is Juliet realizing the Nurse's betrayal of her. It is Romeo driven to kill Paris, the "good gentle youth." It is Juliet facing her father's fury.

Juliet's suffering is finely discriminated from Romeo's as is her suicide and indeed her experience of love. Love has its own devouring exclusiveness, its own ruthless priorities:

> That "banished", that one word "banished",
> Hath slain ten thousand Tybalts. Tybalt's death
> Was woe enough, if it had ended there;
> Or, if sour woe delights in fellowship
> And needly will be ranked with other griefs,
> Why followed not, when she said "Tybalt's dead",
> Thy father, or thy mother, nay, or both,
> Which modern lamentation might have moved?
> (III.ii.119–126)

But what is a frantic probing of new and overwhelming experience in Juliet is a shocking violence of repudiation in Capulet's "hang, beg, starve, die in the street" (III.v.204). Essentially Juliet's suffering is the realization of lone-liness and isolation. The nurse's repudiation ("Romeo's a dishclout to him") of all that she believed understood between them, follows her father's and is the more painful as the relationship of confidante was the more intimate.

I think you are happy in this second match,

> For it excels your first; or if it did not,
> Your first is dead—or 'twere as good he were
> As living here and you no use of him
>   (III.v.230–238)

undermines her confidence in every seeming friend so that to the fear naturally attending the taking of the drug is added a terrible suspicion of the
Friar's motives. The poison speech is masterly in its rendering of horror
enacted in imagination; the source of its great strength lies in the imaginative pressing to an issue of her knowledge that "my dismal scene I needs must
act alone." It is not of death or of being dead that she is afraid. She is afraid,
of course, of a miscarriage of the plan; but her terror is for that moment
when she may find herself imprisoned and alone with the appalling dead.
What her imagination projects is an image of the ultimate aloneness, the
maximum distance which can be travelled by a human being from the
sustaining and comforting presence of his kind. That she is ready for this is
a measure of her fidelity, not an indication that death is "the one kind of
marriage that Eros was ever able to wish for."

    The height of Romeo's anguish is when he sees himself betrayer of his
friend to death, and cries in self-reproach and loss of faith, "Thy beauty has
made me effeminate" (III.i.114); and the lowest point of his degradation (as
the Friar is quick to define it) is his total abandonment to despair at the news
of his banishment. The relation therefore of their suffering to their love is
the consequential relation of tragedy—the relation which will produce a
catharsis of pity and terror. They are exposed to the evil and ignorance of the
world, and involved in the evil and ignorance of the world, by virtue of the
very gifts of imagination which mark them out as the vessels of tragic
suffering.

    From the wreckage tragedy depicts, something that is of the spirit
survives to effect our reconciliation to the heart-shaking emotions of pity and
terror. The scene of their death is the recognition of that survival. Their love
has involved them in misfortune, guilt, deprivation, sorrow, and betrayal but
it has survived—survived even Mercutio's death, and Tybalt's. It is affirmed
by Romeo: "For here lies Juliet, and her beauty makes / This vault a feasting
presence full of light" (V.iii.85–86) and enacted with the most direct
simplicity by Juliet: "O churl! drunk all, and left no friendly drop to help me
after?" (V.iii.163–164). It is not true to the facts of the play to say that they
are married only in death, for their marriage is consummated before Romeo
leaves for Mantua. What one can say is that marriage forms their view of
their relations with each other from the very first balcony scene, so that death
itself is robbed of its sting, is even made welcome, under this figure. This is

the effect of the conjugal and erotic imagery of their final scene. The Elizabethan pun contains manifold possibilities and Juliet's "This is thy sheath; there rest, and let me die" (V.iii.175) is without doubt a metaphorical sexual act. But it is an act undertaken because she is in love with Romeo, not because she is in love with death. Nor is their death a sacrifice of love, as certain of the Christianizing critics would have it.

Their death is an act of freedom and of fidelity; hence an affirmation of the reality, vitality, and value of their experience. Nor do we reconcile ourselves to their deaths because they have become immortal in literature whereas "they would have become old and worldly in time." We reconcile ourselves to our pity and terror because we have witnessed one complete cadence of the human spirit, enacted to the full, rendered entirely intelligible. What reconciles us is not what could possibly reconcile us in life. Only achieved art can so order and satisfy our appetencies, our perceptions, and our insights. Shakespeare's dramatic reticence in the context of boldly erotic imagery gives the scene the suggestiveness of an analogue: we glimpse something of the resources of tenderness and gaiety, freedom and self-possession, which lie in the power of an idealized sexual relation to discover. It is with precisely these higher possibilities that a romance tragedy will leave us. For the lovers, all losses are restored and sorrows end. The elders must make of it what sense they can.

ROSALIE L. COLIE

Othello *and the Problematics of Love*

It was not altogether easy to make a tragedy of a love story, traditionally the stuff of comedy. We are so accustomed to *Romeo and Juliet*, for instance, and to *Othello* and *Antony and Cleopatra*, that we tend to forget that there were technical problems for the playwright in making sufficiently serious as tragedies the domestic problems of love. "Love" existed in the Renaissance in important literary shapes, but on the whole these were not tragic—indeed, if anything, the conjunctive powers of love were regarded, in drama, as suited rather to comic solutions than to high tragic decisiveness. Further, love itself is an unstable element: it is flighty, and as such a proper subject for farce, not for tragedy—at best, romantic comedy, ending in beautiful conciliations, offered a proper generic habitat for tales of love.

Outside of drama, literary love tended to take two major shapes, one of them, the romance, was closely related to comedy, its organization owing much to comic conventions and feeding back into Renaissance comic formulations. The other, the love-lyric, presents quite a different world of love: from Dante's forceful presentation onward, love in lyric form seemed to be of a higher sort than the love presented in either comedy or romance, a private experience in a world—as opposed to the world of comedy or romance—sparsely populated, with a few figures all enjoying notably intense emotions. In the lyric poetry of love, poets began all kinds of explorations

From *Shakespeare's Living Art.* © 1974 Princeton University Press.

into themselves, so that in literature if not in life, psychological self-explo-
ration and self-description were normally practised, and a vast reservoir of
topoi of self-inspection became the inheritance of the great Renaissance
writers of songs and sonnets.

In particular, the sonnet cycle offered possibilities for developing the
lyric themes of love. Dante set the tone and Petrarca confirmed it, to influence writers of lyric cycles and sonnet cycles throughout the long Renaissance, who in turn added their own variations and contributed their own
insights to a genre elevated by those Italian models to something far
beyond the ordinary love-lyric. By the time Shakespeare tried his hand at a
love-tragedy, he had already worked in several of the major literary love-
forms of the Renaissance. His sonnets are a major document in the lyric
tradition, and several early comedies served him as preparations for his
major love-tragedies, *Romeo and Juliet* and *Othello*: *Two Gentlemen of Verona*
offered one kind of pre-study for *Romeo and Juliet*, *Much Ado* is in part a
comic dress-rehearsal for *Othello*. Without *Romeo and Juliet*, I think, Shakespeare would have had greater difficulties with the problems raised by
Othello.

It is, then, with that early play that I wish to deal first. With *Romeo and
Juliet*, its plot deriving from a sad and rather sordid novella, Shakespeare
attempted his first love-tragedy. How did an ambitious and experimental
author go about this task? First of all, he drew upon types officially "comic,"
types which had already colonized the prose narratives of the Renaissance.
He peopled his play in a perfectly familiar way, with figures from the comic
cast: the young girl; her suitor *(adulescens amans)*, whom her father does not
favor; another *adulescens* (County Paris), whom the father approves; a father,
senex, who becomes, naturally, *senex iratus* when crossed by his daughter; a
nurse, not only the customary *nutrix* but a particular subtype, *nutrix garrula*.
Our hero is accompanied by a friend, indeed by two friends, Benvolio and
Mercutio; in a comedy, for symmetry, presumably Juliet would have had two
school-fellows with her, to be disposed of at the play's end to the two young
men. Here, though, she is unaccompanied; and because the play is a tragedy,
Mercutio can be killed off and Benvolio fall out of the play without our
wondering why or lamenting the absence of appropriate girls to be given
away to Romeo's "extra" friends.

Comedies take place in cities; this tragedy is very city-bound; even
Friar Lawrence's cell is within walking distance of the famous two houses.
When Romeo flees Verona, he does not take to the woods, as a proper
romance-hero might have been expected to do (and as Orlando does), but
settles in nearby Mantua, to outwait, as he hopes, his troubles. As befits a
comic city-scene, we have splendid servants of different sorts, baiting each

other and irritating as well as serving their betters, providing relief for what turns out to be a very grim sequence of actions.

So far, so good; but how to turn the play into a tragedy of love? What language, for example, to use? From the first spoken words of *Romeo and Juliet*, the Chorus' speech in sonnet-form, we are directed to a major source for the play's language, the sonnet tradition, from which, as we see at once, Romeo had drunk deep; like the young men at Navarre's court, Romeo knew the literary modes of the Renaissance young gentleman. Critics of the play speak again and again of the sonnets in the play itself, sometimes even a full fourteen lines spoken by a speaker alone or by two speakers in consort—the great sonnet exchange between Romeo and Juliet at their meeting is a sign both of their rhetorical sophistication and of their union with one another. Some of the sonnets have an extra quatrain or even sestet; once an octave stands alone, several times a sestet stands alone. All this sonnet-formality must draw our attention to what the playwright was up to—that is, his deepening of events by a language habitually associated with a particular kind of high-minded and devoted love. By his borrowing of devices and language from another genre for his tragedy, he cues us to the kind of love involved in his play. Of all the lyric forms, indeed of all the literary forms, of love, the sonnet-sequence honors the profound seriousness of the emotion: love is central to the life and existence of the sonnet-persona, who gives himself over to the delicious exigencies of his condition, which he celebrates with all the force of his soul and of his poetical powers. As more transitory love-lyrics do not, the sonnet-sequence also provides opportunities for deep and faceted self-examination, as the sonneteer considers and reconsiders his ever-changing emotional state, recording as carefully as possible his perceptions of his own shifting progress and regress along his path.

We are introduced to Romeo, typed as a melancholy lover before he appears onstage, who enters speaking "distractedly" in the proper Petrarchan rhetoric of oxymoron. He runs through the rhetorical exercises of the love-poet with extraordinary facility. He sets his own text—"Here's much to do with hate, but more with love" (I.i.173)—and amplifies it:

> Why then, O brawling love! O loving hate!
> O anything, of nothing first create!
> O heavy lightness! serious vanity!
> Mis-shapen chaos of well-seeming forms!
> Feather of lead, bright smoke, cold fire, sick health!
> Still-waking sleep, that is not what it is!
> This love feel I, that feel no love in this.
>
> (I.i.174–80)

Shortly after this comical though splendid display of his reading in Petrarchan figure, Romeo defines love, in the manner, says one French theorist, of
the *blason*, or (as English critics tended to say) of the definition:

> Love is a smoke rais'd with the fume of sighs;
> Being purg'd, a fire sparkling in lovers' eyes;
> Being vex'd, a sea nourish'd with loving tears.
> What is it else? A madness most discreet,
> A choking gall, and a preserving sweet.
>
> (I.i.188–92)

He runs through the repertory—the oxymora, so casually tossed off, the variations upon a hundred sonnets in the official mode. His *epideixis* is clear—
"Why then," and "What is it else?" introduce a spate of words in the right
key, uttered by an energetic youth creating his own role according to the best
literary models.

Romeo's Rosaline, always invisible to us, is made up of whole cloth, the
texture of which is classical reference:

> she'll not be hit
> With Cupids' arrow. She hath Dian's wit,
> And in strong proof of chastity well arm'd,
> From Love's weak childish bow she lives unharm'd.
> She will not stay the siege of loving terms,
> Nor bide th'encounter of assailing eyes,
> Nor ope her lap to saint-seducing gold.
> O she is rich in beauty; only poor
> That, when she dies, with beauty dies her store.
>
> (I.i.206–14)

Romeo's clichés play upon the Epicurean argument for love, using the
themes of *carpe diem* and productivity so familiar from love-lyrics (and the
second familiar from Shakespeare's own remarkable sequence of sonnets).
Romeo continues in language remarkably close to those sonnets:

> For beauty, starv'd with her severity,
> Cuts beauty off from all posterity.
>
> (I.i.217–18)

The next couplet points to its own artificiality, with its ostentatious opposition of bliss and despair, again a sonnet-cliché. That couplet then leads to a
familiar paradox:

> She is too fair, too wise, wisely too fair,
> To merit bliss by making me despair.
> She hath forsworn to love, and in that vow
> Do I live dead that live to tell it now.
>   (I.i.219–22)

Even in the familiar self-denial of the sonneteer, self-critical and self-indul-gent at once, Romeo the lover maintains decorum.

Decorum or no, what we are asked to see in this Romeo is the lover by the book, the lover *too* decorous, who adopts the Petrarchan role and lives it to the utmost—in his rhyme, in his solitary nightlife, in the moping melan-choly that so worries his mother. And Romeo sticks to the rules of his loving: when Benvolio urges him to Capulet's feast, hoping that he will there find another lady to fall in love with, Romeo is shocked—but in a sestet:

> When the devout religion of mine eye
> Maintains such falsehood, then turn tears to fires;
> And these, who, often drown'd, could never die,
> Transparent heretics, be burnt for liars!
> One fairer than my love! The all-seeing sun
> Ne'er saw her match since first the world begun.
>   (I.ii.88–93)

Romeo's hyperbolical fidelity leaves much to be desired, since he falls in love with Juliet the instant he claps eye on her and rhymes his new love at once, in familiar language most beautifully disposed:

> O, she doth teach the torches to burn bright!
> It seems she hangs upon the cheek of night
> As a rich jewel in an Ethiop's ear . . .

and on and on, to

> Did my heart love till now? Forswear it, sight;
> For I ne'er saw true beauty till this night.
>   (I.v.42–44, 50–51)

Both Romeo and Juliet are quick at this kind of language; their sonnet, with its "extra" quatrain at the end, spoken in turn by the two of them, is a marvelous sublimation of the witty exchange of young people meeting and trying each other out. Romeo speaks the first quatrain, Juliet the second; they divide the sestet, Juliet setting the rhyme and Romeo matching it. As Juliet

notes, Romeo knows the rules of love—"You kiss by the book"—and so does
she, certainly, for she is capable of very conventional wit in terms of love, as,
it turns out later, she is also capable of conventional comment on hate.

Mercutio offers a critical voice against Romeo's softer one: as the young
men go to the dance, Mercutio teases Romeo, challenging him to exchanges
of wit much like those to which Benvolio had earlier challenged Romeo. All
three young men knew their rhetorical alternatives and chose their styles
freely: Mercutio mocks Romeo in terms of his love-learned language:

> Romeo! humours! madman! passion! lover!
> Appear thou in the likeness of a sigh;
> Speak but one rhyme and I am satisfied;
> Cry but "Ay me!" pronounce but "love" and "dove" . . . ,
> (II.i.7–10)

to pass on to a wonderfully punning salaciousness about the true purpose of
loving. Mercutio provides at these points an Ovidian voice, that of the high-
spirited libertine whose awareness of the physical delights of love balance the
sweetness, the near-namby-pambyness of the Petrarchan traditional
language. In his later exchange with Mercutio, Romeo answers in kind,
thereby convincing his friend that he is once more "sociable," which is to say,
out of love and a sane man again. Romeo has altered his decorum, as
Mercutio notes—"Thy wit is a very bitter sweeting; it is a most sharp
sauce"—from his melancholy sonneteering to the man-about-town, man-
among-men style of the epigrammatist; he sharpens Mercutio's Ovidian
voice to something nearer Martial's tone. And this of course is what fools
Mercutio into believing that his friend has fallen out of love, for no man in
the lover's pose can make the jests of II.iv. about sexuality. We of course know
better: Romeo is finally and at last in love—and, dutiful to convention, has
fallen in at first sight. This prescription of love's proper origin is written into
the action, given reality, unmetaphored, in the scene at the feast: both young
people recognize, too, what is happening to them, though they obey the rules
of courteous wordplay, which detonates their passion, as well as observing
the rules of courtly loving.

Romeo by no means abandons sonnet-language because he has in fact
fallen truly in love—again and again in his speeches to and about Juliet,
conventional sonnet-topics turn up. To his new love, seen at her window, he
offers the conventional likeness of eyes to stars:

> Two of the fairest stars in all the heaven,
> Having some business, do entreat her eyes

To twinkle in their spheres till they return.
What if her eyes were there, they in her head?
The brightness of her cheek would shame those stars,
As daylight doth a lamp; her eyes in heaven
Would through the airy region stream so bright
That birds would sing, and think it were not night.
                                             (II.ii.15–22)

Which is to say, her eyes are not like stars, but like suns; Romeo is a
conceited poet, who draws out his conceits to utter hyperbole—as we shall
see, his Juliet can do the same. He borrows other stock-elements from the
sonneteer; in the orchard he wishes to be a glove on her hand to feel her
cheek leaning against that hand, in Mantua he wishes to be a mouse, the
humblest beast about the house, so as to catch sight of Juliet in Verona.
Again, he combines two common sonnet-images, that of the lover as skipper
and that of the lady as merchandise, in three pretty lines:

I am no pilot; yet, wert thou as far
As that vast shore wash'd with the farthest sea,
I should adventure for such merchandise.
                                             (II.ii.82–84)

   As critics are fond of saying, Juliet's language is less artificial than
Romeo's, which seems to point to her greater simplicity in love than his, to
her greater realism about their situation than his. But she too has had her
training in the love-rhetoric: her Romeo will "lie upon the wings of night/
Whiter than new snow on the raven's back" (III.ii.18–19) She too can pursue
a conceit to its ultimate, absurd conclusions:

                  when he shall die,
Take him and cut him out in little stars,
And he will make the face of heaven so fine
That all the world will be in love with night,
And pay no worship to the garish sun.
                                             (III.ii.21–25)

It is worth noting that Juliet's metaphoric daring is greater than Romeo's: she
solves the sun-stars problem firmly and defiantly in favor of her image, while
his imagery was less committed, less precise, and less extreme: he speaks,
more than she, by the book. Her conceit of "little stars," which shall trans-
late Romeo to classical immortality in a constellation, sends us back to his

likeness of her to the sun. Her language honors the darkness in which her love is conceived, and its ugliest, most forceful image ("cut him out in little stars") forebodes that love's violent end.

When the Nurse comes in with the news of Tybalt's death at Romeo's hands, Juliet bursts into oxymoron, violently denouncing her lover in a passage as rhetorically extreme as anything Romeo had uttered in his period of self-persuaded, false love:

> O serpent heart, hid with a flow'ring face!
> Did ever dragon keep so fair a cave?
> Beautiful tyrant! fiend angelical!
> Dove-feather'd raven! wolfish-ravening lamb!
> Despised substance of divinest show!
>   (III.ii.73–77)

On she goes, in this language, until her reason returns to remind her that of the two, she would far rather have lost Tybalt than Romeo. With that realization, she returns to the simpler poetry more characteristic of her utterance. It may be, as Levin has suggested, that Juliet's linguistic extravagance marks her estrangement from Romeo—certainly it marks her loss of herself in passionate outrage; on the other hand, the images she uses in this passage are linked both to those she had earlier used to try to express her large love for Romeo, and to those he used of her. Even here, the conjunction between the lovers is maintained in their language.

As we look back over the lovers' utterance, we can see very plainly the problem of expression: petrarchan language, *the* vehicle for amorous emotion, can be used merely as the cliché which Mercutio and Benvolio criticize; or, it can be earned by a lover's experience of the profound oppositions to which that rhetoric of oxymoron points. When Romeo and Juliet seek to express their feelings' force, they return constantly to petrarchanisms hallowed with use—but, having watched their development as lovers, an audience can accept as valid the language upon which they must fall back. When Romeo readies himself to die, he does so in the proper sonnet-imagery, to which he has earlier had recourse—

> Thou desperate pilot, now at once run on
> The dashing rocks thy sea-sick weary bark.
>   (V.iii.117–18)

After this crisis and the acknowledgment that ends it, the love of Romeo and Juliet resumes its course, to express itself in the familiar dawn-song of medieval tradition, a song which the lovers speak in dialogue. At this point, one might note a general feature of this play, of which the *aubade* is a splendid example: it is full of set-pieces of different kinds. Lady Capulet and the Nurse speak a duet about the County Paris's charms; at Juliet's supposed death, Lord and Lady Capulet, the Nurse, and Paris utter a quartet. There are many double exchanges—Juliet's sonnet-exchange with Romeo at the dance, Romeo's exchanges with Benvolio and Mercutio, Juliet's stichomythy with Paris at Friar Lawrence's cell. Arias as well: Juliet's great prothalamic invocation to night, with its Ovidian echoes, "Gallop apace, you fiery-footed steeds"; her schematic meditation on death and the charnel-house just before she takes the drug; Mercutio's inventions on the subject of dreams. The effect of these passages is greatly to draw our attention to the poetry of this play, to the evocativeness of its language, but also to do something else, risky in a play though ideal in a lyric, to arrest the action for the sake of poetic display.

When we look at the play from some distance and in terms of fairly stock rhetorical patterns, we can see how formalized, how static, much of its organization is, how dependent upon tableaux and set-pieces. The Chorus begins the play with his sonnet, then one party enters, then the other (from, we presume, "houses" demarcated in the stage-architecture). The two parties engage in a mock-version of the vendetta which, with Tybalt's entrance onstage, quickly transforms the action into real violence, and ends with the Prince's order for the maintenance of peace. At the play's end, one party enters to lament the death of a child, then the other, lamenting the death of the other child; both parties stand to hear Friar Lawrence's unraveling of the plot and the Prince's strictures. Each bereaved father promises the other, appropriately, a sepulchral statue of his child in commemoration of child, of love, and of the ultimate sad settlement of the long feud. With a final moral-izing sestet, the Prince, a dignified *deus ex machina*, ends the action alto-gether. The lyric interludes, so important to the tone and psychology of the whole play, are of a piece with the pageant-like dramaturgy. Though they reveal the conditions of the speaker's mind, they do so in language rather dictated by the situation than obedient to the complexity of the plot, char-acter, or action. The language loosens itself in many ways from the sonnet-substance from which it draws so much, but in *Romeo and Juliet* it is never so free as in *Othello*, where the same body of conventional language is managed to fit the characters and the plots' needs without drawing undue attention to itself.

Romeo and Juliet is in many ways an apprentice-play: there the poet first met the real problems involved in turning lyrical love into tragedy. The Chorus must tell us at the outset that these lovers are star-crossed, and, in case we should forget that this is so, Romeo says later, rather awkwardly, "my mind misgives / Some consequence, yet hanging in the stars, / Shall bitterly begin his fearful date / With this night's revels" (I.iv.106–109). Friar Lawrence's *sententiae* reinforce the notion of rash haste, but they do not increase our sense of tempo—rather, in the way of *sententiae*, they do just the opposite. Rash haste and star-crossing are the rigid *donnée* of the action, which we are not invited to question or to consider. Love is unhappy, deeply-felt, beautifully expressed; youth is wasted at the behest of irrational old age, but the involvements of tragic behavior have not found their language in this play, although the spectacular oppositions of the petrarchan rhetoric have been enlarged into plot, as well as into the emotional and social structure of the play.

All the same, *Romeo and Juliet* makes some marvelous technical manipulations. One of the most pleasurable, for me, of Shakespeare's many talents is his "unmetaphoring" of literary devices, his sinking of the conventions back into what, he somehow persuades us, is "reality," his trick of making a verbal convention part of the scene, the action, or the psychology of the play itself. Love-at-first-sight is here made to seem entirely natural, set against the artificiality and unreality of Romeo's self-made love for Rosaline; its conventionality is forgotten as it is unmetaphored by action. Again, the *aubade* is indeed a dawn-song sung after a night of love, when the lovers must part, but a dawn-song of peculiar poignancy and relevance because of the way in which these lovers must part on this particular day. Another brilliant, natural unmetaphoring is the *hortus conclusus*, which by metaphoric convention a virgin is, and where also pure love naturally dwells, according to the Song of Songs and a host of subsequent poems and romances. Juliet's balcony simply opens upon such an orchard, a garden enclosed, into which Romeo finds out the way. The virgin is, and is in, a walled garden: the walls of that garden are to be breached by a true lover, as Romeo leaps into the orchard.

Still more important is the much-noticed manipulation of light and dark in the play; for Romeo and Juliet, ordinary life is reversed, with darkness the only safe time, when love between them is really possible. They meet at night, their marriage lasts one night, until light parts them. When they finally come together, it is at night in a tomb, which becomes their tomb in actuality. Their second night together is not *nox perpetua una dormienda*. A conventional figurative setting in lyric tradition becomes the "real" setting, carrying with it a specific symbolic significance for the play.

The common juxtaposition and contrast of love and war are also involved in *Romeo and Juliet*, thought not as simile merely. In Verona, love emerges as involved with warfare: the love of Romeo and Juliet is set in contrast to brawling and feud, but its poignancy comes from the bitterness of

the unexplained vendetta. In their lives the lovers speak for peace and reconciliation and at their death are turned into symbols of that reconciliation,
into sepulchral statues. Love and war are both real enough, but they do not
and cannot coexist in this play's world: the one destroys the other. The
conjunction of love and death, commonly linked in the metaphors of lyrical
tradition, make this play unmistakably non-comic; death is the link between
the love-theme and the war-theme, the irreversible piece of action that
stamps the play as tragic. Still, Romeo and Juliet die as much by accident as
Pyramus and Thisbe do, to whose story the narrative of their death owes
much. Indeed, the lovers are preserved in a nearly Ovidian way, not as plants,
but in an *ecphrasis*, as memorial statues exemplifying a specific lesson to
future generations.

By the time he came to write *Othello*, Shakespeare had learned to cope
with some of the problems still open in *Romeo and Juliet*, and could do so
without losing any advantages of his working out in the earlier play a
wonderfully heightened language of love. *Othello* is a remarkably integrated
play, its action compressed, its imagery consistent, its language profoundly
connected with the personalities of the various characters, as well as
subservient to the needs of plot, action, and theme. In *Othello*, it seems, the
different aspects of the play have been deeply driven into one another, to be
separated by some narrow critic only at grave danger to the play as a whole.
I know that this is so, and since my way of working in this exercise necessarily
stresses certain elements at the expense of others, I shall try to strike my
subject as lightly as I can and, wherever possible, to indicate the connection
of my stress-points to other parts of the play.

Othello is a play about love and its relation to the rest of life. *Antony and
Cleopatra* aside, it is difficult to find another major English Renaissance
tragedy in which love is so frankly central, so stripped and so exposed. In this
play, the lovers are not star-crossed, but crossed by their own personalities,
by their own natures, so excellently fine, and by the peculiarities of the small,
intimate society in which they carry on their lives. Like *Romeo and Juliet*, this
play makes use of a situation and of characters habitually associated with the
classical comic tradition. From a slightly different perspective, the play's
elements can be seen to be those of the city comedy. An elderly man, a black-
amoor even, marries a young wife and is jealous of his young assistant. We
do not commonly think of *Othello* as a tale of January and May, though Iago
and Othello are quick enough to accept such an interpretation of the situation. Actually, Shakespeare has turned that triangle of *senex*, *puella*, and
adulescens upside down. Desdemona loves the *senex* with unqualified devotion, and though Cassio certainly admires Desdemona, and his language to

and about her is in the classic courtly tradition, his affections are clearly occupied elsewhere. Othello fears that he is mocked by the public for being a January deceived by may; in fact, the public admires him the more for his achievement of so lovely a wife. The stock characters in the play are not at all what we might expect, either: the prostitute Bianca, for instance, stationed on an island where transient military and naval men are always ready for her favors, turns out to love Cassio "really," far beyond her rights as a stock figure.

With the major characters Shakespeare performs splendid tricks. Othello is a Moor, by stage convention expected to be both lecherous and violent, as well as servile; so Moors appear on the English stage, one of them Aaron, cast by Shakespeare himself as a typical eastern villain. What has happened in this play is that at the outset the Moor is introduced to the audience in terms of such extraordinary nobility as to erase the stereotype from the audience's mind. Later we are forced to discover that it is just the stereotyped qualities of emotionalism, volatility, and gullibility from which Shakespeare finally derives Othello's tragic breaking—after he has bred us away from expecting them in such a hero. By these means, as so often elsewhere, Shakespeare gets it both ways: he breaks the traditional presentation and exploits it at its most conventional points, after having quite cleaned the situation of stereotypical implications. Othello *is* noble, but in his nature reside those qualities of which he is most afraid, exactly the violence, the trickery, the gullibility of the stock-Moor. As was his custom in the great tragedies, Shakespeare chose heroes of startling eccentricity—Hamlet, a thoughtful prince cast as revenger; Lear, an old madman, conspicuously foolish and unjust; Macbeth, corrupted early in the play, whose corruption plays itself out during the action; Antony, proud, careless, and sensual, linked to a cheating, trivial, sensual partner both with him and against him; Coriolanus, cold, proud, passionate, and unreasonable. Not the least daring was Othello, a Moor in Venice, a warrior turned lover, a primitive more civilized than the super-subtle Venetians.

In *Othello* there is much unmetaphoring, largely in relation to medieval and Renaissance romance and lyric traditions; I want to deal especially, though not exclusively, with Shakespeare's use in this play of the sonnet-tradition. First of all, the appearance of hero and heroine: traditionally, the lady-love is fair, both in coloring and in spirit; golden hair and white skin are so typical for the role of beloved that Sidney made the point that his individuated Stella's eyes were black, and Shakespeare could appear original in loving a brunette. Desdemona is fair, within and without. The less fair, less spiritually refined qualities attributed to the standard courtly lover-poet have in fact been written into Othello's background and appearance. He *is* black, and, when pressed, the Venetians remind him of it. Though we are led to expect the opposite, Othello's external blackness turns out to match one segment of his inner life, as well of course as his external behavior to his wife. By taking literally conventional fairness and darkness, Shakespeare has given a new dimension to an artificial arrangement so trite as to appear meaningless: part of the shock involved in this marriage relies upon literary as well as upon social conventions. The relations of lover and beloved conventional in romance and lyric—she morally superior to him—have also been deepened to mean in this play something more than a traditional compliment to a lady. Mere *compliment* is indeed irrelevant: in *Othello* the conventions have been translated into consequential moral fact.

As in *Romeo and Juliet*, in *Othello* much is made of the difference between light and dark, between night and day, here tightly connected to the emblematic fairness and darkness of heroine and hero. As in *Romeo and Juliet*, crucial scenes in *Othello* are night-pieces. The abrupt and brilliant beginning, when Othello's bridal night is interrupted by the news of the Turk; a second interrupted bridal night on Cyprus; the sacrificial murder—each has its language of light and dark reinforcing the conjunction of fair heroine and dark hero, of moral clarity and psychological darkness. Other kinds of contrast occur, one of which has not received its notice due—the more remarkable because it is so obvious. Recently, much has been made of "Venice" as a way of life, in this play as in *The Merchant of Venice*. We know, perhaps even better than the Elizabethan audience did, how appropriate Venice is as the setting for this sort of scene. We know why the merit-system worked to Othello's benefit and to Iago's annoyance, why strangers were in Venice at all, and why strangers, however favored, had difficulty in coming to terms with their difference in the city. We know the social exclusiveness of the class from which Desdemona came, and why Venetian patricians were willing to pay so much to keep war at a distance from their lives ("Why this is Venice; my house is not a grange"). Othello's usefulness to the state, in protecting it from warfare on its shores, was sufficient to override even a patrician's rights in his daughter's marriage. The source aside, which made clear that the story was a Venetian one, Shakespeare made excellent use of his locus, contrasting the comfort and materialism of the great trading city with the intangible values of Othello's courage and Desdemona's purity.

Another way of saying all this is that Shakespeare contrasted materialist Venetian ways with those of love—or, to take love's most obvious location, Venetian with Cyprian ways. In spite of its distance from Venice, the island of Cyprus was, like Rhodes, crucial to the strategic defense of the city against the Turk. In realistic terms, Cyprus was a familiar name on the Venetian tongue. Othello and Iago had seen action there before the events of the play began; the Venetians murmur about Cyprus and Rhodes before the danger is made "certain then for Cyprus." Once Othello and Desdemona arrive on the island, all the action of the play takes place there, and appropriately, when we consider that the rites of Venus, with actual and metaphorical sacrifices, were centered on that island. For Cassio, Cyprus is "this worthy isle"; for Iago, "this warlike isle" and "this fair island." It is peopled by "generous islanders," for whom on their deliverance and his wedding-night Othello is glad to proclaim holiday. Cinthio's story had established Cyprus as the cite of the complicated murder of a Venetian wife by a Moor and a machiavel, but Cinthio made no particular reference to the symbolism implicit in the site. Shakespeare deepens the references to Cyprus, drawing out the island's latent power as the primary locus of love, the island to which, after her birth from the sea-foam, Aphrodite was wafted on her pearly shell. In Cassio's approach to Desdemona coming ashore on the island, the significance of the place is made plain: his heralding of her, "our great captain's captain," turns into a welcoming benediction of the lady, "The divine Desdemona" (II.i.73), coming like the goddess from the sea. *O dea certe*:

> O, behold,
> The riches of the ship is come ashore!
> Ye men of Cyprus, let her have your knees:
> Hail to thee, lady! And the grace of heaven,
> Before, behind thee, and on every hand,
> Enwheel thee round!
>
> (II.i.82–87)

That the island is sacred to love, Cassio had made clear a few lines earlier in his invocation for Othello's protection at sea:

> Great Jove, Othello guard,
> And swell his sail with thine own powerful breath,
> That he may bless this bay with his tall ship,
> And swiftly come to Desdemona's arms,
> Give renew'd fire to our extincted spirits,
> And bring all Cyprus comfort. . . .
>
> (II.i.77–82)

Quite without Iago's suggestiveness, Cassio simply celebrates the ritual love proper to the occasion, the characters, and the island; in his turn, Othello disembarks with love's rites on his mind, speaking to his wife in a speech of marvelous hyperbole, interrupted by his memory of his duty as commander, and by his courteous greeting of his "old acquaintance of the isle."

Love is rarely simple, and only at first blush does Aphrodite appear to provide uncomplicated satisfactions. The island dedicated to her is not, as the play makes clear, so well-fortified as Rhodes; Othello, we are told, knew "the fortitude of the place" from his stays on the island earlier. Actually, in its metaphoric sense, "the fortitude of the place" is what Othello did *not* know— the enormous secret strength of Aphrodite was what overthrew him, his sexual jealousy (in the existence of which he could not believe) coming to dominate his mind and finally his personality. All the references to Cyprus— and there are many more, some of Iago's with considerable *double-entendre*— make perfectly good superficial sense within the literal arrangements of the play; taken with their undertone of symbolic reference, their meaning is even more deeply sunk into the central preoccupation of *Othello*, the problematics of what is called "real" love.

The island is almost magically restored from the threat of war to peace, but it remains ringed about by war and rumors of war. As Ovid put it, war is a proper metaphor, even the proper habitat, for love:

> Militat omnis amans, et habet sua castra cupido;
> Attice, crede mihi, militat omnis amans.
>
> (*Amores* I.ix)

In that poem, the extended metaphor is of love and war, lover and warrior. Both soldier and lover keep vigil, both lie upon the ground, both do great feats in the line of duty, both lay siege to defended places, both find it practical to attack while the enemy sleeps. Donne's version of Ovid's elegy, "Loves Warre," outdoes Ovid in complicating the extended metaphor, outdoes him so readily because the image had such good use in the centuries between Ovid and Donne. In Donne's poem, love and war are not merely paired in metaphor; they are also deeply intermixed by argument so as to seem entirely interdependent conditions. Othello's greeting to Desdemona as he comes ashore at Cyprus—"O my fair warrior"—and Cassio's "Our great captain's captain," as well as Iago's harsher "Our general's wife is now the general," all honor one Petrarchan formula, "O dolce mia guerrera!" by which the lady becomes her lover's commander, his "domina," "donna," his lady as the feudal lord was his master. Again and again the theme runs in the sonnets; Spenser's *Amoretti* LVII, "Sweet warriour, when shall I have peace with you?" is but one of many examples. In *Romeo and Juliet*, love and war co-existed but were always held in rigorous contrast to each other. Throughout *Antony and Cleopatra* and *Troilus and Cressida*, the interrelations of love and war are explored: Helena parries with Parolles on the subject; Adonis wars with his boar instead of frolicking with his goddess.

In *Othello*, as in Donne's elegy, the war-world invades the love-world to make the metaphor not a far-fetched stylization but the literal truth; in this play, love is inconceivable without war. Not that this is really so surprising—Venus, of whom I have spoken much, classically played out her great love-affair with the god of war; indeed, she has much of the stock character of comedy about her. Matched with an elderly and un-beautiful husband, she took a lusty young warlike lover. Vulcan turned his shame to advantage, forging in his miraculous fire a net of gold so strong that from it his wife (*puella*) and her *adulescens* could not escape being hauled off to Olympus and displayed to divine ridicule. Love and war are matched throughout western literature; love began the war that destroyed civilization in the *Iliad*; in medieval romance, the knight was characteristically ennobled and elevated by his love, to become more puissant in war for his lady's dominant sake.

Sometimes a lover was unmanned by Venus: a test of his consistency was his capacity to resist ladies, even the ladies he loved, lying naked as needles beside him. Caught in uxoriousness, Erec felt his manhood threatened, as did also Romeo after Mercutio's death. Like Erec, who went on an immense errand, taking on all comers in his own proof, Romeo turned to fighting and managed to dispose of Mercutio's killer. Something of this tradition lies behind the exchange before the Duke over Desdemona's desire to accompany her husband to his wars. Acceding to his wife's request, Othello takes care to clear himself of the imputation of effeminate preoccupation with love:

> I therefore beg it not
> To please the palate of my appetite,
> Nor to comply with heat, the young affects
> In me defunct, and proper satisfaction,
> But to be free and bounteous of her mind;
> And heaven defend your good souls that you think
> I will your serious and great business scant,
> For she is with me. . . .
>
> (I.iii.261–68)

There is much in this speech to betray Othello's self-deception, his apparent ignorance of the body's proper sway in love. Suffice it simply to note that Othello *is*, or says he is, aware that love can overwhelm a man, turning him in a direction other than the one his occupation dictates. The speech goes on to insist upon Othello's capacity to regulate his own weakness:

> no, when light-wing'd toys,
> And feather'd Cupid, foils with wanton dullness

My speculative and active instruments,
That my disports corrupt and taint my business,
Let housewives make a skillet of my helm,
And all indign and base adversities
Make head against my reputation!

(I.iii.268–74)

The conjunction of "light wing'd toys," "feather'd Cupid," and "a skillet of my helm" suggests a common Ovidian source, again and again portrayed in the visual arts, of Venus resting complacently beside an exhausted Mars, reduced almost to coma by his encounter with her. Venus' troop of *amorini* often make game of the war-god's armor; in Botticelli's picture now in London, Mars' huge helmet quite covers the imp trying it on.

As in *Romeo and Juliet*, there are many uses of "medieval' romance conventions—the fatal handkerchief is a common guerdon exchanged between lady and knight; Iago's crude reference to Cassio and Desdemona in bed together raises one standard test of control on courtly romance, "naked abed, and not mean any harm!" Iago himself is a figure of many literary origins; as Mr. Spivack laboriously demonstrates, he is a type of morality Vice closely connected with the devil himself; he is another old Nick, the stage-machiavel; he is the presenter of the interlude, as well as the manipulating parasite of Roman comedy. He is, also, an Ovidian or libertine voice, speaking to undermine true love, which has its medieval parallel in the figure of the *losengeour*, the voyeuristic deceiver and liar about lovers' relations with one another.

In Iago's exchange with Cassio about Desdemona, one can see two love-rhetorics in conflict, the *losengeour*'s derogation of the whole business, and the plain man's acceptance of honest love:

Iago: . . . our general cast us thus early for the love of his
        Desdemona, who let us not therefore blame: he
        hath not yet made wanton the night with her; and
        she is sport for Jove.
Cass.: She is a most exquisite lady.
Iago: And I'll warrant her full of game.
Cass.: Indeed she is a most fresh and delicate creature.
Iago: What an eye she has! Methinks it sounds a parley
        of provocation.
Cass.: An inviting eye, and yet methinks right modest.
Iago: And when she speaks, 'tis an alarm to love.
Cass.: It is indeed perfection.

(II.iii.14–25)

Iago uses images commonly applied to sexuality—of the hunt ("full of game") and of war ("parley of provocation," "alarm to love")—in his attempt to lead Cassio into indelicacy about Desdemona; but Cassio rejects the invitation to lewdness, continuing to praise Desdemona in fairly abstract terms—"a most exquisite lady," "a most fresh and delicate creature," "methinks right modest," "indeed perfection."

Cassio does not speak in petrarchan, or petrarchistic, hyperbole here; his attitude to his general's wife is respectful and affectionate, but generalized and never passionate. It is Othello who speaks of and to Desdemona with the magniloquence of the sonnet-lover; Othello who, disclaiming rhetorical control, displays the powerful effects of his rhetoric whenever he comes to Venice. This trick is worth noting—it is the disclaimer of Ronsard, of Sidney, of Shakespeare himself, who in their sonnets deny literary eloquence precisely while most self-consciously exploiting its resources. Compared to *Romeo and Juliet*, where the sonnet-language is highly stylized, even over-audible, the sonnet-language of *Othello* is muted, does not draw attention to itself, but is nonetheless very important indeed, not only in shaping our reactions to these lovers and this love, but also in opening upon their attitudes to each other and their love for each other. The two scenes where sonnet-language is most telling are those between Othello and Desdemona at Othello's disembarkation, and just before the murder. Into the first incident, there has been an interpolation by Shakespeare of an element absent from Cinthio's narrative, the detail of the storm separating the lovers' ships on their way to the island. That storm has many analogues in Renaissance love-poetry. Wyatt, for instance, has a beautiful storm:

> After great stormes the cawme retornes,
>   And pleasanter it is thereby . . . ;

Petrarca:

> Non d'atra e tempestosa onda marina
> fuggio in porta gia mai stanco nocchiero,
> com'io dal fosco e torbido pensero
> fugge ove 'l gran desio mi sprona e 'inchina.

We have noted Cassio's beautiful language about the storm and the safe haven of the ship that carries Othello to Desdemona's arms, again an unmetaphoring, the realization in fictional "fact" of a conventional image.

Within the context of the play's action, Othello's address to Desdemona, filled with the imminence of their bitter future, reverses the usual poetic procedure: instead of making up an imaginary storm, a metaphor for a psychological stage of love, Othello associates the real storm to his condition:

> O my soul's joy,
> If after every tempest come such calms,
> May the winds blow, till they have waken'd death,
> And let the labouring bark climb hills of seas,
> Olympus-high, and duck again as low
> As hell's from heaven.
>
> (II.i.184–89)

At the play's end, the sea-imagery flows back with peculiar force, as Othello realizes the enormity of his mistake, to know what his own end must be, the distance of hell from heaven. Over Desdemona's body he says,

> Here is my journey's end, here is my butt,
> And very sea-mark of my utmost sail. . . .
>
> (V.ii.268–69)

"O my fair warrior" echoes Petrarca's "dolce mia guerrera," picked up by so many sonneteers: Ronsard to Cassandre, "ma guerrière Cassandre," Sidney to Stella, "dear Captainesse." Cyprus has been spoken of, its meaning as Venus' isle deepening Othello's greeting to his wife, "Honey, you shall be well desir'd in Cyprus." Of sonnets more is made in this play: Petrarca and Ronsard particularly refer to Venus as the Cyprian, calling their ladies Cyprians and Venusses too. Ronsard's "Vœu à Venus. Pour garder Cypre contre l'armée du Turc" has particular poignancy in relation to this play, though of course no direct connection with it:

> Idalienne, Amathonte, Erycine,
> Garde des Turcs Cypre, ton beau séjour;
> Baise ton Mars, et tes bras à l'entour
> De son col plie, et serre sa poitrine.
>
> Ne permets point qu'un barbare Seigneur
> Perde ton isle et souille ton honneur;
> De ton berceau chasse autre part la guerre.

Surrey's poem about Cyprus makes clear the island's power, as well as the power of love in general:

> In Cypres springes, wheras dame Venus dwelt,

A well so hote that who so tastes the same,
Were he of stone, as thawed yse should melt,
And kindled fynde his brest with secret flame;
Whose moist poison dissolved hath my hate.
This creping fier my cold lymms so oprest
That in the hart that harbred fredom late
Endles dispaire long thraldom hath imprest.
One eke so cold in froson snow is found,
Whose chilling venume of repugnaunt kind
The fervent heath doth quench of Cupides wound,
And with the spote of change infects the mynd;
 Whereof my deer hath tasted to my payne.
 My service thus is growne into disdayne.

Of this darker side of love, Othello has no inkling. His exalted idea of himself, in view of his relations with Desdemona, so much more conventional than her view of the same connection, took into account only his "perfection" as warrior and noble soul, ignoring the potential seriousness of love's disruption. In Othello's imagery, much is presaged in just his speech of welcome on Cyprus:

    If it were now to die,
'Twere now to be most happy, for I fear
My soul hath her content so absolute,
That not another comfort, like to this
Succeeds in unknown fate.
       (II.i.189–93)

As in so many love-poems, the rhetoric of supreme happiness in life turns poets' minds to its opposite, annihilation in death, in this passage so clearly expressed. Immediately after this imagery of joy and death, Othello turns to musical metaphors, kissing Desdemona and saying,

And this, and this, the greatest discord be
That e'er our hearts shall make!
       (II.i.199–200)

Iago picks up the metaphor at once, making discord of their harmony, in an image active and manipulative like himself:

O, you are well tun'd now,

> But I'll set down the pegs that make this music,
> As honest as I am.
>
> (II.i.200–202)

The image of harmony, so important in love-poetry from Dante on, stems from Plato's image of cosmic harmony, traditionally instituted by love's ordering of chaos. Though the image is a commonplace in literature as in thought, the sonneteers made the most of it, their love creating harmony when it was happy, reducing all things to chaos when it was not. As Othello looks after his wife, departing from him for a moment, he speaks of chaos in terms that remind us that he had, at the peak of his contentment, used the imagery of heaven and hell in his great passage about the storm:

> Excellent wretch, perdition catch my soul,
> But I do love thee, and when I love thee not,
> Chaos is come again.
>
> (III.iii.91–93)

Interestingly enough, this speech, sandwiched between Iago's insinuations, is the last spoken out of Othello's conviction of his own invulnerability, the last with the ever-so-slightly megalomaniac overtones of a man invincible in his content—as if *his* love, like the deity's or the sonneteer's, could order chaos! Ronsard's lines, set in the context of the lover's declaration, provide an instructive parallel to Othello's:

> Or, s'il te plaist, fay moy languir en peine,
> Tant que la mort me de-nerve et de-veine,
> Je seray tien. Et plus-tôt le Chaos
>   Se troublera de sa noise ancienne,
> Qu'autre beauté, qu'autre amour que la tienne,
> Sous autre joug me captive le dos.

In Ronsard's poem, chaos is entirely conventional—the fact that the poet considers another beauty, another love, as possible, makes probable the defection so hyperbolically denied. His Cassandre, one knows even in this poem, is one mistress in a series. Othello's language admits no quarter; it points directly to his actual future within the play's plot, his life and his world dependent upon his love.

Other echoes of the hyperbole of literary love-traditions sound in Othello's language. "My life upon her faith" is conventional enough, but in a less committed, or a more experienced, lover need not have led so absolutely to its fulfillment as in Othello's case, who took the words at their literal value. His emphasis on Desdemona's lovely smell, his likening of her to a rose, are all familiar enough from the sonnet-tradition—and, incidentally, serve to stress for us not only the enormous physical appeal Desdemona's person had for her husband, but also his very conventional view of what love ought to be. Yet more: these references underline Othello's self-deception, his pleasure in the sense-experiences which he himself tries to argue away. "Thou smell'st so sweet, that the senses ache at thee," he cried out in the midst of his diatribe against Desdemona. At the end of the play, the traditional image of *carpe diem*, the rose, comes with an awful exactitude. Othello does pluck the day and the rose with it:

> when I have pluck'd the rose,
> I cannot give it vital growth again,
> It must needs wither; I'll smell it on the tree,
> A balmy breath. . . .
>
> (V.ii.13–16)

So lightheartedly gathered, from the Greek Anthology on, the rose of love tended to lose specificity, in the common usage it was accorded; in Othello's speech, the familiar metaphor alters into something actual, into something far more charged than it usually is. Abruptly, all the implications of the image, folded into the rose-petals, unfold again—once plucked, *all* roses wither. Indeed, all roses wither anyway, even if left unplucked upon the tree. Once destroyed, nor roses, nor light, nor love, nor life can be "relum'd." Ronsard's

> Pren ceste rose aimable comme toy
> Qui sers de rose aux roses les plus belles,
> Qui sers de fleur aux fleurs les plus nouvelles,
> Dont la senteur ma ravist tout de moy. . . .

ends on the flower's death. In another poem, he describes the marvelously seductive odor of the opening rose, dying after so brief a blooming:

> La grace dans sa feuille, et l'amour se repose
> Embasmant les jardins et les arbres d'odeur;
> Mais batue ou de pluye, ou d'excessive ardeur,
> Languissante elle meurt, feuille à feuille declose . . .
> Pour obsèques reçoy mes larmes et mes pleurs. . . .

The extraordinary sweetness of the rose often mingles with other images for marvelous sweetness—the phoenix and its sweet-smelling locus, Arabia; or Laura's sweetness, greater than all the nards of the East; other sonnet-ladies' sweetness, then, outdoing Laura's. At Desdemona's death, Othello becomes such an eastern tree; his

> subdued eyes,
> Albeit unused to the melting mood,
> Drop tears as fast as the Arabian trees
> Their medicinal gum. . . .
>
> (v.ii.349–52)

Another sort of imagery, that of jewels, was also standard in the description of beloved ladies, as of Juliet, "like a rich jewel in an Ethiop's ear." There are several jewel-references to Desdemona, beginning with Brabantio's terrible leave-taking:

> for your sake (jewel),
> I am glad at soul I have no other child. . . .
>
> (I.iii.195–96)

and ending on Othello's far more terrible description of himself as Desdemona's killer:

> one whose hand,
> Like the base Indian, threw a pearl away,
> Richer than all his tribe. . . .
>
> (v.ii.347–49)

The jewels come from cases of conventional compliment; but Othello's word "tribe" reminds us of the difficulties in his own life, and the way in which, so bitterly, he turns out to manifest just the passions attributed to that "tribe," which he had so long, and apparently so successfully, struggled to suppress in himself. Petrarca's sonnet 51, furthermore offers the image-cluster of jewel, old man, and Moroccan darkness: the lady is the changeless precious stone. So Desdemona's value can be measured by that "one entire and perfect chrysolite," with all its cosmic radiance, for which her husband would not have sold her.

Other themes in Othello's last speeches offer commentary on the customary languages of literary love. Traditionally, ladies are "cold," as diamonds, as the springs of Helicon, as snow, as ice. Beatrice and Laura were both chilly; even Ronsard's willing ladies were occasionally "froides." Desdemona, we know, was not cold in her lifetime, but only in her death:

> cold, cold, my girl,
> Even like thy chastity.
>
> (v.ii.276–77)

Once more, the metaphor is made real, thrust back into brutal actuality: Desdemona is at last made "cold."

The imagery of light and dark, playing in many contexts, comes to its climax in the great speech before Desdemona's murder. By her marriage, Desdemona had evidently come to terms with Othello's blackness, as her explanation of her unfilial behavior makes plain. But Othello, it turns out, had not, whatever he may have thought. As Iago's insinuations bore into him, Othello seeks reasons why Desdemona should not love him:

> Haply, for I am black,
> And have not those soft parts of conversation
> That chamberers have, or for I am declin'd
> Into the vale of years,
>
> (III.iii.267–70)

he says, pathetically and ambiguously explaining things to himself. And a bit later, in a rage:

> my name, that was as fresh
> As Dian's visage, is now begrim'd, and black
> As mine own face. . . .
>
> (III.iii.392–94)

Desdemona had spoken for herself when she said, "I saw Othello's visage in his mind"; but as events turn out, his mind can be "begrim'd" and black as his face.

Robert Heilman and others have studied the ways in which Othello's grandiloquence falls into the extravagant, passionate, fragmentary, derogatory language that shares more and more with Iago's choice of syntax and vocabulary. It is interesting to note that even in this degeneration, there are traces of literary love-conventions. Othello ceases to see Desdemona whole: as she loses her integrity for him, he sees her only in parts—and, far more important, his rage is such that he wishes to tear her into bits. It is the passionate rage that strikes us, as it ought, with most force, so that Othello's abusive "Noses, ears, and lips" does not obviously make mock of the catalogue of mistress' separate features so dear to writers of blasons and sonnets. Such literary elements are by the by, of course: they do not insist upon themselves, and we do not insist upon them. What we are to notice is the realistic use by the playwright of this kind of reference, as the disjunction of the parts of Desdemona's face is seen to match the disruption in Othello's mind and feelings about her.

Believing himself wronged, Othello reverses the light-dark imagery, calling Desdemona "thou black weed"—although her fairness never ceases to move him deeply, even at that terrible moment. As he readies himself to take her life, Othello speaks in an image-cluster gathering up all the themes of fairness, coldness, hardness, and death:

> I'll not shed her blood,
> Nor scar that whiter skin of hers than snow,
> And smooth, as monumental alabaster. . . .
>   (V.ii.3–5)

The notion of a tomb, made so concrete in *Romeo and Juliet*, is only glanced at here, its power the greater for its obliqueness. A few lines after these, the rose comes in, to make the contrast between cold and warmth, colorlessness and intensity, death and life. A literary parallel might be Petrarca's sonnet 131, where the rose blooms against the snow and, after its brief life, cannot be revived. To hunt among Petrarca's poems for parallels is reliably rewarding, even precisely to the combinations of light and dark that best fit this play. In Laura, of course, light and fairness combine in exceptional radiance; in her imperfect lover, especially imperfect when absent from his lady, darkness prevails—and, one notes, the very darkest sort of darkness, Petrarca tells us: Moroccan or Moorish darkness.

Other love-poets rang changes on Petrarca's oxymora and oppositions, his freezings in fire, his burnings in ice, his poverty in riches, his "dolce ire," "dolcezza amara," "dolce errore," his love that brightens night, darkens day, embitters honey and sweetens vinegar, his peace unfound after armistice, and so on. Oxymoron and contradiction became official figures, expressing in figural shorthand the internal conflicts surfaced by love's intensity. Worked by generations of lyricists, the figure of oxymoron tended to stretch into longer syntactical forms, sentences expressing contradictoriness and paradox. Othello speaks in such contradictions—"O thou black weed, why art so lovely fair?" is his *odi et amo*, a highly condensed version of the conflicting emotions Shakespeare had far more fully worked out in his own sonnets of obsession. Finally, in the soliloquy before Desdemona's death:

> So sweet was ne'er so fatal: I must weep,
> But they are cruel tears; this sorrow's heavenly,
> It strikes when it does love . . . ,
>
> (v.ii.20–22)

the confusions and contradictions of the language bespeak the degree of his suffering. Paradox takes hold at the end, when Othello is beyond restitution and beyond honor, in an echo from the love-poetry, and, more poignantly, from his own disembarkation speech: "Then in my sense 'tis happiness to die." This time, "dying" fulfills great crimes and great grief, not the overwhelming happiness he had experienced at reunion with Desdemona. Like Romeo, Othello himself dies as the sonnet-lover should, upon a kiss:

> I kiss'd thee ere I kill'd thee, no way but this,
> Killing myself, to die upon a kiss.
>
> (v.ii.359–60)

The metaphor is gone, but its echo remains, to remind us, as it reminds Othello, of what is gone with the loss of that love, with the loss of that lady's life.

What all this language does in *Othello* is what it does in *Romeo and Juliet*: it reminds us of what love-lyrics exist to proclaim, that through all the misunderstandings, the violence, the betrayals and self-betrayals, love is at base the most beautiful of human experiences, its satisfactions so great that loss of love can bring incomparable results. It reminds us that in spite of their fictions, poets can be right—that whatever else happens in a man's life, it is his love which most reveals and strips him, which makes his private life sufficiently important to outweigh his public life. In *Romeo and Juliet* the lovers try to live privately, in a social situation which permits no such privacy; their sonnet-language is properly self-important and self-referential, overriding all other considerations as long as love can. The lyrical language of that play, beautiful and buoyant, is at the same time a very obvious language, as befits the subject and the energies of a youthful play about youth; the lyrical element in *Othello* is so understated, so absorbed into the whole play so that we hardly realize all that it does.

When we do, at last, realize that even the plot of *Othello* is in fact the unmetaphoring of typical sonnet-narrative, it comes both as a surprise and as a revelation. Nonetheless, that is just what it is: the sonnet-sequence plot has been animated into dramatic action. Fair bride and darker lover achieve, after initial difficulties, perfection of happiness, only to have jealousy break in, which in sonnet-narratives may indeed result in love's death, but at most a metaphorical death. The lovers in sonnets generally survive, either to achieve a deeper love after the clearing-up of misunderstanding, or to free the lover from an unworthy obsession. In life, of course, such endings are rare: real misprision, real jealousy, real irrationality sicken love past revival. In ordinary life, the ends of such affairs, even between great spirits, are not heroic and are rarely tragic, merely wasteful and sad. In this play, one conventional sonnet-ending is reached, with the metaphorical death in fact unmetaphored. Love literally dies, then; that act is irreversible, Desdemona and love cannot be revived or recalled. But through all the misunderstanding, a kind of reconciliation is reached: the hero learns that his lady is true and his notion of her false. He recognizes the consistent virtue of his wife, and, by reason of his new understanding, can take the terrible consequences of his error. We accept Othello's heroism in part because of the speed and sureness with which he reaffirms his original judgment of Desdemona and of his love for her; after his praise of her stead goodness, he ends his life as judge and executioner of his own criminal self. It is not life-like, perhaps: but the love-fiction has, at Desdemona's death, come to take its consequences, to move onto another moral plane, to become, as tragedy must be, a fiction of responsibility.

In Othello's psychology, too, the *schemata* of official romantic love have left their deep mark. Because his view of love was so stereotyped, he could not see his wife as she actually was, but was fooled into taking her at Iago's fictional assessment. She was in fact generous, frank, and devoted, more openly so than the coy mistress of sonnet-prescription. Her very deviation from romantic type made it easier for Othello to accept Iago's explanation of her, to accept, then, a familiar literary stereotype in place of the (remarkable, it is true) real person. Part of the extraordinary irony of this play is that in one sense, Othello's acceptance of Iago's story is a version of realism, as the world, or the literary world, sees realism. Desdemona's behavior was so romantic, so ideal, that it could indeed seem very unlikely. Iago's interpretation of the world, cheap and cynical though it is, is the version the world tends to take for real—or, Iago's interpretation most persuasively presents the stereotype of realism. Just as with Edmund, whose bastardy speech makes us at first entertain some sympathy for him, but whose behavior reveals, by his own account too, his fundamental lawlessness, so with Iago: the conventions of cynicism, usually protected by fears of romanticism within us, are ultimately revealed as the shoddy things they are. Altogether, we find the problematics of love—the psychology, the language, the behavior of love and its twinned opposite, jealousy—can ultimately be restudied through its expressive stereotypes.

Stereotypes themselves are a problem, because they are at once shoddy and valuable. Their thinness attenuates meaning; their commonplaceness and cliché reiteration make them seem automatic and trivial. All the same, though, stereotypes are developed in the first place because they answer in some measure fundamental needs, either as a simplified version of reality or to give shape to our deep hope that reality can be reinterpreted in some simple way. Artists and writers working with the stereotypes and schemata of their craft must maneuver delicately through the problems so raised, attempting not to say something everyone knows or expects to hear, and yet to speak in terms that everyone can understand.

Shakespeare managed miraculously to bring off his tragic exercise in dramatic sonnetry: by springing the sonnet-plot back into what seems to be reality, he made the effects of love suddenly more patent, more critical, more crucial than they seem to be in their usual habitat, the protected and enclosed garden of love-lyrics. By exploiting the self-examination and self-expression of the lyric lover, especially the sonnet-lover, he made such private feelings seem suddenly almost heroic. By allowing private to move into public life, the profound inwardness of love to work in heroic personalities and thus to open upon tragic possibilities, he raises a lyric plot to tragic scope. Another way of saying this is that the playwright took the literary love-conventions seriously, and by making various literary conventions seem elements in a real situation shows us the power and grievousness of the love they represent.

From literary conventions, he took part of his fable and much of his language. Without the literary conventions at his disposal—and without having practised them in his own earlier works—Shakespeare would have had a hard time convincing us of the importance, especially the tragic importance, of a story so trivial and so sordid as Cinthio's novella. At this play's heart lies a critique of the artificiality built into stylized language and the behavior which that language permits and even encourages. In *Romeo and Juliet*, there is plenty of criticism of the love-language—Mercutio's comments on the numbers that Petrarca and others "flowed in" tell us much—but this criticism never points to the morality beneath the conventions. There, the language points toward emotional condition, but does not reveal its nearly inexpressible complexities. In a fairly standard way, too, the sonnet-ethos is affirmed unquestioned. Juliet, with her language more "real" than her lover's, is to be taken as the nobler, or more mature, character of the two—indeed, in the simplifying of his language, we are to read Romeo's growth through his new love. Desdemona's language is even more direct than Juliet's, both in a comparison between the two women's utterances and within the contexts of the two plays. As a result, Desdemona is obviously less rhetorical, even less poetic, than her husband; her verbal directness displays, we think, the plain "truth" of her nature. Othello's language displays something quite other: it shows us that his concepts of love are less grounded in psychological reality, are far more stereotyped, than those of his wife. Othello, after all, wooed an admitted prize among women; Desdemona studied her husband and chose him at considerable expense to herself. Othello's vulnerabilities show in his enormous pride, to warn us, if not him, of the delicate balance of his personality, especially when it is subjected to peculiar and unfamiliar stress. Less fearful of her senses and fearless of appearing sensual, Desdemona finds it easier to behave with absolute loyalty to Othello than he to her—a loyalty rare in what is called real life. She dies, indeed, upon an act of generosity, trying to clear her husband of the imputation of crime. By convention, the lady is of finer stuff than her lover; by convention, her excellence raises his moral level. Desdemona is fair; she has, in Spenser's words, "The trew fayre, that is the gentle wit,/ and vertuous mind . . . ," and thereby raises the moral level of her lover, at a cost, however, incommensurate with the gain. Love is not a thing to be taken lightly, nor can it be interpreted along conventional lines, even when, as in *Othello*, its conventions turn out to be true. In criticizing the artificiality he at the same time exploits in his play, Shakespeare manages in *Othello* to reassess and to reanimate the moral system and the psychological truths at the core of the literary love-tradition, to reveal its problematics and to reaffirm in a fresh and momentous context the beauty of its impossible ideals.

FRANK KERMODE

Introduction to Romeo and Juliet

*R*omeo and Juliet, though it has always enjoyed popular esteem, has not often been ranked by professional critics with the tragic masterpieces which followed it. A certain unease about the dramatist's intention, some suspicion that, in the early moments of the play at any rate, he lacks that rhetorical control which marks his great period, and—above all—a conviction that he offends against his own criteria for tragedy by allowing mere chance to determine the destiny of the hero and heroine—all these have conspired to limit the critical prestige of *Romeo and Juliet*. It has been admired for its pathetic rather than for its tragic power; and many would agree with Johnson that in this instance anyway Shakespeare's "pathetic strains are . . . polluted with some unexpected depravations."

More recently, however, there has been a tendency to examine the novelty and stress the magnitude of Shakespeare's achievement in this play. For it is experimental; and it belongs to a period when Shakespeare, though the boldness and strength of *Lear* were still some years off, had found ways of realizing much of his power. Few will argue that it equals its great successors; but it may stand as a great play in its own right, proclaiming from its first scene the characteristic skill and intellect of its author.

Although the Nurse's reference to an earthquake eleven years past (I.iii.23) has by some been held to mean that Shakespeare wrote *Romeo and Juliet* that number of years after the London tremor of 1580, most now date

From *The Riverside Shakespeare* © 1974 Houghton Mifflin Company.

it about 1595; it is to be thought of as roughly contemporary with *Richard II* and *A Midsummer Night's Dream*. The story it tells was well known. The use of a sleeping potion as a way out of an unwelcome marriage goes back to the *Ephesiaca* of the Greek novelist Xenophon in the fourth century A.D. Masuccio of Salerno uses it, together with a tale of star-crossed lovers, in *Il Novellino* (1476). Retelling the story in his *Istoria . . . di due nobili Amanti* (c. 1530), Luigi da Porto lays the scene in Verona and names the feuding families the Montecchi and the Cappellati (names he may have got from Dante's *Purgatorio*, vi.105; *Vieni a veder Montecchi e Cappelletti*). His Romeo goes to a Cappellati ball to see a girl whom he loves but who scorns him, and falls in love with Giulietta, as she with him. After a longer courtship than Shakespeare allows, conducted mostly on the girl's balcony, they marry, with the aid of the Franciscan Lorenzo, who hopes that the families will thus be brought together; but Fortune, "enemy of every earthly joy," prevents this outcome by starting up the feud again. The rest of the story is substantially as in Shakespeare. There was a French adaptation by Adrian Sevin in 1542; an Italian poem by Clízia (1553) and a play by Groto (1578) repeat and adapt the story. As a prose *novella* it is told in a novel by Bandello (1554) and again, in French, by Boiastuau in 1559. This last version Painter translated in his *Palace of Pleasure* (1567), a work known to Shakespeare.

Shakespeare's direct source was, however, none of these, but a poem by Arthur Brooke, based on Boiastuau and published in 1562. *The Tragical History of Romeus and Juliet*, 3,000 lines of verse in poulter's measure, is a very dull work. But it had some popularity and was reprinted in 1587. Shakespeare adapts Brooke freely, but he obviously had the poem on his desk or in his head. Brooke takes a very moral tone about the lovers, especially in his *Address to the Reader* (he is kinder to them in the poem itself), and some of this attitude comes through in the play, largely as part of the admonitions of the Friar. Brooke insists, as some of his predecessors had done, on the important part played by Fate in the story; this is another element employed by Shakespeare in his more complex design. Whenever Shakespeare is working largely from a single text, as here and in *The Winter's Tale* and *As You Like It*, in *Othello* and *Antony and Cleopatra*, one observes his readiness to accept and transform a conventional morality, and to find an appropriately limited place in his play for what had struck the author of his source as being the whole moral bearing of the story.

One also recognizes in these cases the essentially theatrical cast of Shakespeare's mind; he thought in terms of plays. To read Brooke with the play in mind is to be struck repeatedly by the easy skill with which Shakespeare has transformed the tale into a dramatic action, altering and compressing to make a sharp theatrical point, telescoping events, expanding such characters as the Nurse and Mercutio, cutting material and inventing new episodes. The effect is not merely to make the story fit "the two hours' traffic of our stage" and to procure significant juxtapositions of event (for Shakespeare obviously enjoyed the possibilities of antithetical love and hate, youth and age, in the tale) but to display in it qualities of passion and intellectual subtlety hidden under the surface of other versions. There are echoes of word and image, and the run of the story is the same; Brooke must have his due. Yet the play, considered in relation to its source, is one of the dramatist's most brilliant transformations.

That mastery of the opening scene which is the hallmark of the mature Shakespeare is as evident here as in *A Midsummer Night's Dream* and *Richard II*. First the formal prologue telling of the feud and—because this is a tragedy, hung in black, with no surprise survivals—announcing the lovers' fate. This choric sonnet Shakespeare owed in part to Brooke, who began in similar fashion; but he makes it mean more than Brooke could. The sonnet form will recur in the play as a hint that love has its formalities as well as death, and that they are in their way tragic. (*Romeo and Juliet* is the kind of tragedy *A Midsummer Night's Dream* hints at when it mentions the possibility that crazy young love is potentially tragic as well as potentially comic; *A Midsummer Night's Dream* chooses comedy, but Shakespeare states the theme in a tragic minor mode at the outset—"So quick bright things come to confusion" (I.i.149)—and repeats it in a farcical major with the Pyramus play at the happy end.)

We pass direct from the sonnet to the idiotic feuding of the Montague and Capulet servants; Tybalt and Benvolio raise it to a more serious level; and, to show that the continuance of this quarrel is the work of the young, the infirm heads of the families display themselves as no longer capable of fight. Only then do we meet Romeo, spinning his melancholy fancies; and in no sense are we led to think that this young man is worth our sympathy, for his first speeches (I.i.171 ff.) are full of remote self-regarding conceits and affectation. We pass on to the Capulet feast, and Romeo's mind undergoes sudden translation from notional to real love; but not before Mercutio has been amusingly indecent on the subject. Youth in this play is a separate nation; its customs are not understood by the old. For the hot blood which makes love at once a matter of rapture and low jokes is the same that keeps warm the obsolete Montague—Capulet feud. The same passions work towards both ends; and Shakespeare remembers this in the masterly moment when Tybalt—mere "goodman boy" to his uncle Capulet—overhears Romeo's first praise of Juliet's beauty:

> This, by his voice, should be a Montague.
> Fetch me my rapier, boy.
>
> (I.v.54–55)

The inability of age to prevent this flow of passion is signified by the unruled nature of Tybalt and Romeo's failure to pacify him, as surely as it is in those other skillful juxtapositions where old Capulet lays his plans with Paris for a sane, cold marriage, while Romeo and Juliet make love in the same house, or when Juliet rapturously invokes the coming night as Tybalt lies dead in the street. One could multiply these instances. From the firm beginning and throughout the main structural design—the use of foreboding dreams, the timing of Romeo's return, not to speak of the skill and plenitude with which difficult moments are turned into richly memorable or psychologically plausible crises (Romeo with the apothecary, Juliet terrified with the potion)—acute dramatic intelligence and imagination develop the plot and explore its potentialities of meaning.

Romeo and Juliet was an experiment in more ways than one. As H. B. Charlton has shown, the Italian dramatist Cinthio was the first to seek new tragic themes appropriate to the modern theatre, to call for stories drawn not from ancient history but from the life of the times. The playwright, he thought, should look for his plots to the novelist (as Shakespeare was later to look to Cinthio's own *novella* about a Moor of Venice). Shakespeare had already written historical tragedies; now he turned to fictional lovers, young aristocrats but not royal—"to choose such folk as these for tragic heroes," observes Charlton, "was aesthetically well-nigh an anarchist's gesture." Little remains of Seneca, save perhaps for the emphasis on Fate, working either through human passion or through the public feud over which the lovers have no control.

More remarkable than the choice of subject are the flexibility and fullness with which Shakespeare developed this apparently narrow tragic theme. It has been objected that the play lacks tragic necessity—that the story becomes tragic only by a trick. Bradley answered this long ago when he called it a rule, from which he did not except *Romeo and Juliet*, that in Shakespearean tragedy "almost all the prominent accidents occur when the action is well advanced and the impression of the causal sequence is too firmly fixed to be impaired." This is true of *Romeo and Juliet*. The completeness and self-surrender of the love between Romeo and Juliet is beautifully rendered; but there is hardly a moment when we are allowed to think that permanence or happiness is part of its nature. The sentences of the Friar are chilled by a sort of benevolent inhumanity—he is not himself familiar with this kind of thing and we are; but nevertheless they sound persistently before the wedding, and the overtones should not be neglected.

> These violent delights have violent ends,
> And in their triumph die.
>
> (II.vi.9–10)

It is the wisdom glanced at by Hermia and Lysander in the opening scene of *A Midsummer Night's Dream*. Before the marriage can be consummated, Tybalt is dead, and the quick bright thing has come to confusion. There is the further point, that Romeo is in distress unmanned: "I thought thy disposition better temper'd," says the Friar (III.iii.115). Shakespeare is using Brooke's unqualified moralism: "to this end . . . is this tragical matter written, to describe unto thee a couple of unfortunate lovers, thralling themselves to unhonest desire, neglecting the authority and advice of parents and friends . . . !" But he is not using it crudely. The love he describes is of itself beautiful and valuable; but just as it is in its very nature the business of the young, with passions hardly controlled, so is it in its very nature associated with disaster and death. Portents, whether of the stars or of dreams, will foretell it. Out of this truth one can make a partial morality; but in this play Shakespeare offers a complex pattern of suffering from which a moral man might as well decide for love as against it. Caught in that tragic swirl of events, Romeo and Juliet say more than Brooke's sermon can. Romeo fluctuates from melancholy to high spirits, from unmanly despair to calm, and moves from a recognition that it is "e'en so" to a kind of adult fatalism. Juliet more strikingly changes from a girl too young to have thoughts of marriage into a mature and suffering woman.

It is in this sense that we should understand the emphasis on Fate. It is represented in the law of the world, which neither the dateless passion of the lovers nor the expedients of Friar Lawrence can alter. Fortune throws the characters into attitudes which ironically belie their fine words; the Friar says "Wisely and slow" but acts in haste, stumbles, leaves Juliet to her unnecessary fate; the lovers who have found the real right thing share but one brief night together; Romeo, seeking to end the feud, is forced to kill Tybalt. These are some of the ways in which Shakespeare manipulates a narrative to show more than two dimensions.

There are others. One curious fact emerges from the labor of writing notes to *Romeo and Juliet*. The language is much more difficult, the thought expressed in more rhetorical and conceited ways, in the early parts of the work. Shakespeare was a master of rhetoric not only in the sense of the textbook, the elaboration of figures appropriate to meaning and mood, but in the wider sense that he understood the mixture of rhetorical levels, the clash of styles, which a complex theme requires. He is like Chaucer, perhaps, making his effects from the contrast between a formal rhetoric based on the book, and a kind of anti-rhetoric, a plainness in itself perhaps as artificial as the ornateness against which it is played off. There is a sudden clearing of the verse, a move from the formality befitting the conventional nature of Romeo's love for Rosaline (as much a convention as the feud itself) to an

apparent denial of formality by plainness; it is summed up by Juliet's words
at her window:

> Fain would I dwell on form, fain, fain deny
> What I have spoke, but farewell compliment!
> (II.ii.88–89)

From the formality of the masque, of the sonnet in which they first speak
together, the lovers move to a direct monosyllabic plainness, as if their minds
were too much occupied with living to have time for mere fantastic speech:

> *Juliet.* I would not for the world they saw thee here.
> *Romeo.* I have night's cloak to hide me from their eyes,
> And but thou love me, let them find me here.
> (II.ii.74–76)

It is only when Juliet is untrue to her faith, upbraiding Romeo for the murder
of Tybalt, that she slips back into the formal rhetoric: "Beautiful tyrant! fiend
angelical!" (III.ii.75 ff.). When all seems and indeed is over, Romeo is hardly
allowing himself a flourish when he says, "Then I defy you, stars!"; but the
true mood of this love is fully established with his "Well, Juliet, I will lie with
thee to-night." The reality of the love relationship is even, by a touch of
genius, contrasted with the relative falsity even of the grief of parents and
Nurse and official lover in the extraordinary passage (IV.v) where the
Capulets vie with Paris' conventional outcries and the absurd lamentation of
the Nurse over Juliet's body: "O woe, O woeful, woeful, woeful day! / Most
lamentable day, most woeful day," etc. There are few more daring rhetorical
adventures in all the tragedies.

In view of this we should beware of supposing that Shakespeare's
sympathies lay strongly in this or that direction; that he was on the Friar's
side when he uttered the conventional condemnation of the lovers in a story
which must always have thrived on their attractiveness; or, on the other hand,
that he was committed to this surreptitious but virtuous passion as in itself of
the highest value. For all the necessary heat of the verse and the pathos of the
theme, Shakespeare maintains a remarkable reserve. That *Romeo and Juliet*
has a strong thematic interest is clear; but Shakespeare has now passed the
stage when one could say, without too much injury to the work, precisely
what that interest may have been. *Romeo and Juliet* is not a simple play; to
suppose that it is would be the most elementary mistake one could make
concerning it.

SUSAN SNYDER

Beyond Comedy: Romeo and Juliet *and* Othello

Both *Romeo and Juliet* and *Othello* use the world of romantic comedy as a point of departure, though in different ways. In the early play a well-developed comic movement is diverted into tragedy by mischance. The change of direction is more or less imposed on the young lovers, who therefore impress us primarily as victims. Othello and Desdemona are victims too, in one sense, but in their tragedy destruction comes from within as well, and comedy is one means by which Shakespeare probes more deeply into his characters and their love. He gives us in the early scenes a brief but complete comic structure and then develops his tragedy of love by exploiting the points of strain and paradox within the system of comic assumptions that informs that structure.

That these two plays are Shakespeare's only ventures into the Italianate tragedy of love and intrigue is no coincidence. The very features that distinguish this subgenre from the more dominant fall-of-the-mighty strain move it closer to comedy: its sources are typically novelle rather than well-known histories, its heroes are of lesser rank, its situations are private rather than public, its main motive force is love. Madeleine Doran, whose designation and description I follow for this kind of tragedy, has pointed out its affinity with comedy: "We are in the region where tragedy and comedy are cut out of the same cloth." The source tales of *Romeo* and *Othello* would, I think, suggest quite readily to Shakespeare the possibility of using comic convention as a springboard for tragedy.

From *The Comic Matrix of Shakespeare's Tragedies.* © 1979 Princeton University Press.

The movement of *Romeo and Juliet* is unlike that of any other Shake-spearean tragedy. It becomes, rather than is, tragic. Other tragedies have reversals, but here the reversal is so complete as to constitute a change of genre. Action and characters begin in the familiar comic mold and are then transformed, or discarded, to compose the shape of tragedy. In this discussion I shall have to disregard much of the play's richness, especially of language and characterization, in order to isolate that shaping movement. But isolating it can reveal a good deal about *Romeo*, and may suggest why this early experimental tragedy has seemed to many to fall short of full tragic effect.

It was H. B. Charlton, concurring in this judgment, who classed the play as "experimental." According to Charlton, Shakespeare in his early history-based tragic plays failed to find a pattern of event and character that would make the dramatic outcome feel inevitable; in *Romeo* he took a whole new direction, that of the modern fiction-based tragedy advocated by the Italian critic Giraldi Cinthio. Certainly dramatic thrust and necessity are unsolved problems in *Titus Andronicus* and *Richard III*, and perhaps in *Richard II* too. But one need not turn to Italian critical theory to explain the new direction of *Romeo*. Given the novella-source, full of marriageable young people and domestic concerns, it seems natural enough that Shakespeare would think of turning his own successful work in romantic comedy to account in his apprenticeship as a tragedian.

We have seen that comedy is based on a principle of "evitability." It endorses opportunistic shifts and realistic accommodations as means to new social health. It renders impotent the imperatives of time and law, either stretching them to suit the favored characters' needs or simply brushing them aside. In the tragic world, which is governed by inevitability and which finds its highest value in personal integrity, these imperatives have full force. Unlike the extrinsic, alterable laws of comedy, law in tragedy is inherent—in the protagonist's own nature and in the larger patterns, divine, natural, and social, with which that personal nature brings him into conflict. Tragic law cannot be altered, and tragic time cannot be suspended. The events of tragedy acquire urgency in their uniqueness and irrevocability: they will never happen again, and one by one they move the hero closer to the end of his own personal time.

Comedy is organized like a game. The ascendancy goes to the clever ones who can take advantage of sudden openings, contrive strategies, and adapt flexibly to an unexpected move from the other side. But luck and instinct win games as well as skill, and I have discussed in the preceding chapter the natural law of comedy that crowns lovers, whether clever or not, with final success. Romeo and Juliet, young and in love and defiant of obstacles, are attuned to the basic movement of the comic game toward marriage and social regeneration. But they do not win: the game turns into a sacrifice, and the favored lovers become victims of time and law. We can better understand this shift by looking at the two distinct worlds of the play and at some secondary characters who help to define them.

If we divide the play at Mercutio's death, the death that generates all those that follow, it becomes apparent that the play's movement up to this point is essentially comic. With the usual intrigues and go-betweens, the lovers overcome obstacles and unite in marriage. Their personal action is set in a broader social context, so that the marriage promises not only private satisfaction but renewed social unity:

> For this alliance may so happy prove
> To turn your households' rancour to pure love.
> (II.iii.91–92)

The households' rancor is set out in the play's first scene. This Verona of the Montague-Capulet feud is exactly the typical starting point of a comedy described by Frye—"a society controlled by habit, ritual bondage, arbitrary law and the older characters." The scene's formal balletic structure, a series of matched representatives of the warring families entering neatly on cue, conveys the inflexibility of this society, the arbitrary barriers that limit freedom of action.

The feud itself seems more a matter of mechanical reflex than of deeply felt hatred. Charlton noted the comic tone of its presentation in this part of the play. The "parents' rage" that sounded so ominous in the prologue becomes in representation an irascible humour: two old men claw at each other, only to be dragged back by their wives and scolded by their prince. Charlton found the play flawed by this failure to plant the seeds of tragedy; but the treatment of the feud makes good sense if Shakespeare is playing on *comic* expectations. At this point, the feud functions in *Romeo* very much as the various legal restraints do in Shakespearean comedy. Imposed from outside on the youthful lovers, who feel themselves no part of it, the feud is a barrier placed arbitrarily between them, like the Athenian law giving fathers the disposition of their daughters which stands between Lysander and Hermia in *A Midsummer Night's Dream*—something set up in order to be broken down.

Other aspects of this initial world of *Romeo* suggest comedy as well. Its characters are the gentry and servants familiar in romantic comedies, and they are preoccupied, not with wars and the fate of kingdoms, but with arranging marriages and managing the kitchen. More important, it is a world of possibilities, with Capulet's feast represented to more than one young man as a field of choice. "Hear all, all see," says Capulet to Paris, "And like her most whose merit most shall be" (I.ii.30–31). "Go thither," Benvolio tells Romeo, who is disconsolate over Rosaline, "and with unattainted eye / Compare her face with some that I shall show" (85–86) and she will be forgotten for some more approachable lady. Romeo rejects the words, of course, but in action he soon displays a classic comic adaptability, switching from the impossible love to the possible.

Violence and disaster are not totally absent from this milieu, but they are unrealized threats. The feast again provides a kind of comic emblem, when Tybalt's proposed violence is rendered harmless by Capulet's festive accommodation.

> Therefore be patient, take no note of him;
> It is my will; the which if thou respect,
> Show a fair presence and put off these frowns,
> An ill-beseeming semblance for a feast.
>   (I.v.69–72)

This overruling of Tybalt is significant because Tybalt in his inflexibility is a potentially tragic character, indeed the only one in the first part of the play. If we recognize in him an irascible humour type, an alazon, we should also recognize that the tragic hero is an alazon transposed. Tybalt alone takes the feud really seriously. It is his *inner* law, the propeller of his fiery nature. His natural frame of reference is the heroic one of honor and death:

> What, dares the slave
> Come hither, cover'd with an antic face,
> To fleer and scorn at our solemnity?
> Now, by the stock and honour of my kin,
> To strike him dead I hold it not a sin.
>   (I.v.53–57)

Tybalt's single set of absolutes cuts him off from a whole range of speech and action available to the other young men of the play: lyric love, witty fooling, friendly conversation. Ironically, his imperatives come to dominate the play's world only when he himself departs from it. While he is alive, Tybalt is an alien.

In a similar way, the passing fears of calamity voiced at times by Romeo, Juliet, and Friar Laurence are not allowed to dominate the atmosphere of the early acts. The love of Romeo and Juliet is already imaged as a flash of light swallowed by darkness, an image invoking inexorable natural law; but it is also expressed as a sea venture, which suggests luck and skill set against natural hazards and chance seized joyously as an opportunity for action. "Direct my sail," says Romeo to his captain Fortune. Soon he feels himself in command:

> I am no pilot; yet, wert thou as far
> As that vast shore wash'd with the farthest sea,
> I should adventure for such merchandise.

The spirit is Bassanio's as he adventures for Portia, a Jason voyaging in quest of the Golden Fleece (*MV* I.i.167–172). Romeo is ready for difficulties with a traditional lovers' stratagem, one which Shakespeare had used before in *Two Gentlemen*: a rope ladder, "cords made like a tackled stair; / Which to the high top-gallant of my joy / Must be my convoy in the secret night" (II.iv.183–185).

But before Romeo can mount his tackled stair, Mercutio's death intervenes to cut off this world of exhilarating venture. Shakespeare developed this character, who in the source is little more than a name and a cold hand, into the very incarnation of comic atmosphere. Mercutio is the clown of romantic comedy, recast in more elegant mold but equally ready to take off from the plot in verbal play and to challenge idealistic love with his own brand of comic earthiness.

> Nay, I'll conjure too.
> Romeo! humours! madman! passion! lover!
> Appear thou in the likeness of a sigh;
> Speak but one rhyme and I am satisfied;
> Cry but 'Ay me!' pronounce but 'love' and 'dove';
> .   .   .   .
> I conjure thee by Rosaline's bright eyes,
> By her high forehead and her scarlet lip,
> By her fine foot, straight leg, and quivering thigh,
> And the demesnes that there adjacent lie.
>
> (II.i.6–20)

He is the best of game-players, endlessly inventive and full of quick moves and countermoves. Speech for him is a constant exercise in multiple possibilities: puns abound, roles are taken up at whim (that of conjuror, for instance, in the passage just quoted), and his Queen Mab brings dreams not only to lovers like Romeo but to courtiers, lawyers, parsons, soldiers, maids.

These have nothing to do with the case at hand, which is Romeo's premonition of trouble, but Mercutio is not bound by events. They serve him merely as convenient launching pads for his flights of wit. When all this vitality, which has till now ignored all urgencies, is cut off abruptly by Tybalt's sword, it must come as a shock to a spectator unfamiliar with the play. In Mercutio's sudden, violent end, Shakespeare makes the birth of tragedy coincide exactly with the symbolic death of comedy. The alternative view, the element of freedom and play, dies with Mercutio. Where many courses were open before, now there seems only one. Romeo sees at once that an irreversible process has begun:

> This day's black fate on moe days doth depend [hang
>   over];
> This but begins the woe others must end.
>
> > (III.i.116–117)

It is the first sign in the play's dialogue pointing unambiguously to tragic necessity. Romeo's future is now determined; he *must* kill Tybalt, he *must* run away, he is Fortune's fool.

This helplessness is the most striking feature of the second, tragic world of *Romeo*. The temper of this new world is largely a function of onrushing events. Under pressure of events, the feud turns from farce to fate; tit for tat becomes blood for blood. Lawless as it seems to Prince Escalus, the feud is dramatically "the law" in *Romeo*. Before, it was external and avoidable. Now it moves inside Romeo to be his personal law. This is why he takes over Tybalt's rhetoric of honor and death:

> Alive in triumph and Mercutio slain!
> Away to heaven respective lenity,
> And fire-ey'd fury be my conduct now!
> Now, Tybalt, take the 'villain' back again
> That late thou gav'st me.
>
> > (III.i.119–123)

Even outside the main chain of vengeance, the world is suddenly full of imperatives. Others besides Romeo feel helpless. Against his will Friar John is detained at the monastery; against his will the Apothecary sells poison to Romeo. Urgency becomes the norm. Nights run into mornings, and the characters seem never to sleep. The new world finds its emblem not in the aborted attack but in the aborted feast. As Tybalt's violence was out of tune with the Capulet festivities in Act II, so in the changed world of Acts III and

IV the projected wedding of Juliet and Paris is made grotesque when Shakespeare insistently links it with death. Preparations for the wedding feast parallel those made for the party in the play's first part, so as to make more wrenching contrast when Capulet must order,

> All things that we ordained festival
> Turn from their office to black funeral:
> Our instruments to melancholy bells,
> Our wedding cheer to a sad burial feast,
> Our solemn hymns to sullen dirges change.
>
> (IV.v.84–88)

The play's last scene shows how completely the comic movement has been reversed. It is inherent in that movement, as we have seen, that the young get their way at the expense of the old. The final tableau of comedy features young couples joined in love; parents and authority figures are there, if at all, to ratify with more or less good grace what has been accomplished against their wills. But here, the stage is strikingly full of elders—the Friar, the Prince, Capulet, Lady Capulet, Montague. Their power is not passed on. Indeed, there are no young to take over. If Benvolio survives somewhere offstage, we have long since forgotten this adjunct character. Romeo, Juliet, Tybalt, Mercutio, and Paris are all dead. In effect, the entire younger generation has been wiped out.

I have been treating these two worlds as separate, consistent wholes in order to bring out their opposition, but I do not wish to deny dramatic unity to *Romeo and Juliet*. Shakespeare was writing one play, not two; and in spite of the clearly marked turning point we are aware of premonitions of disaster before the death of Mercutio, and hopes for avoiding it continue until near the end of the play. Our full perception of the world-shift that converts Romeo and Juliet from instinctive winners into sacrificial victims thus comes gradually. In this connection the careers of two secondary characters, Friar Laurence and the Nurse, are instructive.

In being and action, these two belong to the comic vision. Friar Laurence is one of the tribe of manipulators, whose job it is to transform or otherwise get round seemingly intractable realities. If his herbs and potions are less spectacular than the paraphernalia of Friar Bacon or John a Kent, he nevertheless belongs to their brotherhood. Such figures abound in romantic comedy, as we have seen, but not in tragedy, where the future is not so manipulable. The Friar's aims are those implicit in the play's comic movement: an inviolable union for Romeo and Juliet and an end to the families' feud.

The Nurse's goal is less lofty but equally appropriate to comedy. She wants Juliet married—to anyone. Her preoccupation with bedding and breeding reminds us of comedy's ancient roots in fertility rites, and it is as indiscriminate as the life force itself. But she conveys no sense of urgency in all this. On the contrary, her garrulity assumes the limitless time of comedy. In this sense her circumlocutions and digressions are analogous to Mercutio's witty games and, for that matter, to Friar Laurence's counsels of patience. "Wisely and slow," the Friar cautions Romeo; "they stumble that run fast" (II.iii.94). The Nurse is not very wise, but she is slow. The leisurely time assumptions of both Friar and Nurse contrast with the lovers' impatience, to create first the normal counterpoint of comedy and later a radical split that points us, with the lovers, directly towards tragedy.

Friar Laurence and the Nurse have no place in the new world brought into being by Mercutio's death, the world of limited time, no effective choice, no escape. They define and sharpen the tragedy by their very failure to find a part in the dramatic progress, by their growing estrangement from the true springs of the action. "Be patient," is the Friar's advice to banished Romeo, "for the world is broad and wide" (III.iii.16). But the roominess he perceives in both time and space simply does not exist for Romeo. *His* time has been constricted into a chain of days working out a "black fate," and he sees no world outside the walls of Verona.

Comic adaptability again confronts tragic integrity when Juliet is forced to marry Paris—and turns to her Nurse for counsel, as Romeo has turned to Friar Laurence. In the Nurse's response comedy's traditional wisdom of accommodation is carried to an extreme. Romeo has been banished, and Paris is after all very presentable. In short, adjust to the new state of things.

> Then, since the case so stands as now it doth,
> I think it best you married with the County.
> O, he's a lovely gentleman!
> Romeo's a dishclout to him.
>
> (III.v.217–220)

She still speaks for the life force, against barrenness and death. Even if Juliet will not accept the dishclout comparison, an inferior husband is better than no husband at all: "Your first is dead, or 'twere as good he were / As living here and you no use of him" (225–226).

But her advice is irrelevant, even shocking, in this new context. There was no sense of jar when Benvolio, a spokesman for comic accommodation like the Nurse and the Friar, earlier advised Romeo to substitute a possible love for an impossible one. True, the Nurse here is urging Juliet to violate her marriage vows; but Romeo also felt himself sworn to Rosaline, and for Juliet the marriage vow is a seal on the integrity of her love for Romeo, not a separable issue. The parallel points up the move into tragedy, for while Benvolio's advice sounded sensible in Act I and was in fact unintentionally carried out by Romeo, the course of action that the Nurse proposes in Act III is unthinkable to the audience as well as to Juliet. The memory of the lovers' passionate dawn parting that began this scene is too strong. Juliet and her nurse no longer speak the same language, and estrangement is inevitable. "Thou and my bosom henceforth shall be twain," Juliet vows when the Nurse has left the stage. Like the slaying of Mercutio, Juliet's rejection of her old confidante has symbolic overtones. The possibilities of comedy have again been presented only to be discarded.

Both Romeo and Juliet have now cast off their comic companions and the alternative modes of being that they represented. But there is one last hope for comedy. If the lovers will not adjust to the situation, perhaps the situation can be adjusted to the lovers. This is the usual comic way with obstinately faithful pairs, and we have at hand the usual manipulator figure to arrange it.

The Friar's failure to bring off that solution is the final definition of the tragic world of *Romeo and Juliet*. There is no villain, only chance and bad timing. In comedy chance creates that elastic time that allows last-minute rescues. But here, events at Mantua and at the Capulet tomb will simply happen—by chance—in the wrong sequence. The Friar does his best: he makes more than one plan to avert catastrophe. The first, predictably, is patience and a broader field of action. Romeo must go to Mantua and wait

> till we can find a time
> To blaze your marriage, reconcile your friends,
> Beg pardon of the Prince, and call thee back . . .
> (III.iii.150–152)

It is a good enough plan, for life if not for drama, but it depends on "finding a time." As it turns out, events move too quickly for the Friar. The hasty preparations for Juliet's marriage to Paris leave no time for cooling tempers and reconciliations.

His second plan is an attempt to *gain* time: he will create the necessary freedom by faking Juliet's death. This is, of course, a familiar comic formula. Shakespeare's later uses of it are all in comedies. Indeed, the contrived "deaths" of Hero in *Much Ado*, Helena in *All's Well*, Claudio in *Measure for Measure*, and Hermione in *The Winter's Tale* are more ambitiously intended than Juliet's, aimed at bringing about a change of heart in other characters.

Time may be important, as it is in *Winter's Tale*, but only as it promotes repentance. Friar Laurence, more desperate than his fellow manipulators, does not hope that Juliet's death will dissolve the Montague-Capulet feud, but only that it will give Romeo a chance to come and carry her off. Time and chance, which in the other plays cooperate benevolently with the forces of regeneration and renewal, work against Friar Laurence. Romeo's man is quicker with the bad news of Juliet's death than poor Friar John with the good news that the death is only a pretense. Romeo himself beats Friar Laurence to the tomb of the Capulets. The onrushing tragic action quite literally outstrips the slower steps of accommodation before our eyes. The Friar arrives too late to prevent one half of the tragic conclusion, and his essential estrangement from the play's world is only emphasized when he seeks to avert the other half by sending Juliet to a nunnery. This last alternative means little to the audience or to Juliet, who spares only a line to reject the possibility of adjustment and continuing life: "Go, get thee hence, for I will not away" (V.iii.160).

The Nurse and the Friar show that one way comedy can operate in a tragedy is by its irrelevance. Tragedy is tuned to the extraordinary. *Romeo and Juliet* locates this extraordinariness not so much in the two youthful lovers as in the love itself, its intensity and integrity. As the play moves forward, our sense of this intensity and integrity is strengthened by the cumulative effect of the lovers' lyric encounters and the increasing urgency of events, but also by the growing irrelevance of the comic characters.

De Quincey saw in the knocking at the gate in *Macbeth* the resumption of normality after nightmare, "the re-establishment of the goings-on of the world in which we live, [which] first makes us profoundly sensible of the awful parenthesis that had suspended them." I would say, rather, that the normal atmosphere of *Macbeth* has been and goes on being nightmarish, and that it is the knocking episode that turns out to be the contrasting parenthesis, but the notion of sharpened sensibility is important. As the presence of other paths makes us more conscious of the road we are in fact traveling, so the Nurse and the Friar make us more "profoundly sensible" of the love of Romeo and Juliet and its tragic direction.

The play offers another sort of experiment in mingled genres that is less successful, I think. It starts well, in IV.iv, with a striking juxtaposition of Capulet preparations for the wedding with Juliet's potion scene. On the one hand is the household group in a bustle over clothes, food, logs for the fire— the everyday necessaries and small change of life. On the other is Juliet's tense monologue of fear, madness, and death. It is fine dramatic counterpoint, and its effect is stronger in stage production, as Granville-Barker observed, when the curtained bed of Juliet is visible upstage during the cheerful domestic goings-on. The counterpoint, of course, depends on the Capulets' ignorance of what is behind those curtains. It comes to an end when in scene v Nurse and the others find Juliet's body. But Shakespeare keeps the comic strain alive through the rest of the scene. The high-pitched, repetitive mourning of the Nurse, Paris, and the Capulets sounds more like Pyramus over the body of Thisbe than a serious tragic scene. Finally Peter has his comic turn with the musicians. What Shakespeare is attempting here is not counterpoint but the *fusion* of tragic and comic. It doesn't quite work. S. L. Bethell suggests that the mourners' rhetorical excesses direct the audience to remain detached and thus to reserve their tears for the real death scene that will shortly follow. This makes good theatrical sense. It is also possible that the musicians' dialogue, modulating as it does from shock to professional shop to dinner, was meant to set off the tragic action by projecting a sense of the ongoing, normal life that is denied to Romeo and Juliet. Still, the scene tends to leave spectators uneasy—if, in fact, they get to see it at all: often the mourning passages are cut and the musicians' business dropped altogether. Shakespeare's hand is uncertain in this early essay at fusing tragic and comic. Mastery was yet to come, first in the gravediggers' scene in *Hamlet* and then more fully in *King Lear*.

The structural use of comic conventions does work. The result, however, is a particular kind of tragedy. Critics have often remarked, neutrally or with disapproval, that external fate rather than character is the principal determiner of the tragic ends of the young lovers. For the mature Shakespeare, tragedy involves both character and circumstances, a fatal interaction between man and moment. But in *Romeo and Juliet*, although the central characters have their weaknesses, their destruction does not really stem from those weaknesses. We may agree with Friar Laurence that Romeo is rash, but it is not rashness that propels him into the tragic chain of events. Just the opposite, it would seem. In the crucial duel between Mercutio and Tybalt, Romeo is trying to keep the combatants apart, to make peace. Ironically, this very intervention leads to Mercutio's death.

> *Mer.* Why the devil came you between us? I was hurt
>   under your arm.
> *Rom.* I thought all for the best.

(III.i.99–101)

If Shakespeare had wanted to implicate Romeo's rash, overemotional nature in his fate, he handled this scene with an ineptness difficult to credit. Judging from the resultant effect, what he wanted was something quite different: an ironic dissociation of character from the direction of events.

Perhaps this same purpose lies behind the elaborate development of comic elements in the early acts before the characters are pushed into the opposed conditions of tragedy. To stress milieu in this way is necessarily to downgrade the importance of individual temperament and motivation. At the crucial moment Romeo displays untypical prudence with the most upright of intentions—and brings disaster on himself and Juliet. In this unusual Shakespearean tragedy, it is not what you are that counts, but the world you live in.

Shakespeare may have been dissatisfied with his experiment. At any rate, he wrote no more tragedy for several years, and he never again returned to the comedy-into-tragedy structure. He came closest to it in *Othello*, where comic success precedes tragic catastrophe, but the effect is very different. Character and fate, dissociated in *Romeo and Juliet*, are completely intertwined in this mature tragedy of love. Once again a novella source, with its love motive and deception plot, seems to have prompted the dramatist to shape his material in ways that would remind his audience of comic conventions. But here external forces do not defeat the comic, as in *Romeo*; destruction comes from inside, both inside Othello and inside the assumptions of romantic love. *Othello* develops a tragic view of love by looking more penetratingly at some of those strains and contradictions I have pointed out within the comic convention, a tragic view adumbrated already in some of Shakespeare's lyric poetry. The personalities and situations of *Othello* are such as to put maximum pressure on those areas of thin ice, until the ice breaks and the treacherous currents below are released.

To see how this is so, we need to look in more detail at the conventional comic treatment of love outlined in the preceding chapter, and at Shake-speare's own romantic comedies of the decade and more before he wrote *Othello*. What is pertinent is not the explicit themes of these plays but their common underlying assumptions about love.

The *value* of love and of its proper fruition, marriage, is a basic premise of all Shakespeare's comedies, which invariably present as all or part of their initial situation individuals in a single and unsatisfied state and direct them through plot complications toward appropriate parings-off at the end. Unanimous approval extends from supernatural Oberon to bumpkin Costard; Jaques is the only significant dissenter, and even he is made to bless the Arden marriages (one of which he actively promoted: *AYL* III.iii) before bowing out of society to brood in his hermitage. Indeed, Jaques' election to live permanently in the forest has a certain irony, for his real adversary in this debate is nature itself.

We have observed that in comedy, law and conventional morality generally must give way before nature. The "winners" in comedy are those in tune with the natural forces of life-renewal. Shakespeare is explicit about the naturalness of mating in some comedies (*Love's Labour's Lost*, for example); the notion is implicit in all of them. Those that promote release and resolution of conflicts by moving the characters to some out-of-bounds locale—described for us spatially by Frye's "green world" and temporally by Barber's "holiday"—give structural reinforcement to this sense of nature as love's ally. For all of the artificial and magical elements in the forests of *Two Gentlemen*, *Midsummer Night's Dream*, and *As You Like It*, nature in those places is less trammeled and perverted than in the polite, treacherous court of Milan, or in Theseus's lawbound Athens, or in the dominions where Duke Frederick sets the ethical standard by crimes against his own kindred. Turned out or self-exiled from civilization, the lovers are righted and united in the woods.

Love is natural, then, as well as right. But comedy also affirms that love is irrational and arbitrary. "To say the truth," muses Bottom, "reason and love keep little company together now-a-days. The more the pity that some honest neighbours will not make them friends" (*MND* III.i.131–133). He speaks for comedy in general, not just *Midsummer Night's Dream*. Oberon's potent flower can be seen as an emblem for the unreasonable passions of Titania, Lysander, and Demetrius, but also for those that immediately enslave Orlando to Rosalind (but not Celia), Oliver to Celia (but not Rosalind), Navarre and his friends to the Princess and *her* friends (with balletic tidiness), and, less fortunately, Phebe to Rosalind, Proteus to Silvia, Olivia to Viola-Cesario. If some of these sudden obsessions seem slightly less arbitrary than those of, say, Ariosto's characters as they veer from one course to another with each sip from the fountains of love and hate, it is only that Shakespeare has provided for his *final* couplings an acceptable degree of compatibility in sex, rank, and temperament. But there is no suggestion that this compatibility was reasonably appraised by the lovers or that it influenced their decisions—if they can be called that—at all.

This insistence that anything so vital as the love-choice is totally beyond rational control does not bother comic characters. Bottom is untroubled by his pronouncement, and by the fairy queen's amazing dotage that provokes it. Lovers generally abandon what reason they have without a struggle, and this course seems to be the approved one. When one of them attempts to rationalize his new emotions, as Lysander does when the misapplied love-juice compels him to love Helena, the result fools no one.

> *Lys.* Not Hermia but Helena I love:
>   Who will not change a raven for a dove?

The will of man is by his reason sway'd,
And reason says you are the worthier maid.
Things growing are not ripe until their season;
So I, being young, till now ripe not to reason;
And touching now the point of human skill,
Reason becomes the marshal to my will,
And leads me to your eyes . . .

    .   .   .   .

Hel. Wherefore was I to this keen mockery born?

It is only in the security of comedy's natural law that we can dismiss with laughter Lysander's attempts to reconcile love with reason. Comedy provides no "honest neighbour" to make them truly friends.

The convention of ending comedies with marriage promised, or marriage celebrated, or marriage ratified emotionally and socially (*Taming of the Shrew, Merchant of Venice, All's Well*), has a further corollary. Comedies in this dominant pattern by implication locate the important stresses and decisions of love in the courtship period. Their silence about shifts of direction after marriage suggests that there will be none, that once Jack has Jill, nought can go ill—or, if couples like Touchstone and Audrey seem headed for less than perfect harmony, at least that the "story" is over.

To sum up: Shakespeare's comic forms and conventions assume, first, the value of engagement with a mate, and second, the cooperation of forces beyond man, natural and otherwise, in achieving this mating and forestalling the consequences of human irrationality and malice, as well as plain bad luck. To call these "assumptions" does not, of course, mean that Shakespeare or his audiences accepted them as universally true. Rather, the dramatist's use of the comic formulas and the playgoers' familiarity with them directed which aspects of their diverse perception of experience should be brought forward—wish as well as belief—and which should be held in abeyance.

To the extent that Shakespeare allowed bad luck to defeat love in *Romeo and Juliet*, we may see him as questioning comic assumptions in that play, but the questioning does not go very deep. The lovers' relationship is presented as natural and right in itself. If it makes them irrationally impetuous, it is nevertheless not this rashness that precipitates the tragedy. In *Othello*, however, Shakespeare subjects the comic assumptions about the love union, nature, and reason to a radical reassessment, and in so doing exposes the roots of tragedy.

Just as such a scrutiny logically comes *after* the first unquestioning acceptance, so Othello's and Desdemona's story is deliberately set up as postcomic. Courtship and ratified marriage, the whole story of comedy, appear in *Othello* as a preliminary to tragedy. The play's action up until the reunion of Othello and Desdemona in Cyprus (II.i) is a perfect comic structure in miniature. The wooing that the two of them describe in the Venetian council scene (I.iii) has succeeded in spite of barriers of age, color, and condition of life; the machinations of villain and doltish rival have come to nothing; the blocking father has been overruled by the good duke; and nature has cooperated in the general movement with a storm that disperses the last external threat, the Turks, while preserving the favored lovers. Othello's reunion speech to Desdemona underlines this sense of a movement accomplished, a still point of happiness like the final scene of a comedy:

> If it were now to die,
> 'Twere now to be most happy; for I fear
> My soul hath her content so absolute
> That not another comfort like to this
> Succeeds in unknown fate.
>
> (II.i.187–191)

But at the same time that Othello celebrates his peak of joy so markedly, his invocations of death, fear, and unknown fate make us apprehensive about the postcomic future. Desdemona's equally negative mode of agreement ("The heavens forbid / But that our loves and comforts should increase . . .") indirectly reinforces this unease, and Iago's threat does so directly: "O, you are well tun'd now! / But I'll set down the pegs that make this music." In these few lines Shakespeare prepares us for tragedy, in part by announcing the end of comedy. The happy ending is completed, and Othello and Desdemona are left to go on from there.

If I am right to see the tragedy of *Othello* developing from a questioning of comic assumptions, then the initial comic movement ought to make us aware of unresolved tensions in this successful love. And it does, in various ways. Othello's account of their shy, story-telling courtship, however moving and beautiful, is in retrospect disturbing. "She lov'd me for the dangers I had pass'd; / And I lov'd her that she did pity them" (I.iii.167–168). Is it enough? Some critics have on this hint proclaimed the Moor totally self-centered, incapable of real love. This is surely too severe. Nevertheless, in his summary their love has a proxy quality. "The dangers I had pass'd" have served as a counter between them, a substitute for direct engagement or, at best, a preliminary to something not yet achieved. Twice before, Shakespeare had used comedy to explore the inadequacies of romantic courtship, cursorily in *Taming of the Shrew* and more thoroughly in *Much Ado*. In the latter play,

Claudio and Hero move through the paces of conventional wooing, depending on rumors and go-betweens, without direct exploration of each other's nature. Thus, Hero can be traduced and Claudio can believe it, lacking as he does the knowledge of the heart that should counteract the false certainty of the eyes. *Much Ado* is a comedy, and thus the presiding deities give time for Dogberry's muddled detective work and provide in the Friar a benevolent countermanipulator against Don John. The love of Othello and Desdemona has the same vulnerability, but no time is given; and instead of Friar Francis, Iago is in charge.

Iago is the most obvious potential force for tragedy in the early part of the play. We see him thwarted in his first plot against Othello but already, at the end of Act I, planning the next. His speech at this point suggests in both overt statement and imagery the thrust beyond the comic, the germination out of the first failure of a deeper evil:

> I ha't—it is engender'd. Hell and night
> Must bring this monstrous birth to the world's light.
> (I.iii.397–398)

It was Bradley, expanding on suggestions from Hazlitt and Swinburne, who compared Iago in his first two soliloquies to a playwright in the early stages of writing a new play—"drawing at first only an outline, puzzled how to fix more than the main idea, and gradually seeing it develop and clarify as he works upon it or lets it work." Bradley's parallel highlights the unexpected kinship between Iago and the magicians and friars of comedy, who arrange "fond pageants" in which other characters play unaware the parts assigned to them, and who dispose events toward the desired ending as a dramatist does. The implication that a single human being can control persons and change realities, exhilarating within the safe parameters of comedy, is sinister here.

So is the holiday from reason that comedy proclaims for romantic love. Iago is the most intelligent character in the play, and reason—or the appearance of reason—is his chief means of controlling others. The *power* of the rational view, in the comedies so easily dismissed with laughter or overruled by emotion, is grimly realized in Iago's accurate estimates of character

> The Moor is of a free and open nature
> That thinks men honest that but seem to be so;
> And will as tenderly be led by th' nose . . .
> (I.iii.393–395)

his telling arguments from experience

In Venice they do let God see the pranks
They dare not show their husbands . . .

.   .   .   .

She did deceive her father, marrying you
                              (III.iii.206–210)

his plausible hypotheses

That Cassio loves her, I do well believe it;
That she loves him, 'tis apt and of great credit
                              (II.i.280–281)

and his final triumph in converting Othello to the philosophy of "ocular proof" (III.iii.364). Against him the love of Othello and Desdemona is vulnerable, rooted as it is not in rational evaluation of empirical knowledge but in instinctive sympathy. The same scene that underlines how indirect was their courtship (I.iii) also brings out the peculiar strength of their love that is a weakness as well:

Des. I saw Othello's visage in his mind.
                                             (252)

Oth. My life upon her faith!
                                             (294)

There is a core of power in this instinctive mutual recognition that survives Iago's rational poison and in a sense defeats it, but this victory comes only in death. In his posing of Iago against Othello and Desdemona, Shakespeare fully explores the conventional dichotomy between reason and love and uncovers its deeply tragic implications.

If reason's opposition to love is traditional, nature in *Othello* appears to have changed sides. Love's ally is now love's enemy, partly because the angle of vision has changed: nature as instinctual rightness gives way to nature as abstract concept, susceptible like all concepts to distortion and misapplication. Brabantio, Iago, and finally Othello himself see the love between Othello and Desdemona as *un*natural—"nature erring from itself" (III.iii.231). But there is more to it than this. In key scenes of *Othello* a tension develops between two senses of *nature*, the general and the particular.

It is to general nature, the common experience and prejudice by which like calls only to like, that Brabantio appeals in the Venetian council scene. An attraction between the young white Venetian girl and the aging black foreigner, since it goes against this observed law of nature, could only have been "wrought" by unnatural means.

> She is abus'd, stol'n from me, and corrupted,
> By spells and medicines bought of mountebanks;
> For nature so preposterously to err,
> Being not deficient, blind, or lame of sense,
> Sans witchcraft could not.
>
> (I.iii.60–64)

The other sense of *nature* is particular and personal. What Iago means in his soliloquy at the end of this scene when he says the Moor "is of a free and open nature" is individual essence: the inscape of Othello. Brabantio tries to bring in this nature to support the other in his appeal against the marriage. He says that Desdemona is essentially timid, thus by nature (her own) cannot love the fearsome Moor.

> A maiden never bold,
> Of spirit so still and quiet that her motion
> Blush'd at herself; and she—in spit of nature,
> Of years, of country, credit, every thing—
> To fall in love with what she fear'd to look on!
> It is a judgment maim'd and most imperfect
> That will confess perfection so could err
> Against all rules of nature.
>
> (I.iii.94–101)

But this personal nature is the very ground of Desdemona's love. In her answer to her father and the Venetian Senate she tells how, penetrating through the blackness and strangeness, she saw Othello's true visage in his mind and subdued her heart to that essence, his "very quality."

For Desdemona, then, nature as individual essence is not the enemy of love. But Iago has the last word in this scene, and his conclusion is ominous: Othello's very generosity and openness will make him take the appearance of honesty for the fact. That is, Othello will act instinctively according to the laws of his own nature rather than according to reasoned evaluation (which would perceive that most liars pretend to be telling the truth). This internal law of nature, then, implies the same vulnerability that we have seen in the instinctive, nonrational quality of Othello's and Desdemona's love.

Brabantio's general nature is implicitly reductive in that it derives rules for individuals from the behavior of the herd. Iago's is explicitly reductive. For him "the herd" is no metaphor, and the view he expounds to Roderigo has no place for human values or ethical norms. Natural law for Iago, as for Edmund in *King Lear*, is Hobbesian—a matter of animal appetites promoted by cleverness, with the strongest and the shrewdest winning out. Desdemona, he assures Roderigo, will tire of Othello because the appetite requires fresh stimuli:

> Her eye must be fed; and what delight shall she have to look on the devil? When the blood is made dull with the act of sport, there should be—again to inflame it, and to give satiety a fresh appetite—loveliness in favour, sympathy in years, manners, and beauties—all which the Moor is defective in. Now for want of these requir'd conveniences, her delicate tenderness will find itself abus'd, begin to heave the gorge, disrelish and abhor the Moor; very nature will instruct her in it, and compel her to some second choice.
>
> (II.i.221–233)

Compel her—here is yet another "law," generalized from the ways of animal nature. The context is wholly physical, as the persistent images of eating and disgorging keep reminding us. Iago has begun the discussion by prodding on the hesitant lover Roderigo with a bit of folk wisdom: "They say base men being in love have then a nobility in their natures more than is native to them" (212–214). But he does not pretend to believe it himself. Love is rather "a lust of the blood and a permission of the will"; Roderigo, in love or not, is a snipe; our natures are "blood and baseness." In Iago's determined animalism there is another unexpected reminder of comedy, this time of the antiromantic servant or rustic whose imagination is bounded by the physical. It is perhaps because this view can be destructive when actually *acted out* against idealized love that the clowns of comedy are kept largely apart from the plot, as onlookers. Iago is a clown without good humor and (what underlies that lack) without self-sufficiency, who must therefore prove his theories on other people. Interestingly, this transfer of the debunking low-life perspective to the service of active malevolence seems to have left no function for the play's official clown. His feeble essays at bawdry and wordplay have nothing conceptual to adhere to, and after a second brief appearance in Act II he departs unmourned.

In Shakespeare's portrayal of Iago we can see a version of the clash I have been describing. In spite of his reductive general view, he can recognize the essential goodness of Othello ("free and open nature," "constant, loving, noble nature") as well as Desdemona's generosity and the daily beauty of

Cassio's life. Critics have complained of the inconsistency, and if *Othello* were naturalistic drama, they would be right to do so. But Iago is not just an envious spoiler; he is the symbolic enemy of love itself. The play's conception demands that the weapons of both "natures," like those of reason, be put in his hands.

In his great self-summation at the play's end, Othello says he was "wrought" from his true nature, and so he was. His own nature, noble and trusting, gave him an instinctive perception of Desdemona's, a perception which breaks forth at the sight of her even while Iago is poisoning his mind: "If she be false, O, then heaven mocks itself! / I'll not believe it" (III.iii.282–283). But Iago is able to undermine that trust with false rationality, the insistence that Desdemona's honor, which is "an essence that's not seen," be made susceptible of ocular proof. He succeeds, where Brabantio failed, in using both conceptions of nature against Othello. The Moor's own generous nature, Iago suggests, makes him an easy dupe. "I would not have your free and noble nature / Out of self-bounty be abus'd; look to 't" (203–204). Taught to look from the outside instead of trust from the inside, Othello soon sees Desdemona's choice of him as an aberration, nature erring from itself. Iago quickly advances the other nature, the law of all things, to reinforce the idea:

> Ay, there's the point: as—to be bold with you—
> Not to affect many proposed matches
> Of her own clime, complexion, and degree,
> Whereto we see in all things nature tends—
> Foh! One may smell in such a will most rank,
> Foul disproportion, thoughts unnatural.
>   (232–237)

And so Othello violates his own peculiar essence and internalizes Iago's law of the many. Desdemona soon realizes uneasily that he is altered ("My lord is not my lord": III.iv.125) and, in an ironic reflection of Othello's confusion, seeks the explanation in a generalization about "men": "Men's natures wrangle with inferior things, / Though great ones are their object" (145–146). Later the Venetian visitors gaze horrified at the change in that nature that passion could not shake, as Othello strikes his wife and then exits mumbling of goats and monkeys. He has taken into himself Iago's reductive view of man as animal. In the next scene (IV.ii) he will see Desdemona in terms of toads coupling and maggots quickening in rotten meat.

The love that in comedies was a strength in *Othello* is vulnerable to attacks of reason, arguments from nature. More than that: vulnerability is its very essence. Before falling in love with Desdemona, Othello was self-suffi-cient, master of himself and of the battlefield. After he believes her to be false, his occupation is gone. Why? Because love has created a dependency, a yielding of the separate, sufficient self to incorporation with another. What comedy treated as a liberating completeness becomes in *Othello* the heart of tragedy. Even in the play's comic phase there are signs of this new and poten-tially dangerous vulnerability. Othello's images for his love-commitment are not of expansion but of narrowing and confining:

> But that I love the gentle Desdemona,
> I would not my unhoused free condition
> Put into circumscription and confine
> For the seas' worth.
>
> (I.ii.25–28)

To love totally is to give up the freedom of self for the perils of union, and the expansive great world for an other-centered, contingent one. Othello makes a significant metaphor for Desdemona near the end of the play:

> Nay, had she been true,
> If heaven would make me *such another world*
> Of one entire and perfect chrysolite,
> I'd not have sold her for it.

"My life upon her faith" is literally true. Desdemona has become Othello's world.

It is in this light, I think, that we can best understand why Othello reacts to Iago's insinuations about Desdemona by renouncing his profession. The great aria on military life invokes, not chaos and carnage, but *order*. War is individual passion subordinated to a larger plan, martial harmony, formal pageantry, imitation of divine judgment.

> O, now for ever
> Farewell the tranquil mind! farewell content!
> Farewell the plumed troops, and the big wars
> That makes ambition virtue! O, farewell!
> Farewell the neighing steed and the shrill trump,
> The spirit-stirring drum, th' ear-piercing fife,
> The royal banner, and all quality,
> Pride, pomp, and circumstance, of glorious war!
> And O ye mortal engines whose rude throats

Th' immortal Jove's dread clamours counterfeit,
Farewell! Othello's occupation's gone.
                                                                (III.iii.351–361)

Stylistically and rhythmically, the formal catalogues and ritual repetitions
strengthen this selective picture of war as majestic order. Earlier in this scene
Othello has said that when he stops loving Desdemona, chaos will come
again. Now it has happened. With his world thrown into chaos, his ordering
generalship is gone.

Othello's disintegration of self is the dark side of comedy's rejection of
singleness, its insistence on completing oneself with another. But Shakespeare goes deeper in his exploration of comic assumptions by showing that
the desired merging of self and other is in any case impossible. The more or
less schematized pairings-off of the comedies combine necessary opposition
(male/female) with sympathies in age, background, temperament. It is
enough in comedy to suggest compatibility by outward signs and look no
farther than the formal union. But in *Othello* Shakespeare has taken pains in
several ways to emphasize the separateness of his lovers.

Cinthio's Moor in the source tale is handsome, apparently fairly young,
and a longtime Venetian resident. Apart from sex, his only real difference
from Desdemona is one of color, and Cinthio does not dwell on it much.
Shakespeare dwells on it a great deal. Black-white oppositions weave themselves continually into the verbal fabric of *Othello*. Indeed, the blackness of
Cinthio's hero may have been one of the story's main attractions for Shakespeare. Certainly he altered other details of the story to reinforce this para-
digmatic separation into black and white, to increase Othello's alienness and
widen the gulf between his experience and Desdemona's. Shakespeare's
Moor is a stranger to Venice and to civil life in general; his entire career,
except for the brief period in which he courted Desdemona, has been spent
in camp and on the battlefield (I.iii.83–87). Even Othello's speech reminds us
constantly, if subtly, of his apartness. It is hardly rude, as he claims to the
Venetian Senate, but it is certainly different from theirs. His idiom naturally
invokes Anthropophagi and Pontic seas, roots itself in the exotic rather than
the everyday social life that is familiar to the others but not to him. He knows
as little of Venetian ways as Desdemona knows of "antres vast and deserts
idle," and he is given no time to learn. While Cinthio's Moor and his bride
live for some time in Venice after their marriage, Othello and Desdemona
must go at once to Cyprus—and not even in the same ship. No wonder that,
when Iago generalizes about the habits of his countrywomen ("In Venice
they do let God see the pranks / They dare not show their husbands . . ."),
Othello can only respond helplessly, "Dost thou say so?" (III.iii.206–209).

Shakespeare has deprived him of any common ground with Desdemona on which he can stand to fight back—not only to facilitate Iago's deception, but to heighten the tragic paradox of human love, individuals dependent on each other but unalterably separate and mysterious to one another in their separateness. The two great values of comic convention—love and the fuller self—are seen as tragically incompatible.

To sharpen the contrast, Othello is made middle-aged, thick-lipped—everything Desdemona is not. The image of black man and white girl in conjunction, so repellent to some critics that they had to invent a tawny or café-au-lait Moor, is at the center of the lay's conception of disjunction in love. It gives visual focus to the other oppositions of war and peace, age and youth, man and woman. This disjunction serves the plot: it assists Iago's initial deception, and it provides most of the tension in the period between the deception and the murder, as Desdemona inopportunely pleads for Cassio, and Othello in turn can communicate his fears only indirectly, through insults and degradations. But beyond this plot function the disjunction constitutes a tragic vision of love itself.

What I am suggesting is that the action of *Othello* moves us not only as a chain of events involving particular people as initiators and victims, but also as an acting out of the tragic implications in any love relationship. Iago is an envious, insecure human being who functions as a perverted magician-manipulator, cunningly altering reality for Othello. But he is also the catalyst who activates destructive forces not of his own creation, forces present in the love itself. His announcement of the "monstrous birth" quoted above has special significance in this regard. Coming at the end of a resolved marriage scene, it implies that the monster will be the product of the marriage. Iago says, "It is engender'd," not "I have engendered it," because he is not parent but midwife. "Hell and night," embodied in this demi-devil who works in the dark, will bring the monster forth, but it is the fruit of love itself.

Because *Othello* is a play, and a great one, tragic action and tragic situation are fully fused in it, and it would be pointless to try to separate them. But a look at some of Shakespeare's non-dramatic work may help clarify the paradoxical sense of love as both life and destruction that informs the events of this play. The sonnets present a range of attitudes to love, from joyous assurance to disgust and despair, but they return again and again to a certain kind of tension between lover and beloved. Sonnet 57 is one example.

> Being your slave, what should I do but tend
> Upon the hours and times of your desire?
> I have no precious time at all to spend,
> Nor services to do, till you require.

Nor dare I chide the world-without-end hour,
Whilst I, my sovereign, watch the clock for you,
Nor think the bitterness of absence sour,
When you have bid your servant once adieu;
Nor dare I question with my jealous thought
Where you may be, or your affairs suppose,
But, like a sad slave, stay and think of nought
Save where you are how happy you make those.
   So true a fool is love that in your will,
   Though you do anything, he thinks no ill.

This apparently positive statement belies its own assent to the terms of relationship by double-edged phrases like "no *precious* time" and "Nor *dare* I chide," and by the bitter wordplay of the couplet: "So true a fool" suggests the loyally loving innocent, but also "so absolutely a dupe." "Fool" completes the sonnet's identification of beloved as monarch and lover as slave. He is not just any kind of slave but the king's fool, a hanger-on who is valued for the occasional diversion he provides. The total effect is of a speaker pulled in contrary directions by need of his friend and esteem of himself.

In Sonnet 35, images and syntax convey the cost of commitment in love.

No more be griev'd at that which thou has done:
Roses have thorns, and silver fountains mud;
Clouds and eclipses stain both moon and sun,
And loathsome canker lives in sweetest bud.
All men make faults, and even I in this,
Authorizing thy trespass with compare,
Myself corrupting, salving thy amiss,
Excusing thy sins more than thy sins are;
For to thy sensual fault I bring in sense—
Thy adverse party is thy advocate—
And 'gainst myself a lawful plea commence;
Such civil war is in my love and hate
   That I an accessary needs must be
   To that sweet thief which sourly robs from me.

The poem strives to repair the damaged relationship by creating a new equality between lover and beloved. It does indeed achieve this, but only at the cost of the speaker's own integrity. He manages to absolve his friend of fault by natural comparisons, nature having no moral dimension to justify

blame, and then implicates himself in fault for making those very comparisons—authorizing the trespass with compare. The last part of the sonnet
strains against the first quatrain, and in that strain lies its impact. Can we
accept the absolution given in lines 1–4 if the mode of absolution turns out
to be sinful? The images reinforce this sense of disjunction: those of the first
quatrain are drawn exclusively from the natural world, and those of the
remainder come from the civilized world of moral man, especially the law
courts. "Civil war," finally overt in line 12, is implicit earlier in the like-
sounding antitheses that shape lines 7–10 into a series of tensions. The
couplet, its message of inner division supported by the difficult twisting of
the last line, completes the violation of self that love has required.

The same kind of violation, expressed with less anguish and more wry
acceptance, is the theme of Sonnet 138:

> When my love swears that she is made of truth,
> I do believer her, though I know she lies. . . .

Here is a comic response to the problem of integrity compromised by depen-
dence on another, as *Othello* is a tragic response. In its mutual accommodation reached through lies and pretenses, Sonnet 138 also stresses the other
side of the paradox, the necessary separateness of lovers. Even the more
idealistic sonnets never proclaim complete union. And the most idealistic of
all, Sonnet 116, presents quite an opposite picture, of love persisting on its
own in spite of the beloved's infidelity:

> Love is not love
> Which alters when it alteration finds,
> Or bends with the remover to remove.
>
> .   .   .   .
>
> Love alters not with his brief hours and weeks,
> But bears it out even to the edge of doom.

This is selfless but ultimately single, more like God's love for man than like
any human relationship. Edward Hubler saw in Sonnet 116 Shakespeare's
affirmation of mutuality as the essence of love. It seems to me just the
contrary, a recognition that if love does depend on being requited it will be
neither lasting nor true. It must necessarily bend with the remover, meet
defection with defection.

Enduring mutuality does not seem to be a possibility in the sonnets.
When Shakespeare does address himself to the merging of separate identi-
ties, the result is the rarefied allegory of "The Phoenix and Turtle." Here the

impossibility is even clearer. The phoenix and the turtle dove are perfectly united, but they are dead. Most of the poem is a dirge sung at their funeral, and it ends in complete stasis—triplets with a single rhyme sound asserting that these lovers left no progeny, that what they represented is gone forever.

> Leaving no posterity—
> 'Twas not their infirmity,
> It was married chastity.

> Truth may seem, but cannot be;
> Beauty brag, but 'tis not she:
> Truth and beauty buried be.

What do we make of this? It has been argued that "The Phoenix and Turtle" approaches "pure poetry" in being all vehicle with no tenor. Certainly it is hard to relate these dead birds and their metaphysical-paradoxical union to the affairs of mortal men and women. Do phoenix and turtle die because annihilation is implicit in perfect union, or because their obliteration of distance, number, and individuality offends against natural law, or because such perfection is possible only outside of time? In any case, the poem makes it clear that the idea will never again be realized on earth.

The dead-end quality of "The Phoenix and Turtle" illuminates tragic love in *Othello* in one way, as the sonnets' tensions and compromises do in another. The sonnets, indeed, provide the most succinct statement of the dilemma I have been exploring in *Othello*, in the opening lines of Sonnet 36:

> Let me confess that we two must be twain,
> Although our undivided loves are one.

In his comedies Shakespeare viewed the coming together of incomplete opposites from a certain intellectual distance. In *Othello* he struck a vein of tragedy by focusing on the contradiction within such a conception: denial of self-sufficiency combined with continued isolation in the self. The comic structure at the beginning of *Othello* does not, as in *Romeo and Juliet*, arouse comic expectations. The seeds of tragedy are already there, and Iago threatens in a way that Tybalt could not. Instead, the rather neat comic pattern, glossing over the vulnerabilities and ambiguities in Othello's and Desdemona's love and disposing too opportunely of the implacable forces represented by Iago, sets up a point of departure for what is to follow: the look beyond and beneath comedy.

In calling *Othello* a tragic statement about love in general I do not mean to deny the power and beauty of the relationship between Othello and Desdemona, which the play celebrates fully. The great worth of love is, after all, what makes its internal flaws so painful. Nor do I wish to turn this very human drama into an allegory. But I do suggest that the universal dimension, the wider reverberations that some critics have felt lacking in *Othello*, emerge very clearly when the play is seen from this perspective. We have perhaps spent too much time asking the traditional questions about this play: Is Othello culpable in succumbing to Iago's suggestions? What makes Iago do what he does? These are important questions, but it is also important to look beyond the individual events of *Othello*, the defeat of a more or less noble dupe by an obscurely motivated villain, to the tragic inadequacies and contradictions of love itself.

Shakespeare's two Italianate tragedies offer companion pictures of the vulnerability of love, threatened from without in *Romeo and Juliet*, from within in *Othello*. It is this concentration on vulnerable *love* that distinguishes these plays from two others where love comes to grief, *Troilus and Cressida* and *Antony and Cleopatra*. Both of the latter present their romantic principals with considerable comic distancing and deflation; that is, their emphasis is on the vulnerability of the *lovers*. *Troilus* is so dominated by the debunking vein, which affects the warriors as well as the lovers, that no sense of the heroic survives in it. Confusion over its genre began in Shakespeare's own time—the quarto title pages called it a history, the author of the 1609 preface praised it as a comedy, the First Folio editors apparently planned to place it among the tragedies—and continues in our own. *Antony*, however, is tragic in form and effect. If I had included it in this study, its proper place would have been between *Hamlet* and *King Lear*. Antony, like Hamlet, suffers from his own largeness of spirit and consequent inability to narrow down, choose, discard alternatives. Like Lear, he exemplifies a special version of the heroic which must justify itself in the face of direct comic attack, of intimations of absurdity. But even this attack is adumbrated in *Hamlet*, which looks forward as well as back in its rich exploitation of comic means for tragic ends.

NORTHROP FRYE

Romeo and Juliet

Shakespeare, we remember, got started as a dramatist by writing a series of
plays, four in all, about the period 1422–85, from the death of Henry V to
the accession of Henry VII. During this period England gradually lost all the
land it had conquered in France (except Calais, which it lost a century later),
then suffered a disastrous civil war between Lancastrians and Yorkists, and
finally acquired the Tudors after leaving the last Yorkist king Richard III dead
on a battlefield. The political moral of all those plays seemed clear: once
feuding nobles get out of hand, there's nothing but misery and chaos until a
ruler appears who will do what the Tudors did—centralize authority, turning
the nobles into courtiers dependent on the sovereign. *Romeo and Juliet* is a
miniature version of what happens when feuding nobles get out of hand. The
opening stage direction tells us that servants are on the street armed with
swords and bucklers (small shields). Even if you came in late and missed the
prologue, you'd know from seeing those servants that all was not well in
Verona. Because that means there's going to be a fight: if you let servants
swank around like that, fully armed, they're bound to get into fights. So in
view of Tudor policy and Queen Elizabeth's personal dislike of duels and
brawling, this play would have no trouble with the censor, because it shows
the tragic results of the kind of thing that the authorities thoroughly disap-
proved of anyway.

From *Northrop Frye on Shakespeare* © 1986 Northrop Frye.

The first scene shows Shakespeare in his usual easy command of the situation, starting off with a gabble of dialogue that doesn't contribute much to the plot, but gets over the latecomer problem and quiets the audience very quickly because the jokes are bawdy jokes, the kind the audience most wants to hear. The servants have broadswords: they don't have rapiers and they can't fence; such things are for the gentry. They go in for what used to be called haymakers: "remember thy swashing blow," as one of them says. The macho jokes, "draw thy tool" and the like, are the right way to introduce the theme that dominates this play: the theme of love bound up with, and part of, violent death. Weapons and fighting suggest sex as well as death, and are still doing so later in the play, when the imagery shifts to gunpowder.

Then various characters enter, not at haphazard but in an order that dramatizes the social set-up of the play. The servants are on stage first, then Benvolio and Tybalt, then old Montague and old Capulet, and finally the Prince, who comes in to form the keystone of the arch. This sequence points to a symmetrical arrangement of characters corresponding to the two feuding houses. Later on we meet Mercutio, who "consorts," as Tybalt says, with the Montagues, and Paris, who wants to become a Capulet by marrying Juliet. Both are relatives of the Prince. Then come the two leads, first Romeo and then Juliet, and then the two go-betweens, the Nurse and Friar Laurence.

The scene turns farcical when old Montague and old Capulet dash for their swords and rush out into the street to prove to themselves that they're just as good men as they ever were, while their wives, who know better, keep pulling at them and trying to keep them out of trouble. But something much more serious is also happening. By entering the brawl, they've sanctioned it, because they're the heads of the two houses, and so they're directly responsible for everything that follows. The younger people seem to care very little about the feud: the only one keen on it is Tybalt, and Tybalt, we may notice, is not a Capulet by blood at all; he's expressly said to be a cousin of Lady Capulet. In the next scene, even old Capulet seems quite relieved to be bound over to keep the peace. But once the alarm is given and the reflexes respond, the brawl is on and the tragedy set in motion. After that, even Capulet's very sensible behaviour in restraining Tybalt from attacking Romeo in his own house comes too late. Of course we are never told what the original feud was about.

The Prince begins:

> Rebellious subjects, enemies to peace,
> Profaners of this neighbor-stainèd steel—
> Will they not hear?

> (I.i. 79–81)

The timing is accurate to the last syllable: two and a half lines before they'll stop whacking each other and listen. If it took more, the Prince would seem impotent, stuck with a situation that's beyond his power to control; if it took less, we wouldn't have the feeling of what it would be like to live in a town where that sort of thing could happen at any time. We notice that the crowd is saying what Mercutio is to say so tragically later on: "A plague a both your houses!" They've had it with feuds, and are on the Prince's side, even though they can express their loyalty only by increasing the brawling. After the Prince leaves, the Montagues pick up the pieces, and the conversation seems to get a bit aimless. But we can't skip anything in Shakespeare. Lady Montague says:

> Oh, where is Romeo? Saw you him today?
> Right glad I am he was not at this fray.
> (I.i. 114–15)

It would overload the play to build up the Montagues as much as the Capulets are built up, and these are almost the only lines she gets to speak—certainly the only ones with any punch. But slight as they are they tell us that the sun rises and sets on her Romeo, and so when at the end of the play we're told that she died, offstage, at the news of Romeo's exile, that detail seems less arbitrary and dragged-in than it would otherwise.

The next episode is Paris's suit to the Capulets for Juliet's hand. In the third scene Lady Capulet proposes a family conference to discuss the prospective marriage, and dismisses the Nurse. But, being a conscientious as well as a slightly prissy young woman, she remembers that noble families don't do that to old and trusted servants—or perhaps she realizes that the Nurse is closer to Juliet than she is—so she calls her back again. She soon regrets her concession, because the Nurse goes into action at once with a long reminiscing speech.

This is the kind of speech that looks at first sight like a digression, introduced for comic relief and to give us an insight into the Nurse's character and idiom. But Shakespeare doesn't do things for second-rate reasons: he almost never drags in a scene, and I say "almost" because I can think of only one clear example, the scene about the teaching of Latin to the boy William in his one potboiler, *The Merry Wives of Windsor*. Again, he's not like Dickens or anyone else for whom characterization might be an end in itself. His conventions are different: the action of the play is what is always primary with him, and anything that seems to be a detour in the action is probably advancing that action on another level. Of course the speech *does* give us an insight into the Nurse's character, as well as into that of a man who has died years before the play begins, the Nurse's husband. We know him only from this:

> "Yea," quoth he, "dost thou fall upon thy face?
> Thou wilt fall backward when thou hast more wit;
> Wilt thou not, Jule?"
>
> (I.iii. 41–43)

and that is all we ever want to know about him. As usual with raconteurs of the Nurse's type, we get the punch line four times.

The real reason for the speech, I think, is to sketch in a background for Juliet, whom we see but have barely heard speak yet. We suddenly get a vision of what Juliet's childhood must have been like, wandering around a big house where her father is "Sir" and her mother is "Madam," where to leave she must get special permission, not ordinarily granted except for visits to a priest for confession, and where she is waiting for the day when Capulet will say to his wife, in effect: "I'm sure we've got a daughter around this place somewhere: isn't it time we got rid of her?" Then she would marry and settle into the same mould as her mother, who was married at the same age, about fourteen. Meanwhile, there is hardly anybody for the child to talk to except the Nurse and the Nurse's husband with his inexhaustible joke. Of course there would be a great deal more to be said about her childhood. But there was also, one gathers, a good many deaths ("The earth hath swallowed all my hopes but she," Capulet says to Paris, and the Nurse has lost a daughter as well as a husband), and there would be enough loneliness to throw Juliet on her own resources and develop a good deal of self-reliance. So when, at her crisis in the play, she turns from a frightened child into a woman with more genuine courage and resolution than Lady Macbeth ever had, the change seems less prodigious if we were listening closely to all the overtones in the Nurse's harangue.

After the Nurse finally stops, there's a speech from Lady Capulet which settles into couplets—occasionally a sign in Shakespeare that something is a bit out of key. To the Nurse, marriage means precisely one thing, and she is never tired of telling us what it is. Lady Capulet would like to be a real mother, and say things more appropriate to a well-born girl awaiting courtship and marriage. But she really has nothing to say, communicates nothing except that she approves of the match, and finally breaks down into, "Speak briefly, can you like of Paris's love?" Juliet can only mumble something to the general effect that "It must be all right if you say so: you're looking after these things." If she hadn't seen Romeo, Juliet would probably have been talking in the same way to her daughter fifteen years or so later.

So Capulet gets a chance to throw a party, which he loves doing, and does his best to keep things properly stirred up:

> Welcome, gentlemen! Ladies that have their toes
> Unplagued with corns will walk a bout with you.
> Ah ha, my mistresses! which of you all
> Will now deny to dance? She that makes dainty,
> She I'll swear hath corns. Am I come near ye now?
> (I.v. 16–20)

Well, that gives us the quality of Capulet's humour: it's corny. Meanwhile, a group of Montagues have crashed the party, disguising themselves in masks, as was customary: Romeo sees Juliet, makes his way to her after narrowly escaping death from Tybalt, and the two of them enter into a dialogue that's an exquisitely turned extended (eighteen-line) sonnet. That's not "realistic," of course: in whatever real life may be, lovers don't start cooing in sonnet form. What has happened belongs to reality, not to realism; or rather, the God of Love, as I'll explain in a moment, has swooped down on two perhaps rather commonplace adolescents and blasted them into another dimension of reality altogether. So Capulet's speech and the Romeo-Juliet sonnet, two verbal experiences as different as though they were on different planets, are actually going on in the same room and being acted on the same stage. This is the kind of thing we can get only from Shakespeare.

Romeo and Juliet is a love story, but in Shakespeare's day love included many complex rituals. Early in the Middle Ages a cult had developed called Courtly Love, which focussed on a curious etiquette that became a kind of parody of Christian experience. Someone might be going about his business, congratulating himself on not being caught in the trap of a love affair, when suddenly the God of Love, Eros or Cupid, angry at being left out of things, forces him to fall in love with a woman. The falling in love is involuntary and instantaneous, no more "romantic," in the usual sense, than getting shot with a bullet. It's never gradual: "Who ever loved that loved not at first sight?" says Marlowe, in a line that Shakespeare quotes in *As You Like It*. From that time on, the lover is a slave of the God of Love, whose will is embodied in his mistress, and he is bound to do whatever she wants.

This cult of love was not originally linked to marriage. Marriage was a relationship in which the man had all the effective authority, even if his wife was (as she usually was) his social equal. The conventional role of the Courtly Love mistress was to be proud, disdainful and "cruel," repelling all advances from her lover. The frustration this caused drove the lover into poetry, and the theme of the poetry was the cruelty of the mistress and the despair and supplications of the lover. It's good psychology that a creative impulse to write poetry can arise from sexual frustration, and Elizabethan poets almost invariably were or pretended to be submerged in unhappy love, and writing for that reason.

Back in the thirteenth century, we have Dante, whose life was totally changed by seeing Beatrice at her father's home when he was nine years old. He devoted the rest of his life to her, even though he survived her by many years. But he had no further relations with her, certainly no sexual relations, and his devotion to her had nothing to do with his marrying someone else and fathering four children. His successor in poetry was Petrarch, whose mistress, also out of reach, was Laura, and it was Petrarch who popularized the convention in sixteenth-century England. In the 1590s, when the vogue was at its height, enormous piles of sonnets more or less imitating Petrarch were being written. By Shakespeare's time the convention had become more middle-class, was much more frequently linked to eventual marriage, and the more overtly sexual aspects of such relationships were more fully explored. So "love" in *Romeo and Juliet* covers three different forms of a convention. First, the orthodox Petrarchan convention in Romeo's professed love for Rosaline at the beginning of the play. Second, the less sublimated love for which the only honourable resolution was marriage, represented by the main theme of the play. Third, the more cynical and ribald perspective that we get in Mercutio's comments, and perhaps those of the Nurse as well.

On the principle that life imitates art, Romeo has thrown himself, before the play begins, into a love affair with someone called Rosaline, whom we never see (except that she was at Capulet's party, where she must have wondered painfully what had happened to Romeo), and who tried to live up to the proud and disdainful role that the convention required. So Romeo made the conventional responses: he went around with his clothes untidy, hardly heard what was said to him, wrote poetry, talked endlessly about the cruelty of his mistress, wept and kept "adding to clouds more clouds with his deep sighs." In short, he was afflicted with love melancholy, and we remember that melancholy in Shakespeare's time was a physical as well as an emotional disturbance. More simply, he was something of a mooning bore, his love affair a kind of pedantry, like Tybalt's fighting by the book of arithmetic. Juliet, to her disgust, is compelled to adopt some of the same coy and aloof attitude in her edgy dialogue with Paris in Friar Laurence's cell.

It's obvious that there was no sexual relationship between Romeo and Rosaline, a fact that would have disappointed Mercutio, who takes it for granted that Romeo has spent the night of what we now call the "balcony scene" in Rosaline's arms. Romeo enters the play practically unconscious that he has walked in on the aftermath of a dangerous brawl, and then starts explaining to Benvolio how firm and unyielding his attachment to Rosaline is, even though Rosaline, playing along as best she could, has told him that she has sworn to "live chaste." The dialogue between Romeo and Benvolio seems to us a curiously long one, for the amount said in it, but it's essential to round out the situation Romeo has put himself in.

I said that the Courtly Love convention used an elaborate and detailed parody, or counterpart, of the language of religion. The mistress was a "saint"; the "god" supplicated with so many prayers and tears was Eros or Cupid, the God of Love; "atheists" were people who didn't believe in the convention; and "heretics" were those who didn't keep to the rules. Benvolio suggests that Romeo might get Rosaline into better perspective if he'd compare her with a few other young women, and Romeo answers:

> When the devout religion of mine eye
> Maintains such falsehood, then turn tears to fires;
> And these, who, often drowned, could never die,
> Transparent heretics, be burnt for liars!
>
> (I.ii. 90–93)

This is close to another requirement of the convention, that the lover had to compare his mistress to the greatest heroines of history and literature (heroines from the point of view of love, that is), always to their disadvantage. These included Helen of Troy, Dido in the *Aeneid*, Cleopatra, heroines of Classical stories like Hero and Thisbe, and, of course, Laura. Mercutio, who knows all about the convention even though he assumes that Romeo has taken a different approach to it, says:

> Now is he for the numbers that Petrarch flowed in. Laura, to
> his lady, was a kitchen wench . . . Dido a dowdy, Cleopatra a
> gypsy, Helen and Hero hildings and harlots, Thisbe a grey eye
> or so, but not to the purpose.
>
> (II.iv. 38–43)

However, Romeo takes Benvolio's advice, goes in the Capulet party, sees Juliet, and the "real thing" hits him. Of course, the "real thing" is as much a convention, at least within the framework of the play, as its predecessor, but its effects on both Romeo and Juliet are very different.

Before we examine those effects, though, we have to notice another aspect of the convention that's woven into the play. In the love literature of the time there were very passionate and mutually consuming friendships between men: they also were usually sublimated, and distinguished from "homosexual" attachments in the narrow sense. In fact, the convention often tended to put male friendship even higher than love between men and women, simply because of this disinterested or nonsexual quality in it. Shakespeare himself, in his sonnets, represents himself as loving a beautiful young man even to the point of allowing the latter to steal his mistress, which in this context indicates that neither man has a sexual interest except in women. In this age we'd think of "sexual" much more broadly, but the elementary distinctions are the ones that apply here. The predominance of male friendship over love gets a bit grotesque at the end of a very early comedy, *The Two Gentlemen of Verona*, a puzzling enough play if we try to take it seriously.

In this play the "two gentlemen" are named Valentine and Proteus, which means that one is a true lover and the other a fickle one. Valentine loves Silvia, but is blocked by the usual parental opposition; Proteus loves Julia, but discards her as soon as he sees Silvia. He then deliberately betrays Valentine in order to knock him out as a rival for Silvia; Julia disguises herself as a male page and sets out in pursuit of Proteus. At the end of the play Proteus finds Silvia alone in a wood, tries to rape her, and is baffled when Valentine bursts out of the bushes and says: "Ruffian, let go that rude uncivil touch. . . !" All very correct melodrama, and we wait for Proteus to get the proper reward of his treachery to Valentine. What happens next is so incredible that I can only resort to paraphrase. Proteus says in effect: I know it was a dirty trick to try to rape your mistress; it just seemed too good a chance to miss." And Valentine responds, in effect: "Oh, that's all right, old man, and of course if you really want Silvia so much she's yours." Fortunately, the disguised Julia, who's been following closely behind, puts an end to this nonsense by fainting. They pick her up and see who she is; Proteus now finds her more attractive than he did before, and everything ends happily. So far as all this has a point, the point seems to be that love for women is to be subordinated in a crisis to male friendship.

Getting back to our present Verona gentlemen, Tybalt tries to force Romeo into a duel, which Romeo tries to avoid because he's now more of a Capulet than Tybalt is. Mercutio is disgusted with Romeo's submissiveness and takes Tybalt on for himself. In the duel Romeo makes a bungling effort at interference, and Mercutio gets a fatal wound. When he is dying, he asks Romeo why he interfered, and Romeo can give only the miserably helpless answer, "I thought all for the best." Mercutio says only:

> Help me into some house, Benvolio,
> Or I shall faint.

> (III.i. 103–104)

The name "Benvolio," at the climax of this terrible scene, means that he has turned his back contemptuously on Romeo. At that point Juliet drops out of Romeo's mind, for the first time since he saw her, and all he can think of now is vengeance on Tybalt for his friend's death. Once again, male friendship overrides love of women, but this is tragedy: by killing Tybalt and avenging Mercutio, Romeo becomes irrevocably a tragic figure.

Someone once raised the question of whether Shakespeare's audience would have assumed that Romeo was damned for committing suicide, suicide being regarded by the church as one of the most heinous of sins. The simplest answer is that the question is tedious, and Shakespeare avoids tedium. But it could be said also that the audience would understand that Romeo, as a lover-hero, really belongs to another religion, the religion of love, which doesn't collide with Christianity or prevent him from confessing to Friar Laurence, but nonetheless has different standards of what's good and bad. It also has its own saints and martyrs, those who lived and died for love, and Romeo and Juliet certainly belong in that calendar. Chaucer, two hundred years earlier, had written *The Legend of Good Women*, in which the women chosen, including Helen and Cleopatra and Dido (also Thisbe, whom Mercutio mentions and whom we'll meet again), are "good women" from Eros's point of view: the great erotic saints. When Romeo suddenly feels uneasy just before going into the Capulet party, he says:

> But he that hath the steerage of my course
> Direct my sail!
>
> (I.iv. 112–13)

We are not sure whether he is referring to the God of Love or the Christian God here, and neither, perhaps, is he. But later in the play, when he gets the false feeling of euphoria that so often precedes a tragic catastrophe, and says, "My bosom's lord sits lightly in his throne," he clearly means Eros.

Coming back to the effects of love on the two main characters, the most dramatic change is in their command of language. Before she sees Romeo we hear Juliet making proper-young-lady noises like, "It is an honour that I dream not of" ("it" being her marriage to Paris). After she sees Romeo, she's talking like this:

> Gallop apace, you fiery-footed steeds,
> Towards Phoebus' lodging! Such a wagoner
> As Phaeton would whip you to the west
> And bring in cloudy night immediately.
>
> (III.ii. 1–4)

It appears that Juliet, for all her tender years and sheltered life, has had a considerably better education than simply a technical training to be a wife and mother. The point is that it would never have occurred to her to make use of her education in her speech in the way she does here without the stimulus of her love.

As for Romeo, when we first meet him he's at the stage where he hardly knows what he's saying until he hears himself saying it. We don't hear any of the poetry he wrote about Rosaline (unless the "religion of mine eye" lyric I quoted from a moment ago belongs to it), and something tells us that we could do without most of it. But after he meets Juliet he turns out, to Mercutio's astonishment and delight, to be full of wit and repartee. "Now art thou what thou art, by art as well as by nature," Mercutio says, and even Mercutio knows nothing of the miraculous duets with Juliet in the great "balcony scene" and its successor. When he visits Friar Laurence, the Friar sees him approaching and feels rather apprehensive, thinking, "Oh no, not Rosaline again," and is considerably startled to hear Romeo saying, in effect, "Who's Rosaline?" More important, especially after Juliet also visits him, he realizes that two young people he has previously thought of as rather nice children have suddenly turned into adults, and are speaking with adult authority. He is bound to respect this, and besides, he sees an excellent chance of ending the feud by marrying them and presenting their furious parents with a *fait accompli*.

After disaster strikes with the death of Tybalt and the Prince's edict of banishment, we get very long speeches from both the lovers and from Friar Laurence. The rationale of the Friar's speech is simple enough: Romeo thinks of suicide, and the Friar immediately delivers an involved summary of his situation, trying to show that he could be a lot worse off. The speech is organized on lines of formal rhetoric, and is built up in a series of triads. The point of the length of the speech is its irony: the Friar is steadily adding to Romeo's despair while he is giving reasons why he should cool it. With Romeo and Juliet, the reason for the loosening of rhetorical control is subtler. Take Juliet:

> Hath Romeo slain himself? Say thou but "I,"
> And that bare vowel "I" shall poison more
> Than the death-darting eye of cockatrice.
> I am not I, if there be such an "I"
> Or those eyes' shot that makes the answer "I."
>
> (III.ii. 45–49)

It all turns on puns, of course, on "I," "Ay" (meaning yes, and often spelled "I" at the time), and "eye." But she's not "playing" with words: she's shredding them to bits in an agony of frustration and despair. The powerful explosion of words has nowhere to go, and simply disintegrates. Some critics will tell you that this is *Shakespeare* being immature and uncertain of his verbal powers, because, after looking up the probable dates, they find it's an "early play." Don't believe them. It is true that the earlier plays depend on formal rhetorical figures much more than the later ones: it doesn't follow that the use of such figures is immature. There are other examples of "playing on words" that indicate terrible distress of mind: John of Gaunt's death speeches in *Richard II*, for example.

It is through the language, and the imagery the language uses, that we understand how the *Liebestod* of Romeo and Juliet, their great love and their tragic death, are bound up together as two aspects of the same thing. I spoke of the servants' jokes in the opening scene associating sexuality with weapons, love and death in the context of parody. Soon after Romeo comes in, we hear him talking like this:

> Here's much to do with hate, but more with love.
> Why then, O brawling love! O loving hate!
> O anything, of nothing first create!
>
> (I.i. 173–75)

The figure he is using is the oxymoron or paradoxical union of opposites: obviously the right kind of figure for this play, though Romeo is still in his Rosaline trance and is not being very cogent. From there we go on to Friar Laurence's wonderfully concentrated image of

>   fire and powder
> Which, as they kiss, consume,
>
> (II.vi. 10–11)

with its half-concealed pun on "consummation," and to Juliet's

> Too like the lightning, which doth cease to be
> Ere one can say it lightens.
>
> (II.ii 119–20)

suggesting that their first glimpse of one another determined their deaths as well as their love.

The love-death identity of contrasts expands into the imagery of day and night. The great love scenes begin with Juliet hanging upon the cheek of night and end with the macabre horrors of the Capulet tomb, where we reluctantly can't believe Romeo when he says:

> For here lies Juliet, and her beauty makes
> This vault a feasting presence full of light.
>
> > (V.iii. 85–86)

The character who makes the most impressive entrances in the play is a character we never see, the sun. The sun is greeted by Friar Laurence as the sober light that does away with the drunken darkness, but the Friar is speaking out of his own temperament, and there are many other aspects of the light and dark contrast. In the dialogue of Romeo and Juliet, the bird of darkness, the nightingale, symbolizes the desire of the lovers to remain with each other, and the bird of dawn, the lark, the need to preserve their safety. When the sun rises, "The day is hot, the Capulets abroad," and the energy of youth and love wears itself out in scrambling over the blockades of reality.

The light and dark imagery comes into powerful focus with Mercutio's speech on Queen Mab. Queen Mab, Mercutio tells us, is the instigator of dreams, and Mercutio takes what we would call a very Freudian approach to dreams: they are primarily wish-fulfilment fantasies.

> And in this state she gallops night by night
> Through lovers' brains, and then they dream of love.
>
> > (I.iv. 70–71)

But such dreams are an inseparable mixture of illusion and a reality profounder than the ordinary realities of the day. When we wake we carry into the daylight world, without realizing it, the feelings engendered by the dream, the irrational and absurd conviction that the world as we want it to be has its own reality, and perhaps is what could be there instead. Both the lovers carry on an inner debate in which one voice tells them that they are embarking on a dangerous illusion, and another says that they must embark on it anyway whatever the dangers, because by doing so they are martyrs, or witnesses, to an order of things that matters more than the sunlit reality. Romeo says:

> O blessèd, blessèd night! I am afeard,
> Being in night, all this is but a dream,
> Too flattering-sweet to be substantial.
>
> > (II.ii. 139–41)

Perhaps so, but so much the worse for the substantial, as far as Romeo's actions are concerned.

Who or what is responsible for a tragedy that kills half a dozen people, at least four of them young and very attractive people? The feud, of course, but in this play there doesn't seem to be the clearly marked villain that we find in so many tragedies. We can point to Iago in *Othello* and say that if it hadn't been for that awful man there'd have been no tragedy at all. But the harried and conscientious Prince, the kindly and pious Friar Laurence, the quite likable old buffer Capulet: these are a long way from being villainous. Tybalt comes closest, but Tybalt is a villain only by virtue of his position in the plot. According to his own code—admittedly a code open to criticism— he is a man of honour, and there is no reason to suppose him capable of the kind of malice or treachery that we find in Iago or in Edmund in *King Lear.* He may not even be inherently more quarrelsome or spoiling for a fight than Mercutio. Juliet seems to like him, if not as devoted to his memory as her parents think. Setting Tybalt aside, there is still some mystery about the fact that so bloody a mess comes out of the actions of what seem to be, taken one by one, a fairly decent lot of human beings.

The Nurse, it is true, is called a "most wicked fiend" by Juliet, because she proposes that Juliet conceal her marriage to Romeo and live in bigamy with Paris. But Juliet is overwrought. The Nurse is not a wicked fiend, and wants to be genuinely helpful. But she has a very limited imagination, and she doesn't belong to a social class that can afford to live by codes of honour. The upper class made their names for the lower classes—villain, knave, varlet, boor—into terms of contempt because the people they described had to wriggle through life as best they could: their first and almost their only rule was survival. The deadliest insult one gentleman could give another then was to call him a liar, not because the one being insulted had a passion for truth, but because it was being suggested that he couldn't afford to tell the truth.

Besides, Shakespeare has been unobtrusively building up the Nurse's attitude. On her first embassy to Romeo she is quite roughly teased by Mercutio, and while she is a figure of fun and the audience goes along with the fun, still she is genuinely offended. She is not a bawd or a whore, and she doesn't see why she should be called one. Romeo, courteous as ever, tries to explain that Mercutio is a compulsive talker, and that what he says is not to be taken seriously; but it was said to her, seriously or not, and when she returns to Juliet and takes so long to come to the point in delivering her message, the delay has something in it of teasing Juliet to get even. Not very logical, but who said the Nurse was logical? Similarly when she laments the death of Tybalt and Juliet assumes that she's talking about Romeo, where the teasing seems more malicious and less unconscious. The Nurse has discovered in her go-between role that she really doesn't much like these Montague boys or their friends: as long as things are going well she'll support Romeo, but in a crisis she'll remember she's a Capulet and fight on that side.

The question of the source of the tragic action is bound up with another question: why is the story of the tragic love and death of Romeo and Juliet one of the world's best-loved stories? Mainly, we think, because of Shakespeare's word magic. But, while it was always a popular play, what the stage presented as *Romeo and Juliet*, down to about 1850, was mostly a series of travesties of what Shakespeare wrote. There's something about the story itself that can take any amount of mistreatment from stupid producing and bad casting. I've seen a performance with a middle-aged and corseted Juliet who could have thrown Romeo over her shoulder and walked to Mantua with him, and yet the audience was in tears at the end. The original writer is not the writer who thinks up a new story—there aren't any new stories, really—but the writer who tells one of the world's great stories in a new way. To understand why *Romeo and Juliet* is one of those stories we have to distinguish the specific story of the feuding Montague-Capulet families from an archetypal story of youth, love and death that is probably older than written literature itself.

The specific story of the Verona feud has been traced back to a misunderstood allusion in Dante's *Purgatorio*, and it went through a series of retellings until we come to Shakespeare's main source, a narrative poem, *Romeus and Juliet*, by one Arthur Brooke, which supplied him not only with the main theme, but with a Mercutio, a counterpart of Friar Laurence, and a garrulous nurse of Juliet. Brooke begins with a preface in which he tells us that his story has two morals: first, not to get married without parental consent, and second, not to be Catholic and confess to priests. That takes care of the sort of reader who reads only to see his own prejudices confirmed on a printed page. Then he settles down to tell his story, in which he shows a good deal of sympathy for both the Friar and the lovers. He is very far from being a major poet, but he had enough respect for his story to attract and hold the attention of Shakespeare, who seems, so far as we can tell, to have used almost no other source. Brooke also says he saw a play on the same subject, but no trace of such a play remains, unless those scholars in the guesswork squad are right who see signs of an earlier play being revised in the first Quarto.

But the great story of the destruction of two young lovers by a combination of fate and family hostility is older and wider than that. In Shakespeare's time, Chikamatsu, the Japanese writer of Bunraku (puppet plays), was telling similar stories on the other side of the world, and thousands of years earlier the same story was echoing and re-echoing through ancient myths. Elizabethan poets used, as a kind of literary Bible, Ovid's long (fifteen books) poem called *Metamorphoses*, which told dozens of the most famous stories of Classical myth and legend: the stories of Philomela turned into a nightingale, of Narcissus, of Philemon and Baucis turned into trees, of Daphne and Syrinx. Ovid lived around the time of Christ, but of course the stories he tells are far older. He has many stories of tragic death, but none was more loved or more frequently retold in Shakespeare's day than the story of Pyramus and Thisbe, the two lovers separated by the walls of hostile families, meeting in a wood, and dying by accident and suicide.

In this play we often hear about a kind of fatality at work in the action, usually linked with the stars. As early as the Prologue we hear about "star-crossed lovers," and Romeo speaks, not of the feud, but of "some consequence still hanging in the stars" when he feels a portent of disaster. Astrology, as I've said, was taken quite seriously then, but here it seems only part of a network of unlucky timing that's working against the lovers. Romeo gets to see Juliet because of the sheer chance that the Capulet servant sent out to deliver the invitations to the party can't read, and comes to him for help. There's the letter from Friar Laurence in Verona to Friar John in Mantua, which by accident doesn't get to him, and another hitch in timing destroys Friar Laurence's elaborate plan that starts with Juliet's sleeping potion. If we feel that Friar Laurence is being meddlesome in interfering in the action as he does, that's partly because he's in a tragedy and his schemes are bound to fail. In *Much Ado about Nothing* there's also a friar with a very similar scheme for the heroine of that play, but his scheme is successful because the play he's in is a comedy.

But when we have a quite reasonable explanation for the tragedy, the feud between the families, why do we need to bring in the stars and such? The Prologue, even before the play starts, suggests that the feud demands lives to feed on, and sooner or later will get them:

> And the continuance of their parents' rage,
> Which, but their children's end, nought could remove.

The answer, or part of the answer, begins with the fact that we shouldn't assume that tragedy is something needing an explanation. Tragedy represents something bigger in the total scheme of things than all possible explanations combined. All we can say—and it's a good deal—is that there'd have been no tragedy without the feud.

This, I think, is the clue to one of those puzzling episodes in Shakespeare that we may not understand at first hearing or reading. At the very end of the play, Montague proposes to erect a gold statue of Juliet at his own expense, and Capulet promises to do the same for Romeo. Big deal: nothing like a couple of gold statues to bring two dead lovers back to life. But by that time Montague and Capulet are two miserable, defeated old men who have lost everything that meant anything in their lives, and they simply cannot look their own responsibility for what they have done straight in the face. There's a parallel with Othello's last speech, which ends with his suicide, when he recalls occasions in the past when he has served the Venetian state well. T.S. Eliot says that Othello in this speech is "cheering himself up," turning a moral issue into an aesthetic one. I'd put it differently: I'd say it was a reflex of blinking and turning away from the intolerably blazing light of judgment. And so with Montague and Capulet, when they propose to set up these statues as a way of persuading themselves that they're still alive, and still capable of taking some kind of positive action. The gesture is futile and pitiful, but very, very human.

So far as there's any cheering up in the picture, it affects the audience rather than the characters. Tragedy always has an ironic side, and that means that the audience usually knows more about what's happening or going to happen than the characters do. But tragedy also has a heroic side, and again the audience usually sees that more clearly than the characters. Juliet's parents don't really know who Juliet is: we're the ones who have a rather better idea. Notice Capulet's phrase, "Poor sacrifices of our enmity!" Romeo and Juliet are sacrificial victims, and the ancient rule about sacrifice was that the victim had to be perfect and without blemish. The core of reality in this was the sense that nothing perfect or without blemish can stay that way in this world, and should be offered up to another world before it deteriorates. That principle belongs to a still larger one: nothing that breaks through the barriers of ordinary experience can remain in the world of ordinary experience. One of the first things Romeo says of Juliet is: "Beauty too rich for use, for earth too dear!" But more than beauty is involved: their kind of passion would soon burn up the world of heavy fathers and snarling Tybalts and gabby Nurses if it stayed there. Our perception of this helps us to accept the play as a whole, instead of feeling only that a great love went wrong. It didn't go wrong: it went only where it could, out. It always was, as we say, out of this world.

That's why the tragedy is not exhausted by pointing to its obvious cause in the feud. We need suggestions of greater mysteries in things: we need the yoke of inauspicious stars and the vision of Queen Mab and her midget team riding across the earth like the apocalyptic horsemen. These things don't explain anything, but they help to light up the heroic vision in tragedy, which we see so briefly before it goes. It takes the greatest rhetoric of the greatest poets to bring us a vision of the tragic heroic, and such rhetoric doesn't make us miserable but exhilarated, not crushed but enlarged in spirit.

Romeo and Juliet has more wit and sparkle than any other tragedy I know: so much that we may instinctively think of it as a kind of perverted comedy. But, of course, tragedy is not perverse: it has its own rightness. It might be described, though, as a kind of comedy turned inside out. A typical comic theme goes like this: boy meets girl; boy's father doesn't think the girl good enough; girl's father prefers someone with more money; various complications ensue; eventually boy gets girl. There's a good deal in the Romeo and Juliet story to remind us of such comedy themes. Look at the way the Chorus begins Act II:

> Now old desire doth in his deathbed lie
> And young affection gapes to be his heir.

If we tried to turn the play we have inside out, back into comedy, what would it be like? We'd have a world dominated by dream fairies, including a queen, and by the moon instead of the sun; a world where the tragedy of Pyramus and Thisbe has turned into farce; a world where feuding and brawling noblemen run around in the dark, unable to see each other. In short, we'd have a play very like *A Midsummer Night's Dream*, the one we're going to discuss next.

THOMAS McALINDON

Romeo and Juliet

Titus Andronicus (1593?), Richard III (1593?), and Romeo and Juliet (1595–6), Shakespeare's first attempts in the tragic medium, are strikingly different both from each other and from the tragedies of Shakespeare's maturity in many obvious respects. As I have already indicated, however, it is possible to detect in Titus certain shaping concepts which will prove to be essential in the mature tragedies; and these same concepts can be detected in the other two early tragedies as well. The three plays rest on a common substructure of ideas about the nature of the tragic experience and its relation to reality as a whole.

Titus, we have seen, is the tragedy of a civilised warrior in whom the stable partnership of martial valour and loving-kindness is shattered, so that the violence which had brought honour on the field to 'kind Rome', to his family, and to himself is turned against all three. This tragedy of lost oneness and identity is reflected in the condition of Rome, a city renowned for its combination of civility and martial virtue; its present degenerate state is summed up in the submissive marriage of its emperor to a ruthless barbarian queen. The tragedy of both Ronne and its representative hero are in turn traced to the double nature of 'kind'.

Unlike Titus, Richard Ill is not a creature of double impulse. He is spiritually as well as physically 'deform'd, unfinish'd', sent by 'dissembling

---

From *Shakespeare's Tragic Cosmos*. © 1991 Cambridge University Press.

Nature' into the world 'scarce half made up' (I.i.19–21). His performances as
an amiable friend and kinsman and as a 'jolly thriving wooer' (IV.iii.43) are
fiendish dissembling: his doubleness is perfect duplicity. Wholly without
'tenderness of heart, / And gentle, kind, effeminate remorse' (III.vii.210–11),
he is 'kind in hatred' only (IV.iv.172). The embodiment of domineering
egoism ('I am myself alone'), and an agent of strife and division, he identifies
himself in his opening soliloquy with Mars ('grim visag'd war'), promising to
wreck the peace and pastimes which his war-weary nation is preparing to
enjoy under King Edward (I.i.9). Not for Richard the pursuits of Venus: lute,
dance, my lady's chamber, love's majesty (lines 12–16). The tragedy is his
only in the sense that he 'plots' it (line 32); in the other sense, it is England's
tragedy, that of a nation at war with itself, torn between the rival claims of
the House of Lancaster and the House of York.

In these plays, then, tragic experience is identified with strife, hate,
disunity, and violent change and confusion, and traced to the contrarious
order of nature. This underlying similarity is reinforced by the plays' conclusions. The natural longing for love, peace, and unity which Richard
contemptuously acknowledges at the outset, and exploits in his treacherous
hypocrisies, is answered at the end by Richmond, his conqueror. Lightly
sketched though it is, Richmond's character is that of a man 'full made up'.
He is a good warrior and a good friend, a conquering peacemaker. Through
his marriage to Elizabeth he combines in himself the rival claims of the two
houses; he is a reconciler who will 'unite the white rose and the red' in 'fair
conjunction' (V.v.19–20). So too at the end of *Titus Andronicus*, the dead
hero's brother addresses the people of Rome thus:

> You sad-fac'd men, people and sons of Rome,
> By uproars sever'd, as a flight of fowl
> Scatter'd by winds and high tempestuous gusts,
> O let me teach you how to knit again
> This scatter'd corn into one mutual sheaf,
> These broken limbs into one body.
>
> (V.iii.67–72)

Like all Shakespeare's tragedies, both plays postulate a contrarious natural
order which is cyclical as well as dialectical. The impulse towards unity is
expected to assert itself as inevitably as its opposite, and may even be dependent on it. However terrible the violence which has been unleashed, and
however muted and qualified the hint of reintegration and renewal, these
plays intimate that pure tragedy, like pure comedy, is an image of the world
only half made up. As we shall see, that suggestion is more conspicuous in
Romeo and Juliet than in any other of Shakespeare's tragedies.

Yet to link so exquisitely beautiful a play with *Titus* and *Richard III* might well seem a forced and fruitless exercise. Unlike theirs, its narrative lacks all potential for high tragedy. The story of two very young lovers who lead private lives, and who are driven to suicide by the pointless feuding of their families and the practice of arranged marriages, is potentially very moving; but it is not calculated to present a spectacle of evil and suffering that will stir us profoundly with questions about the human condition. Shakespeare, however, was obviously very conscious of the inherent limitation of the story as material for tragic drama, and addressed himself to the problem with quite remarkable thoroughness and subtlety. In consequence, to treat the play as uncertain, simple, or lacking in generality of implication, or as a tragedy of fate and passive suffering, is quite wrong. Increasing critical emphasis of late on its rare poise and complexity is fully justified.

Essentially, Shakespeare's solution to his problem was to generalise and complicate the tragedy by making the city in which it is set a microcosmic reflection of the great world. 'There is no world without Verona's walls' (III.iii.17), says Romeo, and he is at least right in assuming that Verona is a world in itself. And what matters to Shakespeare in the correspondent relationship between the little and the great world is not their hierarchical but their contrarious structure. Verona is made up of servants, citizens, gentry or nobility, and a princely ruler; but the social fact of prime importance in this hierarchical society is that it is split between two rival families whose mutual hatred erupts periodically into 'black strife' (III.i.175). This hatred has no causal or temporal beginning; it seems to have been always there, like a fact of nature. Its only justification lies in the honour code, with its demand that every slight to one's own or one's family's good name must be violently repudiated. But the honour code, as exemplified in the duelling Tybalt, is shown to be thoroughly irrational; it is male aggressiveness given a veneer of legitimacy, the militarism of chivalry broken loose from the claims of love and peace: '. . . talk of peace! I hate the word / As I hate hell, all Montagues, and thee' (I.i.68–9). A sixteenth-century Italian lawyer spoke of the duel as entirely natural, a manifestation of the hate which permeates the whole physical world; and on the evidence of this play he was right. Shakespeare not only implies that the mutual hostility of the two families was always there (and therefore 'natural'), he also locates it very firmly in the dynamics of a world whose functioning turns off the interaction of Love and Strife (Hate). The tragedy of Romeo and Juliet, who reject hatred and division at the cost of their lives, and whose doomed marriage brings about the 'jointure' (V.iii.296) of their warring families, is fully implicated in the drama of the natural order. This connection is established by means of the play's rich pattern of elemental imagery, and, more overtly, by the Friar's famous set speech on the properties of plants:

The gray-ey'd morn smiles on the frowning night,
Check'ring the eastern clouds with streaks of light;
And fleckel'd darkness like a drunkard reels
From forth day's path and Titan's fiery wheels.
Now, ere the sun advance his burning eye,
The day to cheer and night's dank dew to dry,
I must up-fill this osier cage of ours
With baleful weeds and precious-juiced flowers.
The earth that's nature's mother is her tomb;
What is her burying grave, that is her womb.
And from her womb children of divers kind
We sucking on her natural bosom find;
Many for many virtues excellent,
None but for some, and yet all different.
O, mickle is the powerful grace that lies
In plants, herbs, stones, and their true qualities;
For nought so vile that off the earth doth live
But to the earth some special good doth give;
Nor aught so good but, strain'd from that fair use,
Revolts from true birth, stumbling on abuse:
Virtue itself turns vice, being misapplied;
And vice sometime's by action dignified.
Within the infant rind of this weak flower
Poison hath residence, and medicine power;
For this, being smelt, with that part cheers each part;
Being tasted, slays all senses with the heart.
Two such opposed kings encamp them still
In man as well as herbs—grace and rude will;
And where the worser is predominant,
Full soon the canker death eats up that plant.
                                                    (II.iii.1–30)

The Friar here envisages a spatio-temporal order of great dialectical
complexity (that it is a temporal as well as a spatial order is an important
point habitually missed in critical commentary). Thanks to the regular cycle
of day and night, and of generation and decay, the elements of moisture,
warmth, air and earth combine in a fruitful partnership from which human
art can profit. Human art, however, requires a patient, discriminating awareness of nature's moving, changing, oppositional character. The fruitful earth
yields both poisonous weeds and medicinal flowers. But the flowers may
contain both poison and medicine; furthermore, poison can prove beneficial

and medicine fatal. And in human nature the same laws apply. Each member in every opposition breaks down into a further opposition: contrarious structure and dynamics are inescapable. Here is a view of nature as at once comforting and treacherous, stable and ambiguous. It posits a world where opposites can change places all 'too soon', where confusion and grave error are perennial hazards, and where to 'mean well' (I.iv.48) is seldom enough. Of course the Friar makes no mention of the love–strife or love–hate antinomy; but Romeo, his 'only love sprung from' his 'only hate', enters just as (or just before) the speech ends, and the Friar is soon discussing the possibility of turning 'rancour to pure love' (line 92; I.v.136). It is clear both here and throughout that the play's rich (and much noted) cluster of polarities has nature's most basic opposition at its heart.

II

While it is necessary to observe the underlying affinities between *Romeo and Juliet* and the earlier (and later) tragedies, its unique character must be fully acknowledged. This can be ascribed mainly to its comic and its lyric dimensions. Yet to examine these is to perceive even more clearly the basic elements in Shakespeare's conception of the tragic: violent change and confounding contrariety reflecting a collapse in the tenuous balance and measured pace of nature's oppositional order.

The total effect of the play's richly comic dimension is to counteract the heavily explicit indications of tragic inevitability by suggesting that the story could have ended quite differently. The silliness of the servants and the two paterfamilias in the opening scene, the ludicrous affectations of Romeo in his role as Rosaline's unrequited lover, the ebullient mockeries of Mercutio, the sentimental babblings of old Capulet, and the enchanting garrulity of the Nurse: all these combine to make us feel throughout the first two acts (and in defiance of the Prologue) that the lovers' problem will resolve itself in the time-honoured fashion of comedy—constancy and skilful intrigue will overcome all obstacles, hard-nosed parents will be reconciled to a marriage of true love. Not until the entirely unexpected killing of the great jester in Act III does the atmosphere become genuinely tragic. But even then there is more comedy to come: not just the absurd, nocturnal bustling of Father Capulet as he prepares for the wedding feast, but, more importantly, the entrance of the clown at the end of the funeral lamentations over the presumed-dead Juliet. At this point the comedy clearly becomes part of a general, self-reflexive strategy. When Peter asks the dejected musicians to play him some 'merry dump' (i.e. some merry sad song), and they retort, ''tis no time to play now' (IV.v.105–7), the original audience was to ask itself, 'How shall we find the concord of this discord?' What artistic justification can there be for disregarding so flagrantly the classical and neoclassical insistence on excluding all traces of comedy from tragic drama? The answer has in fact been prepared for in the proleptic ironies that occur in so many of the comic and satiric passages. To take but one example. Romeo's 'He [i.e. Mercutio] jests at scars that never felt a wound' (II.ii.1) anticipates the dying Mercutio's jest on his fatal wound ('No, 'tis not so deep as a well, not so wide as a church door. But 'tis enough, 'twill serve. Ask for me tomorrow, and you shall find me a grave man') (III.i.93–5); and the link tells us that comedy and tragedy cannot be separated without adopting a static and monocular view of a world which is inescapably kinetic and duplex: each genre or mode is the tomb and womb of the other. Old Capulet's lament, however, prepares much more decisively than these early anticipations of generic exchange for the clown's untimely intrusion, and fully involves it in the imaginative design of the whole play:

> All things that we ordained festival
> Turn from their office to black funeral:
> Our instruments to melancholy bells,
> Our wedding cheer to a sad burial feast,
> Our solemn hymns to sullen dirges change;
> Our bridal flowers serve for a buried corse;
> And all things change them to the contrary.
>
> (IV.v.85–91)

Shakespeare implicitly acknowledges that popular demand for clowning in the midst of tragedy results in a 'Mis-shapen chaos of well-seeming forms' (I.ii.177). But he also presents himself as a successful Friar Lawrence, one whose art is effective in producing 'confusion's cure' (IV.v.65): that is, a complex, meaningful unity; a controlled *discordia concors* which holds the mirror up to nature in all its unpredictability.

As I have already remarked, Shakespeare's metadramatic justification for the new mixed mode of tradegy was borrowed from Kyd's *The Spanish Tradegy*, echoes of which are strongly felt throughout this play. However, the audacity and invention with which Shakespeare incorporates the comic element are entirely his own. His use of lyric conventions in such a way as to reinforce the special emphases in this new kind of tragedy was also suggested by Kyd; but again what he accomplishes on the basis of Kydian precedent represents a huge leap in imaginative expressiveness. There are three aspects of lyric convention which call for special attention here. The first and most obvious is the Petrarchan rhetoric of pun, antithesis, paradox, and oxymoron. This is a source of comedy in the posturings of Romeo in Act I; but thereafter it serves to articulate a pervasive sense of tragic duality, conflict, confusion, and swift contrarious change. The sonnet-prologue somewhat ostentatiously foretells this raid on Petrarchan idiom, and moulds it perfectly to the tragic conception. In 'the *two*-hours' traffic of our stage', the audience will see a tragedy set in one place and concerning '*Two* households, *both* alike in dignity'. 'Ancient grudge break[s] to new mutiny.' 'Civil blood [civil war] makes civil [peaceful] hands unclean.' 'From forth the fatal loins of these *two* / Foes, a *pair* of star-cross'd lovers take their life [are born/kill themselves].' Their 'death-mark'd love' (and that alone) serves to 'bury their parents' strife'. As Leonard Forster has remarked, the whole play is devoted to bringing the Petrarchan cliché of the 'dear enemy' to life. By setting that cliché in so firmly dualistic a framework, by insinuating a conception of human nature as both gentle and violent, by postulating a repetitive cycle of peace and violence, by showing the paradoxical interdependence of fundamental opposites, and by repetition of the words 'love' and 'strife', the sonnet-prologue indicates just why the old cliché proves so attractive to the tragic dramatist. But it is not just in rhetorical figures such as paradox, oxymoron, pun, and antithesis that the principle of contrariety affects the expressive mode of the tragedy. It is manifest everywhere: in character contrasts and in opposed attitudes to love, in imagistic and symbolic patterning, and in scenic juxtaposition.

The second inheritance from lyric tradition of special relevance here is the symbolic representation of love as a religion. The imagery of religion serves in the play to characterise love as the supreme value and the one source of redeeming grace; but it also points to the governing principles of contrarious unity and tragic doubleness. It comes into prominence when Romeo sets eyes on Juliet for the first time. A scene of exceptional lyric charm and wit, this is also a highly complex and illuminating microcosm of the given play-world; and religious symbolism is central to it. Romeo has spoken in a previous scene of 'the devout religion of mine eye' (I.iii.88), but this is where the trite Petrarchan phrase becomes meaningful. Indifferent to the dance, a silent watcher holding a candle, Romeo suddenly catches sight of Juliet. From that moment he is transformed, filled with a kind of reverent joy; and in words which evoke the birth of chivalry itself, he asks: 'What lady's that which doth enrich the hand / Of yonder knight?' (I.v.39–40). He feels that if his hand touches hers, a redeeming grace will pass into it: 'I'll watch her place of stand, and touching hers, make blessed my rude hand' (where 'rude' means 'uncivilised' and 'unregenerate', as in the Friar's phrase, 'rude will'). Of course the pair join words as well as hands, and most artfully.

The first fourteen lines of their dialogue constitute a perfect sonnet in which Romeo has the first quatrain and Juliet the second; the sestet is broken up between them, and the concluding couplet is shared. It is obvious that the sonnet form and its complex rhyming scheme is designed to work in conjunction with the music and the dance to establish the idea of opposites harmonised: the concordant discord of a Montague and a Capulet.

What is rather less obvious (or at least has not attracted critical attention) is that nine of the lines in this sonnet refer to the hand: to the profaning of hands, to the joining of hands, to praying hands, and to hands which impart a blessing. There is also a linking pun on 'palmer' (meaning 'pilgrim') and 'palm' which neatly reinforces the significance of the key image and connects it with the fact that Romeo, whose name is an Italian word for 'pilgrim' ('pellegrino che va a Roma'), has come to the masque in the disguise of a palmer (hence the candle). But what completes the significance of the hand image is the visible fact that Romeo, while praying and receiving grace in a perfect communion, is being watched by a very rude young man whose hand (I assume) flies instinctively to his hip in anger and frustration. 'Fetch me my rapier, boy', exclaims Tybalt to his servant (line 53), eager to fulfil the Prologue's prediction: 'civil blood makes civil hands unclean'. Temporarily restrained by Capulet, who cites Romeo's reputation as 'a virtuous and well govern'd youth' (line 66), Tybalt represents himself in soliloquy as the emergent alternative to the meeting of contraries we have just witnessed:

> Patience perforce with wilful choler meeting
> Makes my flesh tremble in their different greeting.
> I will withdraw; but this intrusion shall,
> Now seeming sweet, convert to bitterest gall.
>
> (lines 87–90)

Throughout the play attention is drawn repeatedly to the hand, so that we observe it at work revealing the twin possibilities of human nature. There is the gentle hand that prays, pleads, blesses, appeases, parts antagonists, unites lovers, forgives and makes friends: the hand of palmer, saint, helpless mortal, holy friar, peacemaker, reconciled enemy. And there is the violent hand that strikes, divides, and destroys—'cut[s] . . . youth in twain' (v.iii99): the 'cursed hand' (III.iii.104) not only of the indignant gentleman who would avenge a wrong or an insult ('*He draws*'), but also of the furious patriarch who feels like strangling his daughter when she pleads against his rude will: 'My fingers itch' (III.v.164).

The symbolism of the hand exactly pinpoints the tragedy of Romeo. When he comes married from the Friar's cell ('God join'd my heart and

Romeo's, thou our hands' (IV.i.55)), he is insulted and challenged by 'the furious Tybalt' (III.i.118); but he responds in conciliatory and even loving terms. However, the blessed hand of love (first extended, it would seem, from a kneeling posture) is scorned by the hand of Mars, and twice over:

> Romeo . . . spoke him fair, and bid him bethink
> How nice the quarrel was, and urg'd withal
> Your high displeasure. All this, uttered
> With gentle breath, calm look, knees humbly bow'd,
> Could not take truce with the unruly spleen
> Of Tybalt, deaf to peace, but that he tilts
> With piercing steel at bold Mercutio's breast;
> Who, all as hot, turns deadly point to point,
> And, with martial scorn, with one hand beats
> Cold death aside, and with the other
> Sends it back to Tybalt, whose dexterity
> Retorts it. Romeo he cries aloud
> 'Hold, friends! friends, part!' and, swifter than his tongue,
> His agile arm beats down their fatal points,
> And twixt them rushes; underneath whose arms
> An envious thrust from Tybalt hit the life
> Of stout Mercutio . . .
>
> (lines 150–66)

Tybalt's 'dexterity' is (by way of an etymological pun) his 'right hand' (Latin *dexter);* but the passage seems to suggest that the symbolic distinction between one hand (arm) and the other is quite lost here; and that confusion becomes Romeo's. With Mercutio's death, he abruptly subscribes to the code of honour; momentarily convinced that Juliet's love has 'soft'ned valour's steel' and made him 'effeminate', he calls on 'fire-ey'd fury' to be his 'conduct now' (lines 108–21). And so 'Tybalt is slain'—he 'whom Romeo's hand did slay' (line 149; cf. III.ii.71; III.iii.104, 108). It is perhaps true that 'we *want* him to show himself a man against the detestable 'Tybalt'; but we must also perceive that the decision which proves fatal to both Juliet and himself represents a regression from full humanity as imaginatively defined by the play. It is only at the end, when he kills Paris in self-defence (after having tried conciliation), and then effects a moving atonement (at-one-ment) with his dead rival, that Romeo achieves heroic integrity:

> O, give me thy hand,
> One writ with me in sour misfortune's book!

I'll bury thee in a triumphant grave. . . .
O, what more favour can I do to thee
Than with that hand that cut thy youth in twain
To sunder his that was thine enemy?
Forgive me, cousin.

                                   (v.iii.81–3, 98–101)

III

A third and much more important inheritance from lyric tradition which has
been adapted and developed to fit the play's tragic design is the theme of time
and its associated imagery. In lyric and sonnet, and especially in Shakespeare's own sonnets, Time is the great enemy of both the poet-lover and the
beloved. Capriciously, Time retards his pace when the lovers are separated
and accelerates it when they are together. With his scythe and his frosts, he
destroys the flower of youth and withers the rose of beauty. The poet's lines
are in themselves an attempt to counteract his evil work: they distil the
perfume of the rose before it withers, win fame and lasting memory for rare
beauty and virtue. In the aubade or dawn song, too, Time figures as the
lovers' enemy: the rising sun curtails their secret happiness and contradicts
their sense of ecstatic transcendence.

The extreme youth and immaturity of the doomed lovers in *Romeo and
Juliet* is the chief indication of time's cruel speed. According to Capulet, his
'child is yet a stranger in the world' and has 'not seen the change of fourteen
years' (I.ii.8–9) (she is sixteen in Shakespeare's principal source, and eighteen
in other versions of the story). And when she is found as dead in her bridal
clothes, Capulet speaks of death as lying upon her 'like an untimely frost /
Upon the sweetest flower of all the field'; as 'a flower . . . deflower'd' by Death
(IV.v.28–9, 37). Here, and in Capulet's earlier reference to Juliet as 'the hopeful
lady of my earth' (I.ii.14), Shakespeare implicitly invokes the most poignant of
all the myths of untimely death: that of Proserpina, daughter of Ceres (goddess
of earth's plenty), who was seized while gathering flowers by Pluto, god of
death and of funerals, and taken by him to live as his wife in his infernal
kingdom. Among the most powerful images in the play are those of Death as
Juliet's surrogate husband; they are all echoes of this myth which embodies the
idea of time's intrusion on a timeless, unchanging, paradisal world.

Shakespeare will deploy this myth more overtly and extensively in relation to the love of Perdita and Florizel in *The Winter's Tale* (IV.iv.111–33).
The allusion is pertinent here, since Romeo, like Florizel, is also identified
with the flower of youth. There is even a significant play on his name which

works in the same way as Florizel's: when the Nurse notes that 'rosemary and Romeo begin both with a letter', and implies that he is 'the flower of courtesy' (II.iv.200, v.43), Shakespeare must be recalling that the Spanish word *romero* (= Ital. *romeo*) means both 'pilgrim' and 'rosemary'. But the flower image works comprehensively in the play, and in the final scene is superbly literalised to provide a vivid stage image of time's hostility to almost all Verona's youth. At the end, Benvolio is the only surviving representative of the younger generation: Mercutio and Tybalt are 'yet but green in earth' (IV.iii.42), the bodies of Romeo, Juliet, and Paris (described earlier as 'a very flower' (I.iii.78–80)) are before us, and lying about the stage are the flowers brought by Paris to the tomb and scattered everywhere in the violence of his fight with Romeo.

No less important in relation to the time theme than the floral imagery is the imagery of light (often fiery) and of darkness, amplified in numerous references to day and night, sun, moon, and stars. The function of this complex of images as expressing the transience as well as the splendour of the lovers' passion is strengthened by their own conviction that 'the garish sun' (III.iii.25) is hostile to their secret love, whereas night is friendly, allowing it to shine in all its brilliance. The aubade theme of unwelcome daylight and reluctant parting is introduced after their only night together, and acquires an altogether new force in the circumstances of this particular relationship: if Romeo does not leave before sunrise, he will be killed.

As in *Julius Caesar* and *Othello*, two other tragedies in which time is of unusual significance, a narrative which originally extended over a much longer period is compressed into a very short time frame (here, four days) so as to give the impression of events unfolding with dangerous speed in a highly charged atmosphere. Moreover, the familiar question as to whether or not this is a tragedy of mischance rather than of character arises mainly from the fact that so many of the actions which advance the tragedy are in some way mistimed: asynchrony is almost the determining principle of the action. If the wedding of Juliet to Paris had not been brought forward from Thursday to Wednesday; if Friar Lawrence's message had reached Romeo in time; if Romeo had reached the vault a minute later, or Juliet awakened a minute earlier; or if the Friar had not stumbled as he ran to the vault: if any one of these conditions had been met, then the tragedy would not have occurred. It does indeed seem as if a malignant outside force is responsible for destroying the lovers' happiness. Fortune and the stars are blamed from the start, but their malign influence is incorporate in the more palpable hostility of time: 'O lamentable day! O woeful time!' (IV.v.30); 'Ah, what an unkind hour / Is guilty of this lamentable chance! (V.iii.145–6).

However, anyone coming to the play from a Renaissance epithalamium or marriage masque, or from Spenser's unconventional sonnet sequence,

Amoretti (published with his 'Epithalamion', in 1595), would quickly find evidence to suggest that the typical sonneteer's notion of time as the enemy of human happiness is only half-endorsed by Shakespeare's text. Such an intertextual approach is not at all necessary in order to perceive the wider implications of the time theme, but it certainly seems to have been presupposed by Shakespeare, and it does make one more fully responsive to the play's complex pattern of meaning. The *Amoretti* sequence is the record not of unrequited love but of a courtship which leads to the marriage day of 'Epithalamion'. The sonnet lover frequently complains against Time's cruel protractions and contractions (Sonnets XXV, XXXVI, LXXXVI), but his complaints are woven into the cycle of the seasons, to whose constraining order he painfully submits his passionate impatience. The same tension and reconciliation between time and desire is enacted in the extraordinary mimetic structure of 'Epithalamion', the poem which triumphantly celebrates the culmination of the twelve-months' courtship. The poem consists of twenty-four stanza units; the wedding takes place on midsummer day, and the bride arrives at the church (stanza 12) when the sun, whose progress from dawn to dusk is duly marked, is at its height. It ends with the prayer that 'a large posterity' will be the 'timely fruit of this same night' (lines 404, 417), and with the description of the poem itself as 'an endless monument' erected by the poet to his bride (line 433): permanence is achieved through accommodation to time's cyclical order, and through a poetic art structured on the numbers of time. The poem is born of the assumption that harmony with the rhythm of time is the major pre-condition for enduring happiness in love and for fruitfulness in all undertakings. In his continuation of Marlowe's unfinished tragic narrative, *Hero and Leander*, George Chapman, who assuredly had read this poem as well as *Romeo and Juliet*, rendered Spenser's governing idea quite explicit when he wrote:

> Time's golden thigh
> Upholds the flowery body of the earth
> In sacred harmony, and every birth
> Of men and actions makes legitimate,
> Being us'd aright; *the use of time is fate.*
>
> (III.60–4)

Epithalamic tradition reinforces the comic dimension of *Romeo and Juliet* in that it points to the alternative ending, enhances the sense of waste and loss, and enables us to view the story from the widest possible perspective. The tradition is overtly invoked in Juliet's great soliloquy in III.ii ('Gallop apace')—often referred to as her epithalamium. The epithalamic norm of timeliness and ripeness is expressed on several occasions in the play, twice with specific relation to marriage. As befits a father, Capulet restrains the impatient suitor Paris, tying respect for time to a regard for interpersonal harmony and the ideal of 'multilateral consent' in marriage that was advocated by English moralists from about 1570 onwards:

> Let two more summers wither in their pride
> Ere we may think her ripe to be a bride.
>
> But woo her, gentle Paris, get her heart;
> My will to her consent is but a part,
> And, she agreed, within her scope of choice
> Lies my consent and fair according voice.
> (I.ii.10–11,16–19)

Juliet echoes her father's words when she restrains Romeo and expresses the hope that 'This bud of love, by summer's ripening breath, / May prove a beauteous flower when next we meet' (II.ii.121–3). And if the sun is scorned by the lovers it is referred to by others as 'the worshipp'd sun' (I.i.115) and 'the all-cheering sun' (line 133). Partnered by the moon, its presence is felt throughout, manifesting a dualistic temporal order which is not intrinsically capricious or malign; Juliet speaks of the 'variable' and 'inconstant moon, / That monthly changes in her circled orb' (I.ii.109–11), but her phrasing unintentionally acknowledges that the moon's changes are ordered. And the last image of the sun is as a kindly father grieving over the 'untimely death' (V.iii.233, 258) of the young: 'The sun for sorrow will not show his head' (line 305).

Of course references in *Romeo and Juliet* to the timely order which promises fruitfulness and permanence serve but to highlight the prevailing 'violence'—a key term which denotes both haste and destruction. As its first word indicates, Juliet's 'Gallop apace' soliloquy is not so much an epithalamium as an epithalamium subverted. Central to the meaning of the speech is Juliet's self-identification with Phaeton, the 'runaway' (III.ii.3, 6) son of Phoebus who sought to manage his father's fiery chariot, failed, and brought in 'cloudy night immediately' (line 4); the speech is a superb manifestation of intense, erotic passion verging on willed self-extinction. Juliet herself had anticipated this perception when she warned the much more impulsive Romeo that their contract was 'Too like the lightning which doth cease to be / Ere one can say "It lightens"' (II.ii.119–20). It is in the scene which follows this ominous remark that the lyric image of the flower loses its simple significance (or innocence) by being projected into the contrarious order of all nature: 'Within the infant rind of this weak flower / Poison hath residence, and medicine power.'

However, it is important to avoid undue emphasis on the rashness of the lovers, for a fiery, passionate impatience animates and agitates the whole society into which they have been born. Capulet enjoins patience and

concord on both Tybalt and Paris, but subsequently delights in the speed
with which he sets up an enforced marriage; and he reacts with a frightening
display of rude will and itching hands to the kneeling Juliet's plea for time.
Mercutio 'make[s] haste' to take up the challenge rejected by Romeo: his
bitter, 'I am sped', is a fitting epitaph (III.i.78, 88). And the effect of his death
is that Tybalt and Romeo 'to't . . . go like lightning' (line 169). Paris proves
to be as provocative and furious in quarrel (V.iii.63, 70) as he was impatient
in love. Even the Prince contributes to the prevailing ethos. Distressed by
the death of his kinsman Mercutio, he is 'deaf to pleading and excuses' and
sentences Romeo to exile 'in haste' (III.i.189–92): patient consideration might
have resulted in a more equitable judgement, and averted tragedy. And of
course the Friar becomes deeply involved in the haste he deplored: his
exclamation, 'Saint Francis be my speed! How oft tonight / Have my old feet
stumbled at graves!' (V.iii.121-2), ironically echoes his advice: 'Wisely and
slow. They stumble that run fast' (II.iii.94).

Shakespeare has thus created a hectic environment where fatal accidents brought about by unfortunate mistimings are in the end inevitable.
More important, it is presented as an environment in which haste is a poison
that spreads to infect almost everyone: all references to poison, plague, infection, and pestilence combine to form a central symbol for Verona's passionate
impatience and fatal speed. The Friar speaks of poison in the flower just
before Romeo enters demanding to be married to his new love 'today'
(II.iii.64). Mercutio's 'I am sped' is preceded *and* followed by the famous 'A
plague a both your houses' (III.i.88, 97). Friar Lawrence's messenger is
delayed because he is suspected of having been in 'a house where the infec-
tious pestilence did reign' (V.iii.9–10) (the symbolic intent is evident from the
fact that in Brooke's *Romeus and Juliet* the infected house is in Mantua, not
Verona; and from the synonymity of 'infection' and 'rank poison' at
I.ii.49–50). And Romeo, swiftly opting for suicide obtains from the apothecary 'A dram of poison, such soon-speeding gear / As will disperse itself
through all the veins . . . / As violently as hasty powder fir'd / Doth hurry
from the fatal cannon's womb' (V.i.60-5). We may conclude that although the
rashness of the lovers contributes to their tragedy, it is a pestilence caught
from others. And we have to remember that there is a huge difference
between the impetuosities of love and those of anger and hate—although
they can work tragically towards the same end.

IV

It is apparent, then, that in *Romeo and Juliet* time is not a blind, external force hostile to youth and love but rather a complex ruling order which can be creative or destructive according as men and women are able to function within its inescapable limits. And in that sense the philosophy of the sonnets is heavily qualified. However, it seems to be in the nature of Shakespeare's tragic environment that time is already out of joint, so that the protagonists are compelled, as it were, to journey across a heavily mined battle-field. Furthermore, the greatness of the tragic hero and heroine, and especially of heroic lovers, lies precisely in their need to transcend limits; they can only be fully themselves if they 'soar above a common bound' (I.iv.18) and so court destruction. Around Capulet's house, 'the orchard walls are high and hard to climb; / And the place death' if Romeo is discovered; but he declares that he will 'o'erperch these walls' since 'stony limits cannot hold love out' (II.ii.64–7). Juliet's rejection of limit derives from her eloquently expressed awareness that love's bounty is 'boundless as the sea', 'infinite' (lines 131–5; see also II.vi.32–4).

No less important in the complex vision of this tragedy is the fact that although their own violence and that of their families makes the lovers the victims of time, they are, in the deepest sense, triumphant over time's destructive action. It is this triumph which makes possible the reconciliation of their families; and although we may consider that to be a poor reward for the sacrifice of two such individuals, their resolute refusal to accept change and division when everything conspires to enforce it upon them is itself a thing of supreme value, something that endures like the statue of 'pure gold' which their parents erect in their memory—or like the legend of their loves. This triumph over change is all the more distinct in that it was not a foregone conclusion; somewhat awkwardly, but obviously enough, Shakespeare delineates in their characters and relationship a process of maturing, of fall and recovery, of constancy undermined and restored; and this in turn hints at the paradox that time's destructive action can be seen as part of a creative cycle.

In the orchard scene, Juliet expresses fears about Romeo's constancy, but her own constancy is clearly threatened after Tybalt's death. Her notorious oxymoronic outburst against Romeo ('O serpent heart, hid with a flow'ring face! . . . Beautiful tyrant, fiend angelical' etc.) is intended to disclose a fierce struggle between hatred for the man who killed her cousin and love for her banished husband (III.iii.73–84). It is, however, an artificial crisis; not simply because of the overdone rhetoric, but also and mainly because Juliet's love for Tybalt is not an imagined nor even an imaginable reality—we have never once seen her with that thoroughly unlovable thug. Very different is the test to which she is put when she has to be buried alive in the family vault in order to remain 'an unstain'd wife to my sweet love'

(IV.i.88). The horrors of death and putrefaction engulf her imagination, and the way in which she defeats them comes across very forcefully as a heroic act of love's constancy. It would be reasonable to say that the young girl clearly becomes a woman here. However, the text compliments her in a manner which few women today would deem agreeable, but which must be read in its historical context. The idea is that she transcends her sex, or rather the weakness traditionally ascribed to her sex; she is warned by Friar Lawrence that the whole plan to salvage her marriage will fail if any 'inconstant toy' or 'womanish fear' abates her 'valour' (IV.i.119–20). (We will encounter the same idea in the last act of *Antony and Cleopatra.*)

Characteristically, however, Shakespeare deconstructs the opposition of male constancy and female inconstancy in his delineation of the early Romeo. Romeo makes his debut with a carefully framed act of inconstancy, as ludicrous as anything to be found in the comedies; in the space of seconds, he transfers to Juliet his much publicised devotion to the frosty Rosaline: 'What a change is here!', exclaims the Friar (II.iii.65). This change indicates a kind of maturing, a progress from fanciful to authentic passion. But its main purpose may be to highlight the issue of constancy and to hint at Romeo's potential unworthiness. His eagerness in the orchard scene to swear everlasting fidelity is what provokes Juliet's fear that he will prove 'variable' and 'inconstant', like the moon; and events show that she has good cause to be uneasy. As I have already noted, it is his lapse from love to male 'honour' that brings the world crashing about their heads. And it is finely ironical that he should decide there that her beauty has 'soften'd valour's steel' and made him 'effeminate'; because when he is told of his banishment, he falls weeping and screaming to the floor, and even attempts to commit suicide—thinking only of *his* loss and not of what Juliet will have to endure. The gravity of this moral fall—emblematised, as in a comparable scene in *Othello*, by his prostrate position—is spelt out by the Friar: he is not 'a man'; his 'tears are womanish'; his 'wild acts denote the unreasonable fury of a beast' (III.iii.108–13).

In his recovery, Romeo's growth as a man and as a lover are coincident, interdependent. When the next piece of terrible news (that Juliet is dead) is brought to him, he has been buoyant with the expectation of good news; but now there is no wild ranting. Instantly he decides to die with Juliet, keeps the decision to himself, and gives an astonishing display of quiet stoicism in dealing with the servant who brought the news and must be made to serve his dark purpose. Moreover his dialogue with the wretched apothecary reveals in him a whole lifetime's understanding of human misery. And it is in the role of valiant and gentle manhood that he deals with Paris's insulting provocations: 'Good gentle youth, tempt not a desperate man'; 'Wilt provoke me? Then have at thee, boy!' (v.iii.59, 70). The union of the houses of Capulet and Montague follows logically from the constant oneness—the union of opposites—which the lovers achieve both individually and as a married pair. To consider the 'jointure' of the families in dissociation from that complex oneness is inevitably to devalue it, and, of course, to simplify the play's conclusion.

V

Perhaps the most discussed and problematic of the play's oppositions is that of character and fate. Some critics have taken extreme positions on this issue, either holding that everything in the action is determined by the initial stress on 'star-cross'd lovers', or insisting that the lovers are free agents whose uncontrolled passion brings upon them a morally just punishment. Others have speculated whether the two concepts coexist in a state of pure contradiction or whether they are reconciled. The double perspective originates in Brooke's *Romeus and Juliet*, where the lovers are berated for their irresponsibility in the preface and sympathetically presented in the body of the poem as the victims of a malign fate ('the restles starres', 'the fatall sisters three, and Fortune full of chaunge'). Shakespeare has fully integrated this double view into the play, partly, perhaps, because the dualistic conception which governs the whole could so easily accommodate it.

There will always be disagreement on whether the issue of free will and pre-determination is a resolvable paradox or a pure contradiction we simply have to live with. This disagreement must inevitably be reflected in interpretations of a play which manipulates the question so conspicuously. But two points are worth making here. First, given the whole design of *Romeo and Juliet*, many in Shakespeare's audience would probably have reflected on the issue in the manner of Sir Kenelm Digby, who, in considering the problem of divine foreknowledge and human freedom, argued that liberty and a constrained necessity are mutually compatible and entirely consistent with the creation of a world whose order rests on the concord of contrarious and disagreeing qualities; they might reasonably have felt that in the end the play achieves a *discordia concors* of fatality and responsibility. Second, and as already implied here, insofar as the paradox is resolved within the play, the resolution is accomplished in terms of time, haste, and impatience. When the prince begins the inquiry intended to 'clear these ambiguities' (v.iii. 216), his chief witness is the Friar, who tells a tale of untimely and mistimed actions. Lawrence does not practice astrology, but like Prospero (who does), he is a wise man who uses 'art' (v.iii.242) to control nature; and like Prospero he has the astrologer's awareness that timing—knowing the propitious and the unpropitious moment, and acting accordingly—is of the utmost importance in negotiating the changeful complexities of life ('ruling the stars'). His tale is one of sustained efforts to control a sequence of events whose problematical nature was temporal throughout. From the beginning of the play, we should recall, the hostility of external circumstance to the lovers is expressed in terms both of the stars and of time. Romeo fears that he and his friends will arrive at the Capulets 'too early', for his 'mind misgives / Some consequence yet hanging in the stars' that will lead to 'untimely death' (I.iv.106–11); and Juliet exclaims: 'My only love sprung from my only hate! / Too early seen, and known too late!' (I.v.135–6). Being what they are, however, they rush, and are driven by others, to actualise the fate which they see as prepared for them. For his part, the Friar accepts that he cannot stop Romeo's headlong commitment and accepts it as inevitable; but he also perceives the possibility of turning it to the good. However, when he agrees to the marriage, and yet again when he devises plans to cope with unexpected problems (Romeo's banishment and the Paris–Juliet marriage), he stresses that a happy outcome will depend entirely on exact timing (II.iii.90–4; III.iii.149–71; IV.i.69–117). Increasingly 'desperate' (line 69), his art, as we have seen, is defeated less by accident than by the passionate impatience with which the characters involved in the plot he is trying to control react to changing circumstance. In the end, he declares himself responsible for the tragedy and yet innocent: 'myself condemned and myself excus'd' (V.iii.226). Much the same, perhaps, can be said both of the stars (if literally understood) and of the lovers.

In subsequent tragedies, and especially in *Othello*, we will have the same sense of an inescapable doom working itself out through the choices, passions, and errors of men and women; the same sense, too, that 'the use of time is fate'. The limitation of this play as tragedy is that the compulsion to embrace a fatal destiny is too closely identified with mere haste, and too dependent on verbal and imagistic expression. In the later tragedies, by contrast, it is deeply embedded in character and linked to a capacity for violence and destruction which is truly frightening.

HAROLD BLOOM

Romeo and Juliet

Shakespeare's first authentic tragedy has sometimes been critically under-valued, perhaps because of its popularity. Though *Romeo and Juliet* is a triumph of dramatic lyricism, its tragic ending usurps most other aspects of the play and abandons us to unhappy estimates of whether, and to what degree, its young lovers are responsible for their own catastrophe. Harold Goddard lamented that the Prologue's "A pair of star-cross'd lovers take their life" had "surrendered this drama to the astrologers," though more than the stars in their courses are to blame for the destruction of the superb Juliet. Alas, half a century after Goddard, the tragedy more frequently is surren-dered to commissars of gender and power, who can thrash the patriarchy, including Shakespeare himself, for victimizing Juliet.

Thomas McAlindon in his refreshingly sane *Shakespeare's Tragic Cosmos* (1991) traces the dynamics of conflict in the dramatist back to the rival worldviews of Heraclitus and Empedocles, as refined and modified in Chaucer's *The Knight's Tale*. For Heraclitus, all things flowed, as Empedocles visualized a strife between Love and Death. Chaucer, as I have remarked, rather than Ovid or Marlowe, was the ancestor of Shakespeare's greatest originality, that invention of the human that is my prime concern in this book. Chaucer's ironic yet amiable version of the religion of love, more perhaps in his *Troilus and Criseyde* than in *The Knight's Tale*, is the essential

---

From *Shakespeare: The Invention of the Human*. © 1998 Harold Bloom.

context for *Romeo and Juliet*. Time's ironies govern love in Chaucer, as they will in *Romeo and Juliet*. Chaucer's human nature is essentially Shakespeare's: the deepest link between the two greatest English poets was temperamental rather than intellectual or sociopolitical. Love dies or else lovers die: those are the pragmatic possibilities for the two poets, each of them experientially wise beyond wisdom.

Shakespeare, somewhat unlike Chaucer, shied away from depicting the death of love rather than the death of lovers. Does anyone, except Hamlet, ever fall out of love in Shakespeare? Hamlet denies anyway that he ever loved Ophelia, and I believe him. By the time the play ends, he loves no one, whether it be the dead Ophelia or the dead father, the dead Gertrude or the dead Yorick, and one wonders if this frightening charismatic ever could have loved anyone. If there were an Act VI to Shakespeare's comedies, doubtless many of the concluding marriages would approximate the condition of Shakespeare's own union with Anne Hathaway. My observation, of course, is nonsensical if you would have it so, but most of the Shakespearean audience—then, now, and always—goes on believing that Shakespeare uniquely represented realities. Poor Falstaff never will stop loving Hal, and the admirably Christian Antonio always will pine for Bassanio. Whom Shakespeare himself loved we do not know, but the Sonnets seem more than a fiction and, at least in this aspect of life, Shakespeare evidently was not so cold as his Hamlet.

There are mature lovers in Shakespeare, most notably Antony and Cleopatra, who cheerfully sell each other out for reasons of state, yet return to each other in their suicides. Both Romeo and Antony kill themselves because they falsely think their beloveds are dead (Antony bungles the suicide, as he does everything else). The most passionate marriage in Shakespeare, the Macbeths', subtly appears to have its sexual difficulties, as I will show, and ends in madness and suicide for Queen Macbeth, prompting the most equivocal of elegiac reflections by her usurping husband. "Yet Edmund was belov'd," the icy villain of *King Lear* overhears himself saying, when the bodies of Goneril and Regan are brought in.

The varieties of passionate love between the sexes are endlessly Shakespeare's concern; sexual jealousy finds its most flamboyant artists in Othello and Leontes, but the virtual identity of the torments of love and jealousy is a Shakespearean invention, later to be refined by Hawthorne and Proust. Shakespeare, more than any other author, has instructed the West in the catastrophes of sexuality, and has invented the formula that the sexual becomes the erotic when crossed by the shadow of death, There had to be one high song of the erotic by Shakespeare, one lyrical and tragicomical paean celebrating an unmixed love and lamenting its inevitable destruction.

Romeo and Juliet is unmatched, in Shakespeare and in the world's literature, as a vision of an uncompromising mutual love that perishes of its own idealism and intensity.

There are a few isolated instances of realistic distincts in Shakespeare's characters before *Romeo and Juliet*: Launce in *The Two Gentlemen of Verona*, the Bastard Faulconbridge in *King John*, Richard II, self-destructive king and superb metaphysical poet. The fourfold of Juliet, Mercutio, the Nurse, and Romeo outnumber and overgo these earlier breakthroughs in human invention. *Romeo and Juliet* matters, as a play, because of these four exuberantly realized characters.

It is easier to see the vividness of Mercutio and the Nurse than it is to absorb and sustain the erotic greatness of Juliet and the heroic effort of Romeo to approximate her sublime state of being in love. Shakespeare, with a prophetic insight, knows that he must lead his audience beyond Mercutio's obscene ironies if they are to be worthy of apprehending Juliet, for her sublimity *is* the play and guarantees the tragedy of this tragedy. Mercutio, the scene stealer of the play, had to be killed off if it was to remain Juliet's and Romeo's play; keep Mercutio in Acts IV and V, and the contention of love and death would have to cease. We overinvest in Mercutio because he insures us against our own erotic eagerness for doom; he is the play to some considerable purpose. So, in an even darker way, is the Nurse, who helps guarantee the final disaster. The Nurse and Mercutio, both of them audience favorites, are nevertheless bad news, in different but complementary ways. Shakespeare, at this point in his career, may have underestimated his burgeoning powers, because Mercutio and the Nurse go on seducing audiences, readers, directors, and critics. Their verbal exuberances make them forerunners of Touchstone and Jacques, rancid ironists, but also of the dangerously eloquent manipulative villains Iago and Edmund.

2

Shakespeare's greatness began with *Love's Labour's Lost* (1594–95, revised 1597) and *Richard II* (1595), superb achievements respectively in comedy and in history. Yet *Romeo and Juliet* (1595–96) has rightly overshadowed both, though I cannot quite place it for eminence with *A Midsummer Night's Dream*, composed simultaneously with Shakespeare's first serious tragedy. The permanent popularity, now of mythic intensity, of *Romeo and Juliet* is more than justified, since the play is the largest and most persuasive celebration of romantic love in Western literature. When I think of the play, without rereading and teaching it, or attending yet one more inadequate performance, I first remember neither the tragic outcome nor the gloriously vivid Mercutio and the Nurse. My mind goes directly to the vital center, Act II, Scene ii, with its incandescent exchange between the lovers:

> *Rom.* Lady, by yonder blessed moon I vow,
>   That tips with silver all these fruit-tree tops—
> *Jul.* O swear not by the moon, th'inconstant moon,
>   That monthly changes in her circled orb,
>   Lest that thy love prove likewise variable.
> *Rom.* What shall I swear by?
> *Jul.* Do not swear at all,
>   Or if thou wilt, swear by thy gracious self,
>   Which is the god of my idolatry,
>   And I'll believe thee.
> *Rom.* If my heart's dear love—
> *Jul.* Well, do not swear. Although I joy in thee,
>   I have no joy of this contract tonight:
>   It is too rash, too unadvis'd, too sudden,
>   Too like the lightning, which doth cease to be
>   Ere one can say 'It lightens'. Sweet, good night.
>   This bud of love, by summer's ripening breath,
>   May prove a beauteous flower when next we meet.
>   Good night, good night. As sweet repose and rest
>   Come to thy heart as that within my breast.
> *Rom.* O wilt thou leave me so unsatisfied?
> *Jul.* What satisfaction canst thou have tonight?
> *Rom.* Th'exchange of thy love's faithful vow for mine.
> *Jul.* I gave thee mine before thou didst request it,
>   And yet I would it were to give again.
> *Rom.* Wouldst thou withdraw it? For what purpose, love?
> *Jul.* But to be frank and give it thee again;
>   And yet I wish but for the thing I have.
>   My bounty is as boundless as the sea,
>   My love as deep: The more I give to thee
>   The more I have, for both are infinite.
>   [II.ii.107–35]

The revelation of Juliet's nature here might be called an epiphany in the religion of love. Chaucer has nothing like this, nor does Dante, since his Beatrice's love for him transcends sexuality. Unprecedented in literature (though presumably not in life), Juliet precisely does not transcend the human heroine. Whether Shakespeare reinvents the representation of a very young woman (she is not yet fourteen) in love, or perhaps does even more than that, is difficult to decide. How do you distance Juliet? You only shame yourself by bringing irony to a contemplation of her consciousness. Hazlitt, spurred by a nostalgia for his own lost dreams of love, caught better than any other critic the exact temper of this scene:

> He has founded the passion of the two lovers not in the plea-
> sures they had experienced, but on all the pleasures they had
> *not* experienced.

It is the sense of an infinity yet to come that is evoked by Juliet, nor can we doubt that her bounty is "as boundless as the sea." When Rosalind in *As You Like It* repeats this simile, it is in a tonality that subtly isolates Juliet's difference:

> *Ros.* O coz, coz, coz, my pretty little coz, that thou didst
>   know how many fathoms deep I am in love! But it
>   cannot be sounded. My affection hath an unknown
>   bottom, like the Bay of Portugal.
> *Celia.* Or rather bottomless, that as fast as you pour affec-
>   tion in, it runs out.
> *Rosalind.* No. That same wicked bastard of Venus, that
>   was begot of thought, conceived of spleen and born of
>   madness, that blind rascally boy that abuses everyone's
>   eyes because his own are out, let him be judge how
>   deep I am in love.
>   [IV.i.195–205]

This is the sublimest of female wits, who one imagines would advise Romeo and Juliet to "die by attorney," and who knows that women, as well as men, "have died from time to time and worms have eaten them, but not for love." Romeo and Juliet, alas, are exceptions, and die for love rather than live for wit. Shakespeare allows nothing like Rosalind's supreme intelligence to intrude upon Juliet's authentic rapture. Mercutio, endlessly obscene, is not qualified to darken Juliet's intimations of ecstasy. The play has already made clear how brief this happiness must be. Against that context, against also all of his own ironic reservations, Shakespeare allows Juliet the most exalted declaration of romantic love in the language:

Juliet. But to be frank and give it thee again;
　　　And yet I wish but for the thing I have.
　　　My bounty is as boundless as the sea,
　　　My love as deep: The more I give to thee
　　　The more I have, for both are infinite.
　　　　　　　　　　　　　　　　[II.ii.131–35]

We have to measure the rest of this play against these five lines, miraculous in their legitimate pride and poignance. They defy Dr. Johnson's wry remark on Shakespeare's rhetorical extravagances throughout the play: "his pathetick strains are always polluted with some unexpected depravations." Molly Mahood, noting that there are at least a hundred and seventy-five puns and allied wordplays in *Romeo and Juliet*, finds them appropriate to a riddling drama where "Death has long been Romeo's rival and enjoys Juliet at the last," an appropriate finale for doom-eager lovers. Yet little in the drama suggests that Romeo and Juliet are in love with death, as well as with each other. Shakespeare stands back from assigning blame, whether to the feuding older generation, or to the lovers, or to fate, time, chance, and the cosmological contraries. Julia Kristeva, rather too courageously not standing back, rushes in to discover "a discreet version of the Japanese *Realm of the Senses*," a baroque sado-masochistic motion picture.

Clearly Shakespeare took some risks in letting us judge this tragedy for ourselves, but that refusal to usurp his audience's freedom allowed ultimately for the composition of the final high tragedies. I think that I speak for more than myself when I assert that the love shared by Romeo and Juliet is as healthy and normative a passion as Western literature affords us. It concludes in mutual suicide, but not because either of the lovers lusts for death, or mingles hatred with desire.

3

Mercutio is the most notorious scene stealer in all of Shakespeare, and there is a tradition (reported by Dryden) that Shakespeare declared he was obliged to kill off Mercutio, lest Mercutio kill Shakespeare and hence the play. Dr. Johnson rightly commended Mercutio for wit, gaiety, and courage; presumably the great critic chose to ignore that Mercutio also is obscene, heartless, and quarrelsome. Mercutio promises a grand comic role, and yet disturbs us also with his extraordinary rhapsody concerning Queen Mab, who at first seems to belong more to *A Midsummer Night's Dream* than to *Romeo and Juliet*:

Mer. O then I see Queen Mab hath been with you.
Benvolio. Queen Mab, what's she?
Mer. She is the fairies' midwife, and she comes
　　In shape no bigger than an agate stone
　　On the forefinger of an alderman,
　　Drawn with a team of little atomi
　　Over men's noses as they lie asleep.
　　Her chariot is an empty hazelnut made by the joiner
　　squirrel or old grub,
　　Time out o'mind the fairies' coachmakers;
　　Her wagon-spokes made of long spinners' legs;
　　The cover of the wings of grasshoppers,
　　Her traces of the smallest spider web,
　　Her collars of the moonshine's watery beams,
　　Her whip of cricket's bone, the lash of film,
　　Her waggoner, a small grey-coated gnat,
　　Not half so big as a round little worm
　　Prick'd from the lazy finger of a maid;
　　And in this state she gallops night by night
　　Through lovers' brains, and then they dream of love;
　　O'er courtiers' knees, that dream on curtsies straight;
　　O'er lawyers' fingers who straight dream on fees;
　　O'er ladies' lips, who straight on kisses dream,
　　Which oft the angry Mab with blisters plagues
　　Because their breaths with sweetmeats tainted are.
　　Sometime she gallops o'er a courtier's nose,
　　And then dreams he of smelling out a suit;
　　And sometime comes she with a tithe-pig's tail,
　　Tickling a parson's nose as a lies asleep;
　　Then dreams he of another benefice,
　　Sometime she driveth o'er a soldier's neck
　　And then dreams he of cutting foreign throats,
　　Of breaches, ambuscados, Spanish blades,
　　Of healths five fathom deep; and then anon
　　Drums in his ear, at which he starts and wakes,
　　And being thus frighted swears a prayer or two
　　And sleeps again. This is that very Mab
　　That plaits the manes of horses in the night
　　And bakes the elf-locks in foul sluttish hairs,
　　Which, once untangled, much misfortune bodes.
　　This is the hag, when maids lie on their backs,

That presses them and learns them first to bear,
Making them women of good carriage.
This is she—

[I.iv.53–94]

Romeo interrupts, since clearly Mercutio never stops once started. This mercurial vision of Queen Mab—where "Queen" probably means a whore, and Mab refers to a Celtic fairy, who frequently manifests as a will-o'-the-wisp—is anything but out of character. Mercutio's Mab is the midwife of our erotic dreams, aiding us to give birth to our deep fantasies, and she appears to possess a childlike charm for much of the length of Mercutio's description. But since he is a major instance of what D. H. Lawrence was to call "sex-in-the-head," Mercutio is setting us up for the revelation of Mab as the nightmare, the incubus who impregnates maids. Romeo interrupts to say: "Thou talkst of nothing," where "nothing" is another slang term for the vagina. Mercutio's bawdy obsessiveness is splendidly employed by Shakespeare as a reduction of Romeo and Juliet's honest exaltation of their passion. Directly before their first rendezvous, we hear Mercutio at his most obscenely exuberant pitch:

If love be blind, love cannot hit the mark.
Now will he sit under a medlar tree
And wish his mistress were that kind of fruit
As maids call medlars when they laugh alone.
O Romeo, that she were, O that she were
An open-arse, and thou a poperin pear!

[II.i.33–38]

Mercutio's reference is to Rosaline, Romeo's beloved before he falls, at first glance, in love with Juliet, who instantly reciprocates. The medlar, rotten with ripeness, popularly was believed to have the likeness of the female genitalia, and "to meddle" meant to perform sexual intercourse. Mercutio happily also cites a popular name for the medlar, the open-arse, as well as the poperin pear, at once pop-her-in her open arse, and the slang name for a French pear, the Poperingle (named for a town near Ypres). This is the antithetical prelude to a scene that famously concludes with Juliet's couplet:

Good night, good night. Parting is such sweet sorrow
That I shall say good night till it be morrow.

Mercutio at his best is a high-spiritual unbeliever in the religion of love, reductive as he may be:

> *Ben.* Here comes Romeo, here comes Romeo!
> *Mer.* Without his roe, like a dried herring. O flesh, flesh,
> how art thou fishified! Now is he for the numbers
> that Petrarch flowed in. Laura, to his lady, was a
> kitchen wench—marry, she had a better love to
> berhyme her—Dido a dowdy, Cleopatra a gypsy,
> Helen and Hero hildings and harlots, Thisbe a grey
> eye or so, [. . .]
> [II.iv.37–44]

Obsessed as he may be, Mercutio has the style to take his death wound as gallantly as anyone in Shakespeare:

> *Romeo.* Courage, man, the hurt cannot be much.
> *Mer.* No, 'tis not so deep as a well, nor so wide as a
> church door, but 'tis enough, 'twill serve. Ask for me
> tomorrow and you shall find me a grave man. I am
> peppered, I warrant for this world. A plague o' both
> your houses.
> [III.i.96–101]

That indeed is what in his death Mercutio becomes, a plague upon both Romeo of the Montagues and Juliet of the Capulets, since henceforward the tragedy speeds on to its final double catastrophe. Shakespeare is already Shakespeare in his subtle patterning, although rather overlyrical still in his style. The two fatal figures in the play are its two liveliest comics, Mercutio and the Nurse. Mercutio's aggressivity has prepared the destruction of love, though there is no negative impulse in Mercutio, who dies by the tragic irony that Romeo's intervention in the duel with Tybalt is prompted by love for Juliet, a relationship of which Mercutio is totally unaware. Mercutio is victimized by what is most central to the play, and yet he dies without knowing what *Romeo and Juliet* is all about: the tragedy of authentic romantic love. For Mercutio, that is nonsense: love is an open arse and a poperin pear. To die as love's martyr, as it were, when you do not believe in the religion of love, and do not even know what you are dying for, is a grotesque irony that foreshadows the dreadful ironies that will destroy Juliet and Romeo alike as the play concludes.

4

Juliet's Nurse, despite her popularity, is altogether a much darker figure. Like Mercutio, she is inwardly cold, even toward Juliet, whom she has raised. Her language captivates us, as does Mercutio's, but Shakespeare gives both of them hidden natures much at variance with their exuberant personalities. Mercutio's incessant bawdiness is the mask for what may be a repressed homoeroticism, and like his violence may indicate a flight from the acute sensibility at work in the Queen Mab speech until it too transmutes into obscenity. The Nurse is even more complex; her apparent vitalism and her propulsive flood of language beguile us in her first full speech:

> Even or odd, of all days in the year,
> Come Lammas Eve at night shall she be fourteen.
> Susan and she—God rest all Christian souls!—
> Were of an age. Well, Susan is with God;
> She was too good for me. But as I said,
> On Lammas Eve at night shall she be fourteen.
> That shall she; marry, I remember it well.
> 'Tis since the earthquake now eleven years,
> And she was wean'd—I never shall forget it—
> Of all the days of the year upon that day.
> For I had then laid wormwood to my dug,
> Sitting in the sun under the dovehouse wall.
> My lord and you were then at Mantua—
> Nay I do bear a brain. But as I said,
> When it did taste the wormwood on the nipple
> Of my dug and felt it bitter, pretty fool,
> To see it tetchy and fall out with the dug.
> Shake! quoth the dovehouse! 'Twas no need, I trow,
> To bid me trudge.
> And since that time it is eleven years.
> For then she could stand high-lone. Nay, by th'rood,
> She could have run and waddled all about;
> For even the day before she broke her brow,
> And then my husband—God be with his soul,
> A was a merry man—took up the child,
> 'Yea,' quoth he, 'dost thou fall upon thy face?
> Thou wilt fall backward when thou hast more wit,
> Wilt thou not, Jule?' And, by my holidame,
> The pretty wretch left crying and said 'Ay'.

To see now how a jest shall come about.
I warrant, and I should live a thousand years
I never should forget it. 'Wilt thou not, Jule?' quoth he,
And, pretty fool, it stinted, and said 'Ay'.

[I.iii.16–48]

Her speech is shrewd and not so simple as first it sounds, and comes short of poignance, because already there is something antipathetic in the Nurse. Juliet, like her late twin sister, Susan, is too good for the Nurse, and there is an edge to the account of the weaning that is bothersome, since we do not hear the accents of love.

Shakespeare delays any more ultimate revelation of the Nurse's nature until the crucial scene where she fails Juliet. The exchanges here need to be quoted at length, because Juliet's shock is a new effect for Shakespeare. The Nurse is the person who has been closest to Juliet for all the fourteen years of her life, and suddenly Juliet realizes that what has seemed loyalty and care is something else.

> *Jul.* O God, O Nurse, how shall this be prevented?
> My husband is on earth, my faith in heaven.
> How shall that faith return again to earth
> Unless that husband send it me from heaven
> By leaving earth? Comfort me, counsel me.
> Alack, alack, that heaven should practise stratagems
> Upon so soft a subject as myself.
> What sayst thou? Hast thou not a word of joy?
> Some comfort, Nurse.
> *Nurse.* Faith, here it is:
> Romeo is banish'd, and all the world to nothing
> That he dares ne'er come back to challenge you,
> Or if he do, it needs must be by stealth.
> Then, since the case so stands as now it doth,
> I think it best you married with the County.
> O, he's a lovely gentleman.
> Romeo's a dishclout to him. An eagle, madam,
> Hath not so green, so quick, so fair an eye
> As Paris hath. Beshrew my very heart,
> I think you are happy in this second match,
> For it excels your first; or if it did not,
> Your first is dead, or 'twere as good he were
> As living here and you no use of him.

Jul. Speakest thou from thy heart?
Nurse. And from my soul too, else beshrew them both.
Jul. Amen.
Nurse. What?
Jul. Well, thou hast comforted me marvellous much.
    Go in, and tell my lady I am gone,
    Having displeas'd my father, to Laurence' cell,
    To make confession and to be absolv'd.
Nurse. Marry, I will; and this is wisely done.
Jul. Ancient damnation! O most wicked fiend,
    Is it more sin to wish me thus forsworn,
    Or to dispraise my lord with that same tongue
    Which she hath praised him with above compare
    So many thousand times? Go, counsellor.
    Thou and my bosom henceforth shall be twain.
    I'll to the friar, to know his remedy.
    If all else fail, myself have power to die.
                            [III.v.204–42]

    The more-than-poignant: "that heaven should practise stratagems / Upon so soft a subject as myself" is answered by the Nurse's astonishing "comfort": "it excels your first; or if it did not, / Your first is dead." The Nurse's argument is valid if convenience is everything; since Juliet is in love, we hear instead an overwhelming rejection of the Nurse, proceeding from the eloquent "amen" on to the dry: "Well, thou hast comforted me marvellous much." The Nurse indeed is "Ancient damnation! O most wicked fiend," and we will hardly hear from her again until Juliet "dies" her first death in this play. Like Mercutio, the Nurse moves us at last to distrust every apparent value in the tragedy except the lovers' commitment to each other.

5

Juliet, and not Romeo, or even Brutus in *Julius Caesar*, dies her second death as a prefiguration of Hamlet's charismatic splendor. Romeo, though he changes enormously under her influence, remains subject to anger and to despair, and is as responsible as Mercutio and Tybalt are for the catastrophe. Having slain Tybalt, Romeo cries out that he has become "Fortune's fool." We would wince if Juliet called herself "Fortune's fool," since she is as nearly flawless as her situation allows, and we recall instead her wry prayer: "Be fickle, Fortune." Perhaps any playgoer or any reader remembers best Romeo and Juliet's aubade after their single night of fulfillment:

Jul. Wilt thou be gone? It is not yet near day.
 It was the nightingale and not the lark
 That pierc'd the fearful hollow of thine ear.
 Nightly she sings on yond pomegranate tree.
 Believe me, love, it was the nightingale.
Rom. It was the lark, the herald of the morn,
 No nightingale. Look, love, what envious streaks
 Do lace the severing clouds in yonder east.
 Night's candies are burnt out, and jocund day
 Stands tiptoe on the misty mountain tops.
 I must be gone and live, or stay and die.
Jul. Yond light is not daylight, I know it, I.
 It is some meteor that the sun exhales
 To be to thee this night a torchbearer
 And light thee on thy way to Mantua.
 Therefore stay yet: Thou need'st not to be gone.
Rom. Let me be ta'en, let me be put to death.
 I am content, so thou wilt have it so.
 I'll say yon grey is not the morning's eye,
 'Tis but the pale reflex of Cynthia's brow.
 Nor that is not the lark whose notes do beat
 The vaulty heaven so high above our heads.
 I have more care to stay than will to go.
 Come death, and welcome. Juliet wills it so.
 How is't, my soul? Let's talk. It is not day.
Jul. It is, it is. Hie hence, begone, away.
 It is the lark that sings so out of tune,
 Straining harsh discords and unpleasing sharps.
 Some say the lark makes sweet division.
 This doth not so, for she divideth us.
 Some say the lark and loathed toad change eyes.
 O, now I would they had chang'd voices too,
 Since arm from arm that voice doth us affray,
 Hunting thee hence with hunt's-up to the day.
 O now be gone, more light and light it grows.
Rom. More light and light: more dark and dark our woes.

[III.v.1–36]

Exquisite in itself, this is also a subtle epitome of the tragedy of this
tragedy, for the entire play could be regarded as a dawn song that, alas, is out
of phase. A bemused audience, unless the director is shrewd, is likely to

become skeptical that event after event arrives in the untimeliest way possible. Romeo and Juliet's aubade is so disturbing precisely because they are not courtly love sophisticates working through a stylized ritual. The courtly lover confronts the possibility of a real-enough death if he lingers too long, because his partner is an adulterous wife. But Juliet and Romeo know that death after dawn would be Romeo's punishment, not for adultery, but merely for marriage. The subtle outrageousness of Shakespeare's drama is that everything is against the lovers: their families and the state, the indifference of nature, the vagaries of time, and the regressive movement of the cosmological contraries of love and strife. Even had Romeo transcended his anger; even if Mercutio and the Nurse were not quarrelsome busybodies, the odds are too great against the triumph of love. That is the aubade's undersong, made explicit in Romeo's great outcry against the contraries: "More light and light: more dark and dark our woes."

What was Shakespeare trying to do for himself as a playwright by composing *Romeo and Juliet?* Tragedy did not come easily to Shakespeare, yet all this play's lyricism and comic genius cannot hold off the dawn that will become a destructive darkness. With just a few alterations, Shakespeare could have transformed *Romeo and Juliet* into a play as cheerful as *A Midsummer Night's Dream.* The young lovers, escaped to Mantua or Padua, would not have been victims of Verona, or of bad timing, or of cosmological contraries asserting their sway. Yet this travesty would have been intolerable for us, and for Shakespeare: a passion as absolute as Romeo's and Juliet's cannot consort with comedy. Mere sexuality will do for comedy, but the shadow of death makes eroticism the companion of tragedy. Shakespeare, in *Romeo and Juliet*, eschews Chaucerian irony, but he takes from *The Knight's Tale* Chaucer's intimation that we are always keeping appointments we haven't made. Here it is the sublime appointment kept by Paris and Romeo at Juliet's supposed tomb, which soon enough becomes both her authentic tomb and their own. What is left on stage at the close of this tragedy is an absurd pathos: the wretched Friar Laurence, who fearfully abandoned Juliet; a widowed Montague, who vows to have a statue of Juliet raised in pure gold; the Capulets vowing to end a feud already spent in five deaths—those of Mercutio, Tybalt, Paris, Romeo, and Juliet. The closing curtain of any proper production of the play should descend upon these final ironies, presented as ironies, and not as images of reconciliation. As is *Julius Caesar* after it, *Romeo and Juliet* is a training ground in which Shakespeare teaches himself remorselessness and prepares the way for his five great tragedies, starting with the *Hamlet* of 1600–1601.

Chronology

1564	William Shakespeare christened at Stratford-on-Avon April 26.
1582	Marries Anne Hathaway in November.
1583	Daughter Susanna born, baptized on May 26.
1585	Twins Hamnet and Judith born, baptized on February 2.
1587	Shakespeare goes to London, without family.
1589–90	*Henry VI, Part One.*
1590–91	*Henry VI, Part Two; Henry VI, Part Three.*
1592–93	*Richard III; The Two Gentlemen of Verona.*
1592–93	Publication of *Venus and Adonis*, dedicated to the Earl of Southampton; The *Sonnets* probably begun.
1593	*The Comedy of Errors.*
1593–94	Publication of *The Rape of Lucrece*, also dedicated to the Earl of Southampton; *Titus Andronicus; The Taming of the Shrew.*
1594–95	*Love's Labour's Lost; King John; Richard II.*
1595–96	*Romeo and Juliet; A Midsummer Night's Dream.*
1596	Son Hamnet dies; a coat of arms granted to his father, John.
1596–97	*The Merchant of Venice; Henry IV, Part One;* purchases New Place in Stratford.

1597–98   *The Merry Wives of Windsor; Henry IV Part Two.*

1598–99   *Much Ado About Nothing.*

1599   *Henry V; Julius Cesar; As You Like It.*

1600–01   *Hamlet.*

1601   *The Phoenix and the Turtle;* Shakespeare's father dies.

1601–02   *Twelfth Night; Troilus and Cressida.*

1602–03   *All's Well That Ends Well.*

1603   Death of Queen Elizabeth; James VI of Scotland becomes James I of England; Shakespeare's Company becomes the King's Men.

1604   *Measure for Measure; Othello.*

1605   *King Lear.*

1606   *Macbeth; Antony and Cleopatra.*

1607   Marriage of daughter Susanna on June 5.

1607–08   *Coriolanus; Timon of Athens; Pericles.*

1608   Death of Shakespeare's mother.

1609   Publication, probably unauthorized, of the quarto edition of the *Sonnets.*

1609–10   *Cymbeline.*

1610–11   *The Winter's Tale.*

1611   *The Tempest;* Shakespeare returns to Stratford, where he will live until his death.

1612   *A Funeral Elegy.*

1612–13   *Henry VIII;* The Globe Theatre destroyed by fire.

1613   *The Two Noble Kinsmen* (with John Fletcher).

1616   Marriage of daughter Judith on February 10; Shakespeare dies on April 23.

1623   Publication of the First Folio edition of Shakespeare's plays.

Contributors

HAROLD BLOOM is Sterling Professor of the Humanities at Yale University and Henry W. and Albert A. Berg Professor of English at the New York University Graduate School. He is the author of over 20 books, including *The Anxiety of Influence* (1973), which sets forth Professor Bloom's provocative theory of the literary relationships between the great writers and their predecessors. His most recent book, *Shakespeare: The Invention of the Human* (1998), was a finalist for the 1998 National Book Award. Professor Bloom is a 1985 MacArthur Foundation Award recipient, served as the Charles Eliot Norton Professor of Poetry at Harvard University in 1987–88, and has received honorary degrees from the universities of Rome and Bologna. In 1999, Professor Bloom received the prestigious American Academy of Arts and Letters Gold Medal for Criticism.

ROBERT PENN WARREN (1905–1989) twice won the Pulitzer Prize for his poetry (*Promises, 1957; Now and Then: Poems 1976–1977, 1978*); he also won in 1947 for his novel *All the King's Men*. In 1985, he was named the first Poet Laureate in America. An influential literary critic and theorist, he is the author of *An Approach to Literature, Fundamentals of Good Writing* (with Cleanth Brooks), and *Democracy and Poetry*.

HAROLD C. GODDARD (1878–1950) was for many years head of the English department at Swarthmore College. He is the author of *Studies in New England Transcendentalism* and the editor of an edition of Ralph Waldo Emerson's essays. His book *The Meaning of Shakespeare* was published after his death, in 1951.

JOHN LAWLOR is the author of *Chaucer, Piers Plowman, Elysium Revisited*, and *The Tragic Sense in Shakespeare*.

RUTH NEVO, formerly a professor of English at the University of Jerusalem, is the author of *Tragic Form in Shakespeare, Comic Transformation in Shakespeare*, and *Shakespeare's Other Language*.

ROSALIE L. COLIE taught at Barnard, Oxford, Yale, and Toronto University. At the time of her death in 1972, she was chairman of the Department of Comparative Literature at Brown University. She is the author of *Paradoxia Epidemica: The Resources of Kind, Shakespeare's Living Art, Atlantic Wall and Other Poems*, and *Some Facets of King Lear: Essays in Prismatic Criticism*.

SIR FRANK KERMODE is Professor of English at Cambridge University. Among his best known books are *Romantic Image, The Classic, The Sense of an Ending, Continuities, Sheakespeare, Spenser and Donne: Renaissance Essays, The Uses of Error*, and *The Genesis of Secrecy*.

SUSAN SNYDER is the author of *The Comic Matrix of Shakespeare's Tragedies* and *Pastoral Process: Spenser, Marvell, Milton*.

NORTHROP FRYE (1912–1991), Canadian educator and literary critic. Among his most influential book are *Fearful Symmetry: A Study of William Blake*, and *Anatomy of Criticism*. His later works include books on T.S. Eliot, Milton's epics, Shakespearean comedy and tragedy, English Romanticism, and a study of the mythology and structure of the Bible, *The Great Code: The Bible and Literature*.

THOMAS MCALINDON is the author of the book *Shakespeare's Tragic Cosmos*.

Bibliography

Adams, Barry B. "The Prudence of Prince Escalus." *English Literary History* 35 (1968): 32–50.

Andreas, James. "The Neutering of *Romeo and Juliet*." In *Ideological Approaches to Shakespeare: The Practice of Theory*, ed. Robert P. Merrix. Lewiston, NY: Edwin Mellen Press, 1992.

Andrews, J. F. (ed.). *Romeo and Juliet: Critical Essays*. New York: Garland, 1993.

Belsey, Catherine. "The Name of the Rose in *Romeo and Juliet*." *Yearbook of English Studies* 23 (1993): 125–42.

Black, James. "The Visual Artistry of *Romeo and Juliet*." *Studies in English Literature 1500–1900* 15 (1975): 245–56.

Bond, Ronald B. "Love and Lust in *Romeo and Juliet*." *Wascana Review* 15 (1980): 22–31.

Bryant, James C. "The Problematic Friar in *Romeo and Juliet*." *English Studies* 55 (1974): 340–50.

Carroll, William T. "'We Were Born to Die': *Romeo and Juliet*." *Comparative Drama* 15 (1981): 54–71.

Chang, Joseph S. M. J. "The Language of Paradox in *Romeo and Juliet*." *Shakespeare Studies* 3 (1967): 22–42.

Cribb, T. J. "The Unity of *Romeo and Juliet*." *Shakespeare Survey* 34 (1981): 93–104.

Dickey, Franklin M. *Not Wisely But Too Well: Shakespeare's Love Tragedies*. San Marino, California: Huntington Library Press, 1957.

Estrin, Barbara. "Romeo and Juliet, and the Art of Naming Love." *Ariel* 12, (April 1981): 31–49.

Evans, Bertrand. "The Brevity of Friar Laurence." *PMLA* 65 (1950): 841–65.

Evans, Blakemore G. Introduction to *Romeo and Juliet*, by William Shakespeare, ed. G. Blakemore Evans. Cambridge: Cambridge University Press, 1980.

Everett, Barbara. "*Romeo and Juliet*: the Nurse's Story." *Critical Quarterly* 14 (1972): 169–82.

Faber, M. D. "The Adolescent Suicide of Romeo and Juliet." *Psychoanalytic Review* 59 (1972): 169–82.

Gibbons, Brian. Introduction to *Romeo and Juliet*, by William Shakespeare, ed. Brian Gibbons. *The New Arden Shakespeare*, ed. Harold F. Brooks, Harold Jenkins, and Brian Morris. London and New York: Methuen, 1980.

Farrrel, Kirby. "Love, Death, and Patriarchy in *Romeo and Juliet*." In *Shakespeare's Personality*, ed. Norman N. Holland, Sidney Homan, and Bernard J. Paris. Berkeley: University of California Press, 1989.

Holmer, Joan Ozark. " 'Myself Condemned and Myself Excus'd': Tragic Effect in *Romeo and Juliet*." *Studies in Philology* 88 (1991): 345–62.

Kahn, Coppelia. "Coming of Age in Verona." *Modern Language Studies* 8 (1977–78): 5–22.

Leech, Clifford. "The Moral Tragedy of *Romeo and Juliet*." *English Renaissance Drama: Essays in Honor of Madeleine Doran and Mark Eccles*. Henning, Standish, et al., eds. Carbondale and Edwardsville: Southern Illinois University Press, London and Amsterdam: Feffer and Simons: 1976.

Levenson, Jill L. "The Definition of Love: Shakespeare's Phrasing in *Romeo and Juliet*." *Shakespeare's Studies* 15 (1982): 21–36.

Levin, Harry. "Form and Formality in *Romeo and Juliet*." *Shakespeare Quarterly* 10 (1959): 35–44.

Mahood, M. M. "Romeo and Juliet." In *Shakespeare's Wordplay*. London: Methuen, 1957.

Marsh, Derick R. C. *Passion Lends Them Power: A Study of Shakespeare's Love Tragedies*. Manchester: Manchester University Press: 1976.

Mason, Harold A. *Shakespeare's Tragedies of Love*. 1970.

Moisan, Thomas E. "Rhetoric and Rehearsal of Death: the 'Lamentations' Scene in *Romeo and Juliet*." *Shakespeare Quarterly* 34 (1983): 389–404.

Moore, Olin H. *The Legend of Romeo and Juliet*. Columbus: Ohio State University Press, 1950.

Parker, Douglas H. "Light and Dark Imagery in *Romeo and Juliet*." *Queen's Quarterly* 75 (1968): 663–74.

Porter, Joseph A. *Shakespeare's Mercutio: His History and Drama*. Chapel Hill: University of North Carolina Press, 1988.

Ryan, Kiernan. "*Romeo and Juliet*: the Language of Tragedy." In *The Taming of the Text: Explorations in Language, Literature and Culture*, ed. Willie van Peer. London: Routledge, 1988, pp. 106–21.

Scragg, Leah. *Shakespeare's Mouldy Tales: Recurrent Plot Motifs in Shakespearean Drama*. London: Longman, 1992.

Seward, James H. *Tragic Vision in Romeo and Juliet*. Washington, D.C.: Consortium Press, 1973.

Siegal, Paul N. "Christianity and the Religion of Love in *Romeo and Juliet*." *Shakespeare Quarterly* 12 (1961): 371–92.

Stamm, Rudolf. "The First Meeting of the Lovers in Shakespeare's *Romeo and Juliet*." *English Studies* 67 (1986): 2–13.

Thomas, Sidney. "The Queen Mab Speech in *Romeo and Juliet*." *Shakespeare Survey* 25 (1972): 73–80.

Utterback, Raymond V. "The Death of Mercutio." *Shakespeare Quarterly* 24, No. 2 (Spring 1973): 105–16.

Wallace, Nathaniel. "Cultural Tropology in *Romeo and Juliet*." *Studies in Philology* 88 (1991): 329–44.

Waters, Douglas. *Christian Settings in Shakespeare's Tragedies*. London: Associated University Presses, 1994.

Watts, Cedric. *Romeo and Juliet*. Boston: Twayne, 1991.

Williamson, Marilyn L. "Romeo and Death." *Shakespeare Studies* 14 (1981): 129–37.

Young, Bruce W. "Haste, Consent, and Age at Marriage: Some Implications of Social History in *Romeo and Juliet*." *Iowa State Journal of Research* 62 (1988): 459–74.

Acknowledgments

"Pure and Impure Poetry" by Robert Penn Warren (1942). From *New and Selected Essays*. © 1989 by Robert Penn Warren. Reprinted by permission of William Morris Agency, Inc., on behalf of the author.

"*Romeo and Juliet*" by Harold C. Goddard. From *The Meaning of Shakespeare*. © 1951 by The University of Chicago. Reprinted by permission.

"*Romeo and Juliet*" by John Lawlor. From *Early Shakespeare*. © 1961 Edward Arnold Publishers. Reprinted by permission.

Ruth Nevo. "Tragic Form in *Romeo & Juliet*." *Studies in English Literature, 1500–1900*. [Vol. 9, No. 2 (Spring 1969)], pp. 241–58. © 1969. Reprinted by permission of the Johns Hopkins University Press.

Rosalie L. Colie. "Shakespeare's Living Art." *Othello and the Problematics of Love*. © 1974 by Princeton University Press. Reprinted by permission of Princeton University Press.

"Introduction to *Romeo and Juliet*" by Frank Kermode. From *The Riverside Shakespeare*, first edition. © 1974 by Houghton Mifflin Company. Reprinted by permission.

Susan Snyder, "The Comic Matrix of Shakespeare's Tragedies." *Beyond Comedy: Romeo & Juliet and Othello*. © 1979 by Princeton University Press. Reprinted by permission of Princeton University Press.

Northrop Frye, "Northrop Frye on Shakespeare," *Romeo & Juliet*, published by Yale University Press. © 1986 by Yale University Press.

"*Romeo and Juliet*" by Thomas McAlindon. From *Shakespeare's Tragic Cosmos*. © 1991 Cambridge University Press. Reprinted with the permission of Cambridge University Press.

"*Romeo and Juliet*" by Harold Bloom. From *Shakespeare: The Invention of the Human*. © 1998 by Harold Bloom. Reprinted by permission.

Index

209